AUTHENTIC TRANSCRIPTIONS
WITH NOTES AND TABLATURE

KENNY WAYNE SHEPHERD

LEDBETTER HEIGHTS

PREFACE

It's hard to believe it's been 20 years since the release of my first album, *Ledbetter Heights*. In 1995, I was just a kid and excited that I was being given the opportunity to write and record music and play my guitar for a living. Twenty years later, I still feel the same way. With the release of each new record and the launch of every tour, I am grateful that I'm able do what I love and share my music with my fans. I am very proud of *Ledbetter Heights* and everything that has been accomplished as a result of this first album. When I listen to each one of the songs transcribed in this book a smile comes to my face as I hear a young man pouring his heart and soul into each note, eager to make a name for himself in the world of the music that he adores. I hope each time you listen to this album or play these songs it brings a smile to your face as well. Here's to at least another 20 years of making music for you.

Thanks for your support. Cheers!

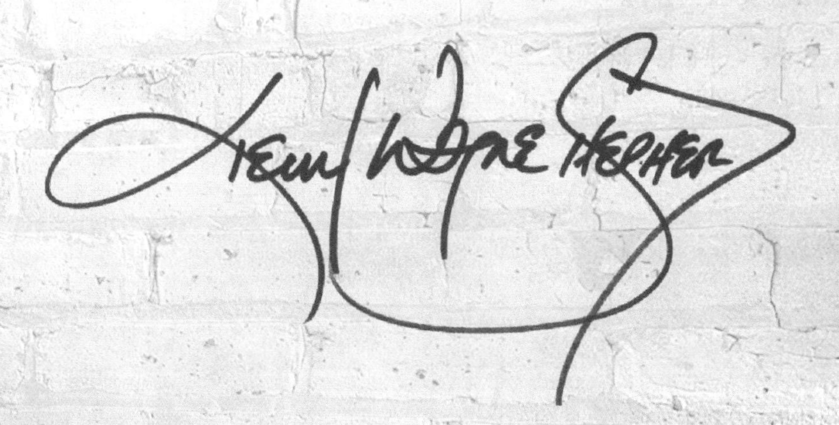

Music transcriptions by Pete Billmann

ISBN 978-1-4950-4529-5

7777 W. BLUEMOUND RD. P.O. BOX 13819 MILWAUKEE, WI 53213

Visit Hal Leonard Online at
www.halleonard.com

KENNY WAYNE SHEPHERD 2015
Photo by Greg Logan

KENNY WAYNE SHEPHERD

LEDBETTER HEIGHTS

Fender

Photo by Ken Shepherd
(Top row, L to R) Chris Layton, Jimmy Wallace – Chris Layton, KWS, Joe Nadeau – Joe Nadeau – Buddy Flett, KWS
(Bottom row, L to R) Chris Layton, Jimmy Wallace, Joe Nadeau, Will Ainsworth – David Z, KWS – Corey Sterling

Photo by Ken Shepherd
Jessie Thomas and KWS

Photo by Rich Masters

Born with a Broken Heart

Words and Music by Danny Tate and Kenny Wayne Shepherd

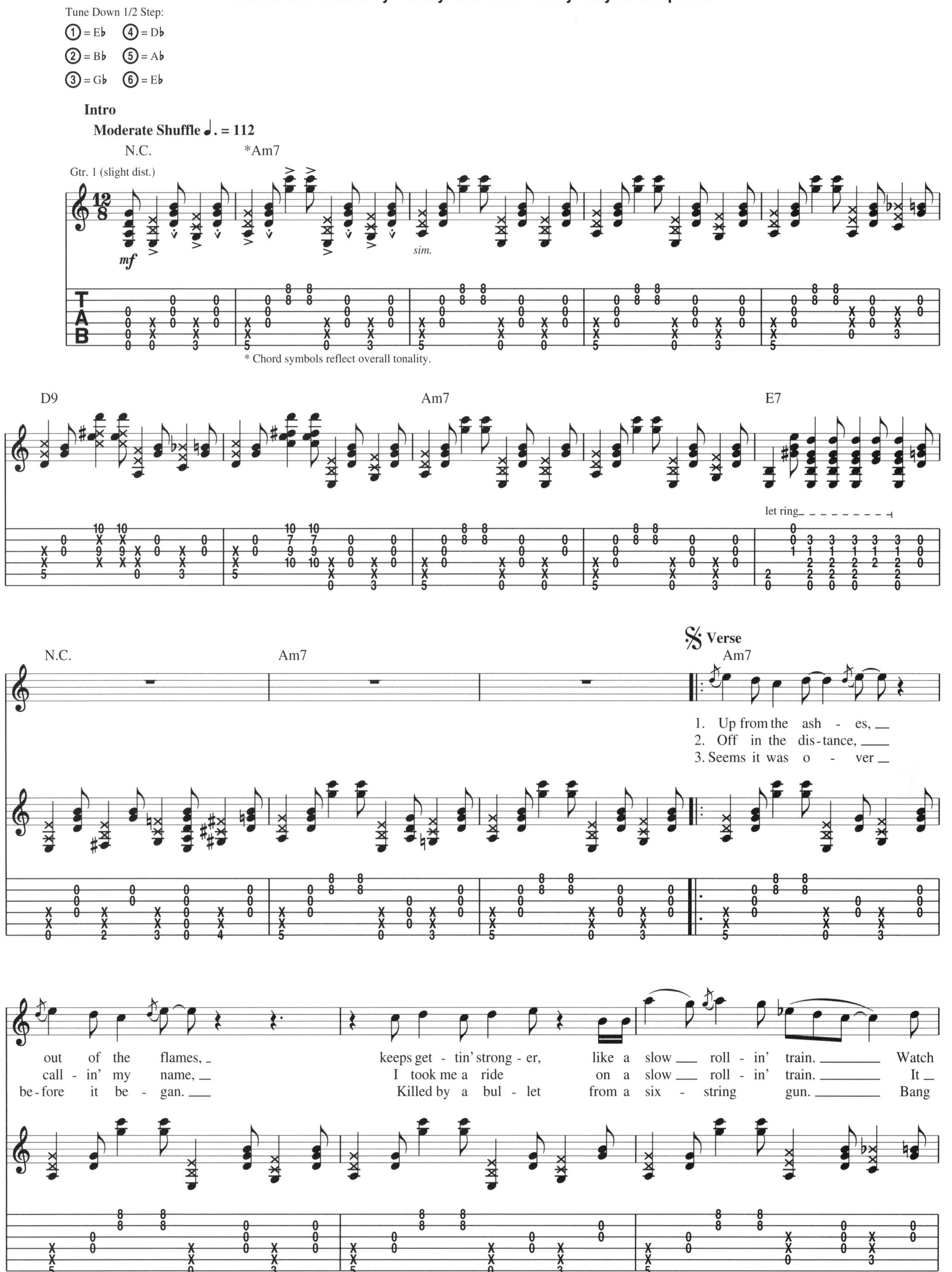

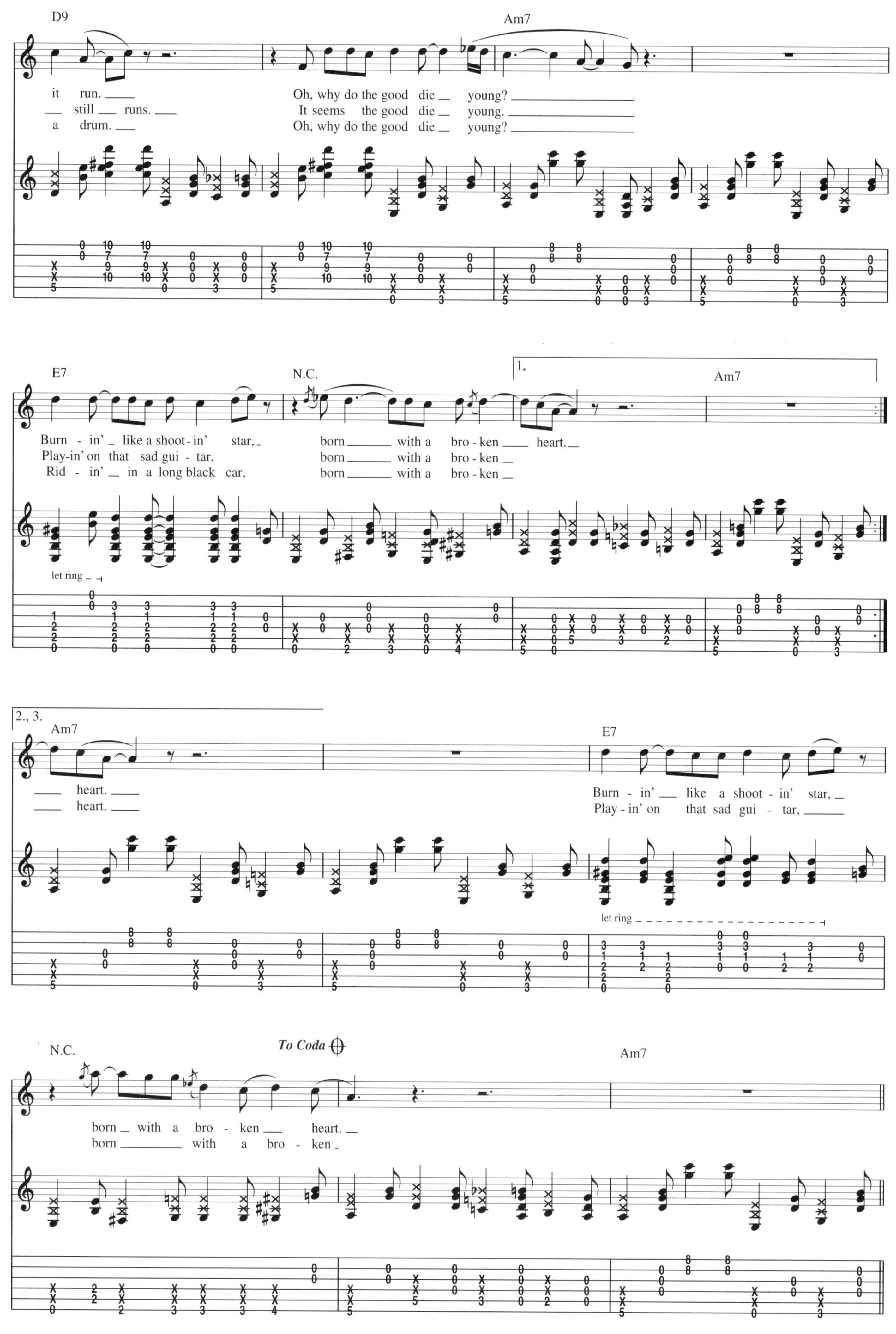
D9
Am7
it run.
still runs.
a drum.
Oh, why do the good die young?
It seems the good die young.
Oh, why do the good die young?
E7
N.C.
1.
Am7
Burn - in' like a shoot - in' star,
Play-in' on that sad gui - tar,
Rid - in' in a long black car,
born with a bro - ken heart.
born with a bro - ken
born with a bro - ken
let ring
2., 3.
Am7
heart.
heart.
E7
Burn - in' like a shoot - in' star,
Play - in' on that sad gui - tar,
let ring
N.C.
To Coda
Am7
born with a bro - ken heart.
born with a bro - ken

Guitar Solo

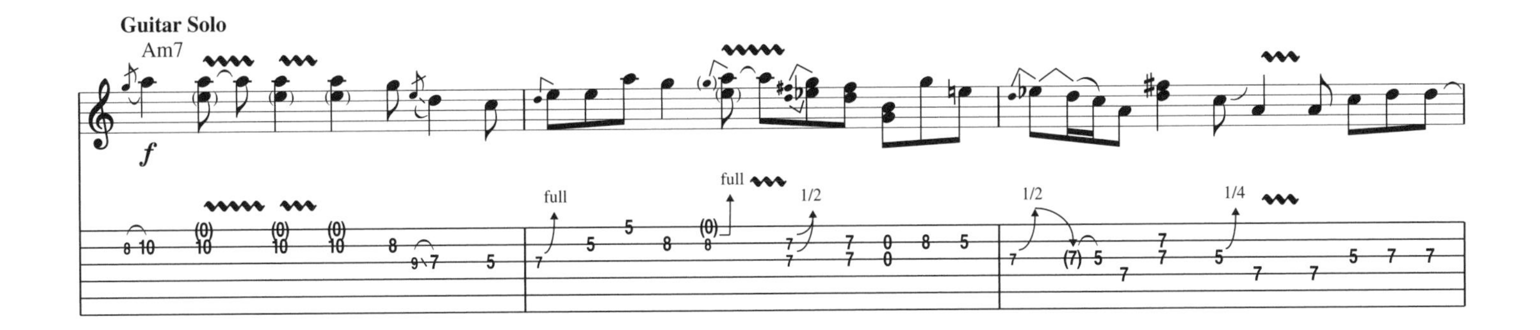
Am7
f
full
full
1/2
1/2
1/4

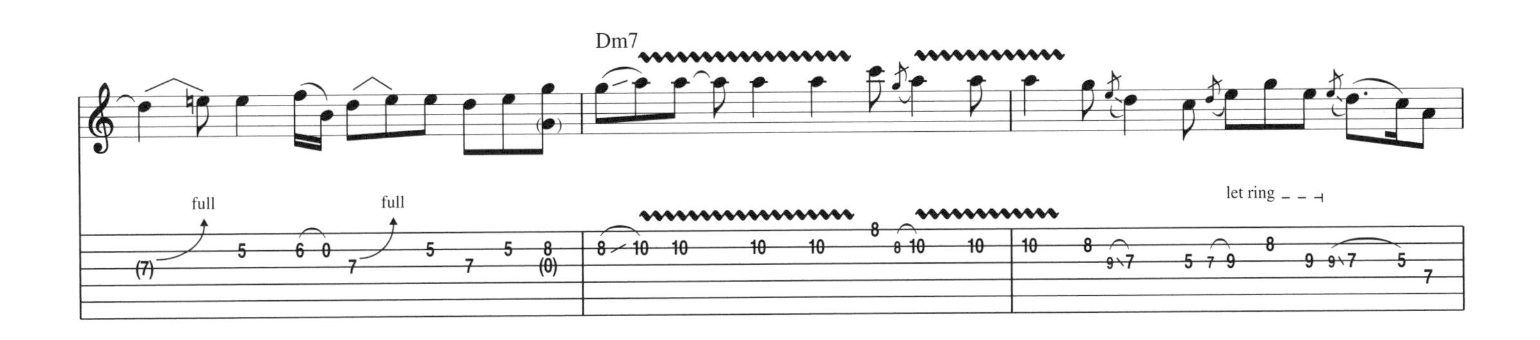
Dm7
full
full
let ring

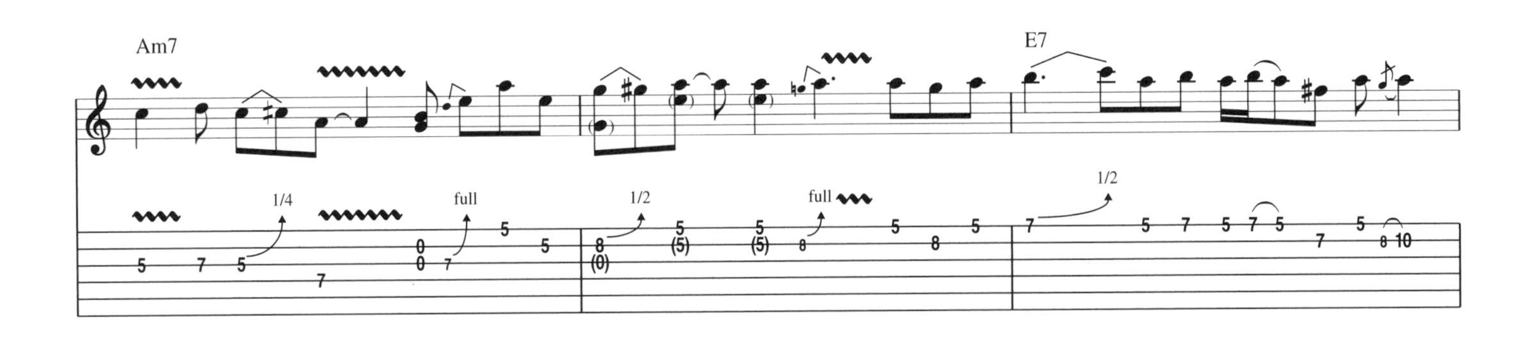
Am7
E7
1/4
full
1/2
full
1/2

Am7
1/4
1/2
1/2

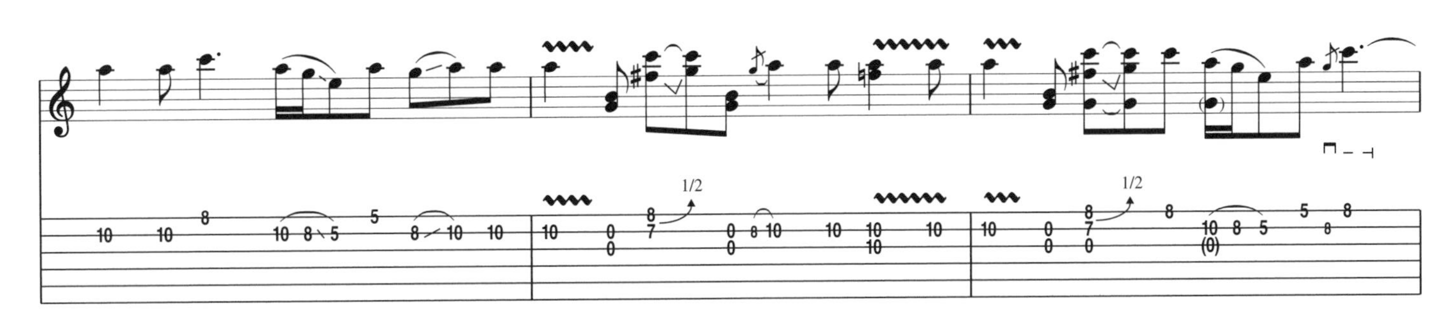
1/2
1/2

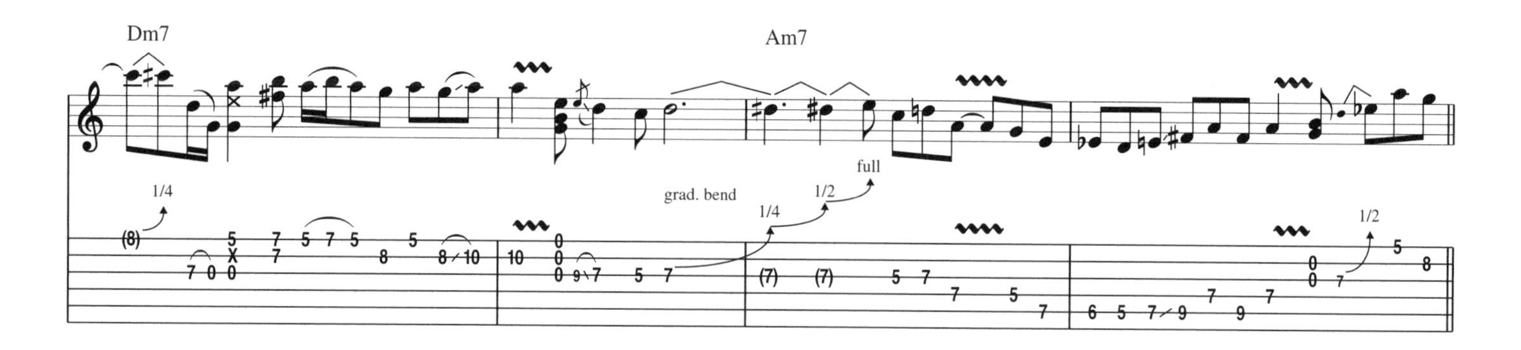
Dm7
Am7
grad. bend
full
1/4
1/2

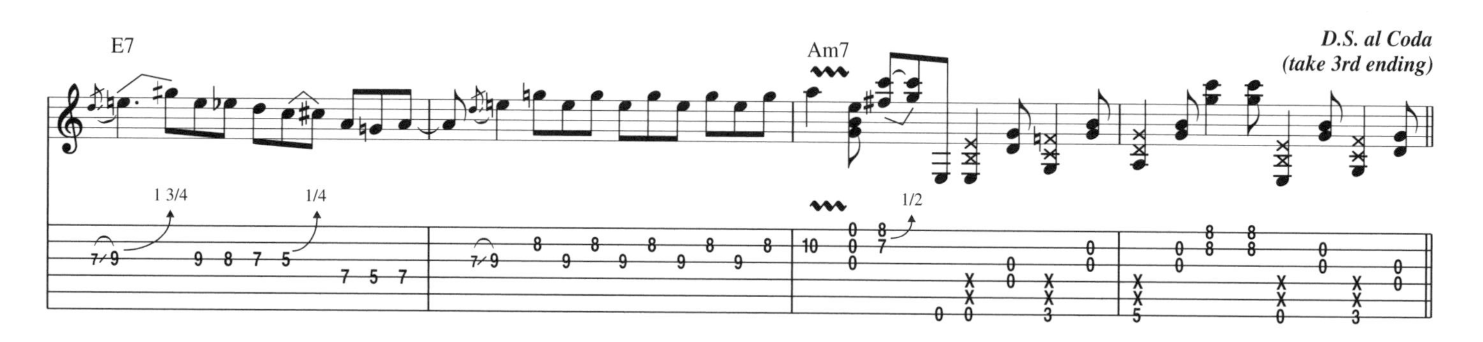
E7
Am7
D.S. al Coda
(take 3rd ending)
1 3/4
1/4
1/2

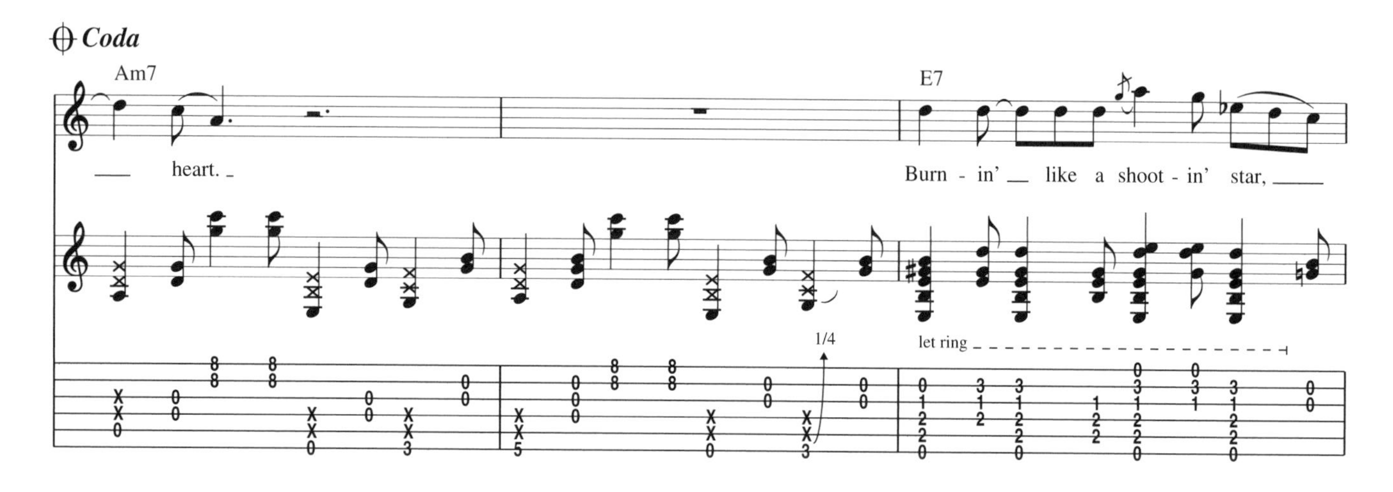
Coda
Am7
E7
heart.
Burn - in' like a shoot - in' star,
let ring
1/4

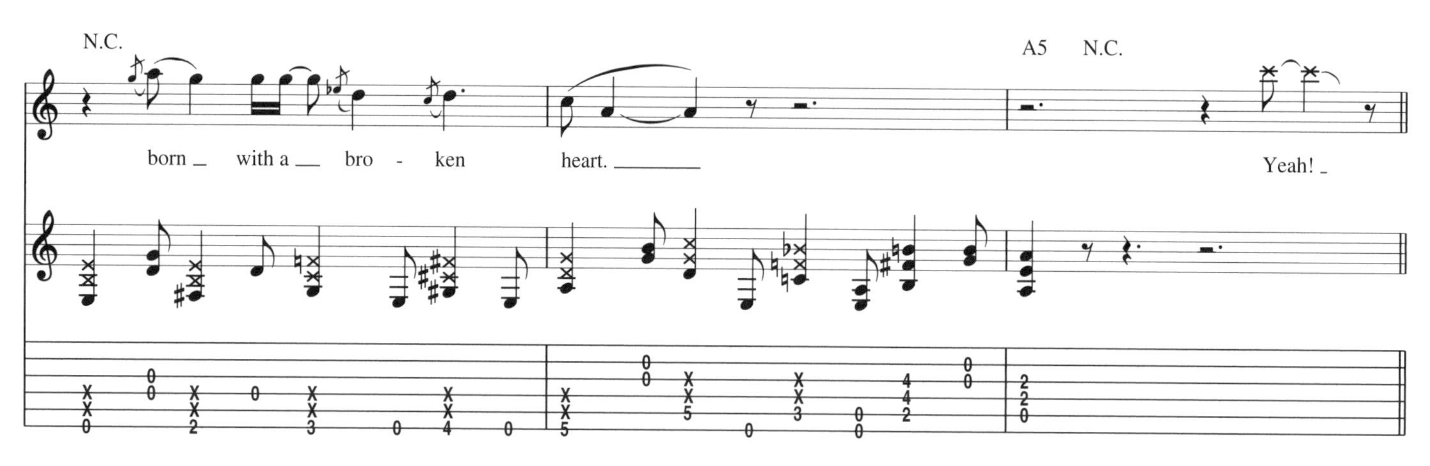
N.C.
A5
N.C.
born with a bro - ken heart.
Yeah!

Outro-Guitar Solo
Am7
grad. bend
full
1/2
1/4
3/4

grad. bend
3/4
1/4
1/2

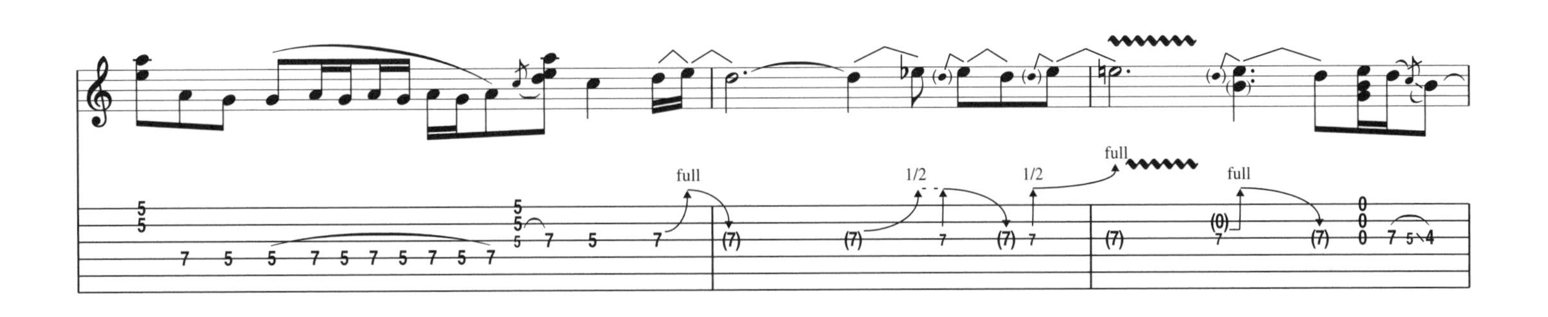
full
1/2
1/2
full
full

1/2
1/2
1/4
3/4
full

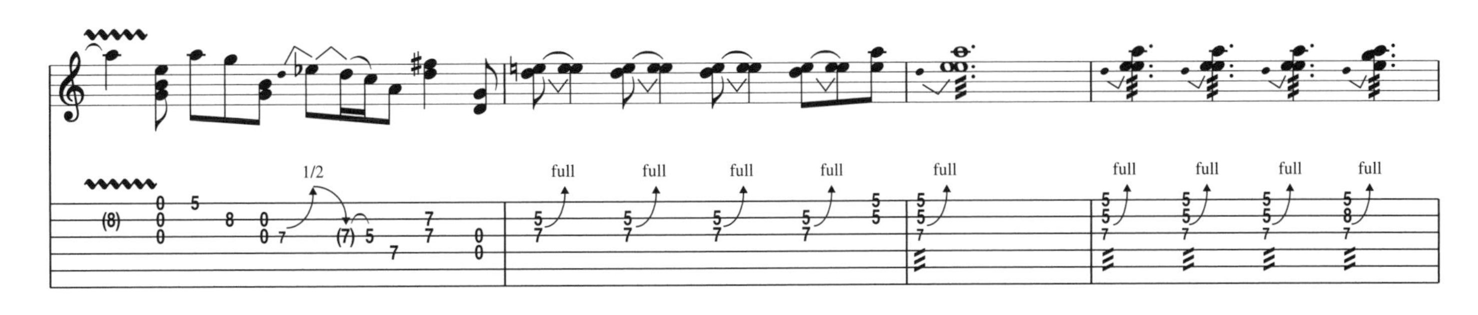
1/2
full
full
full
full
full
full
full
full
full

full
1/4
1/2
1/4
1 1/2
1/4
1/4

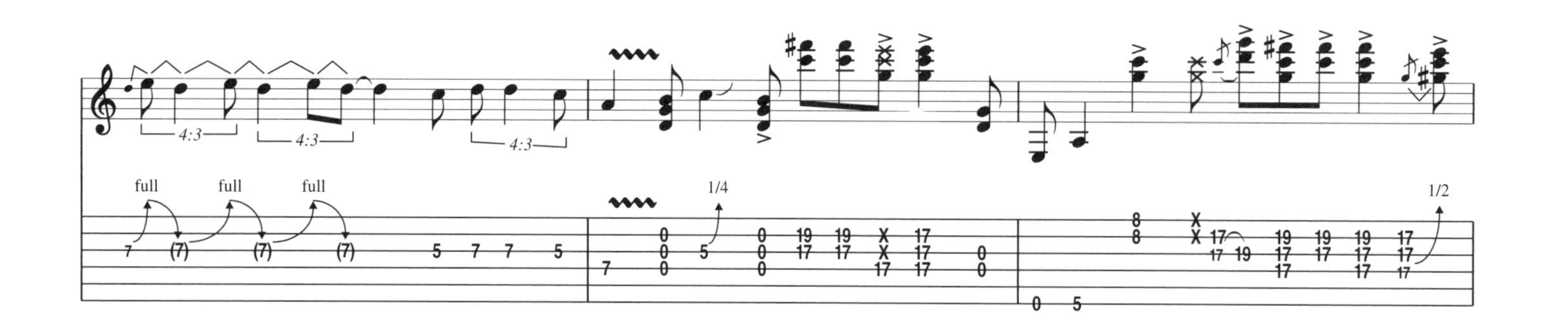
4:3
4:3
4:3
full
full
full
1/4
1/2

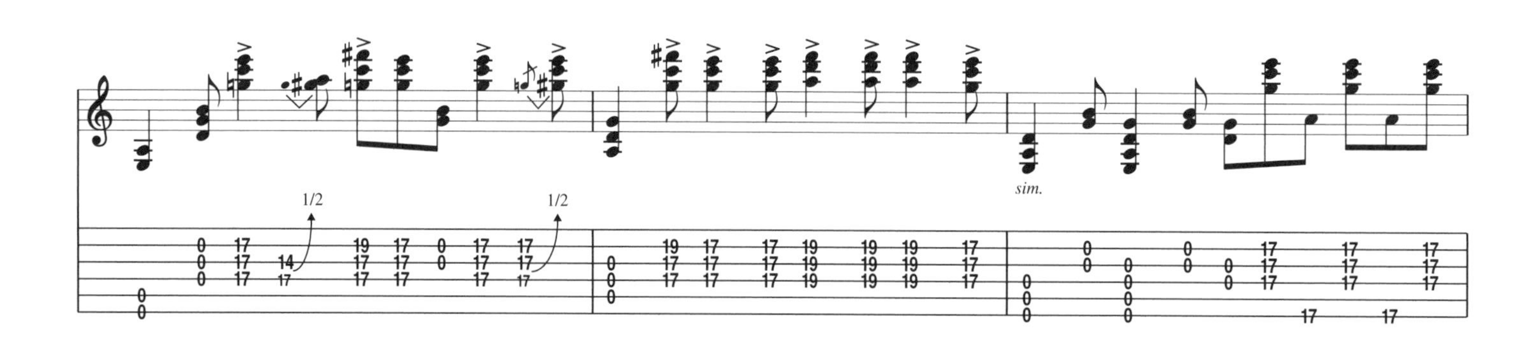
1/2
1/2
sim.

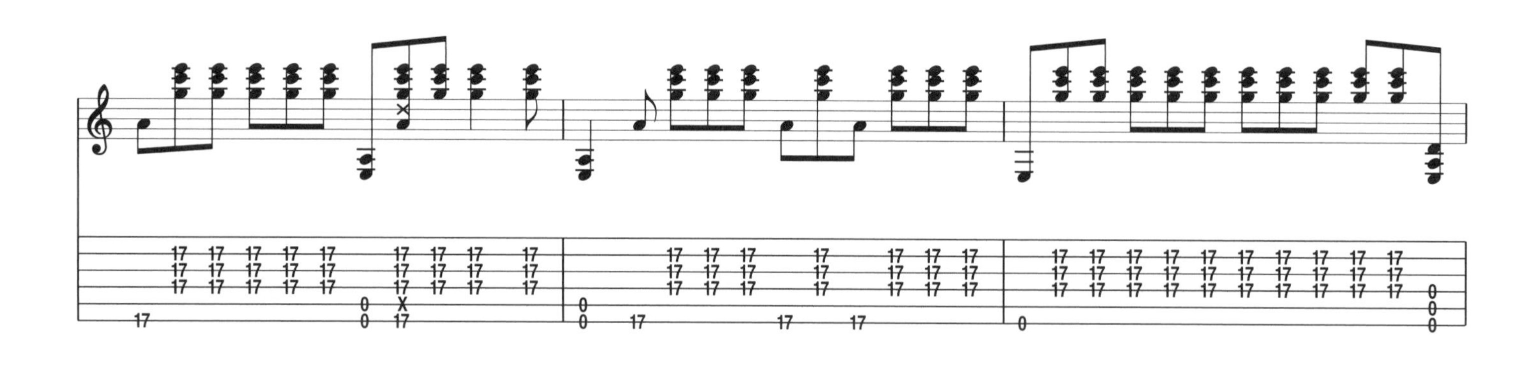

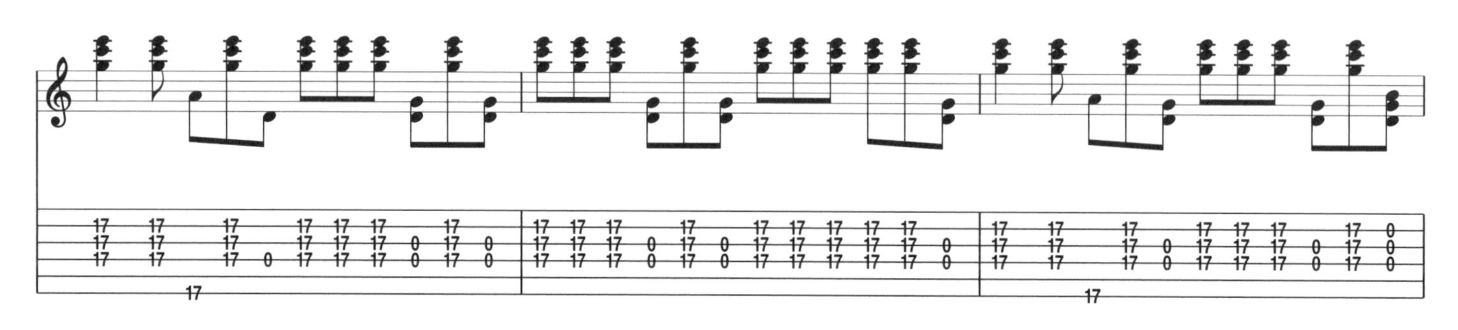

sim.
sim.

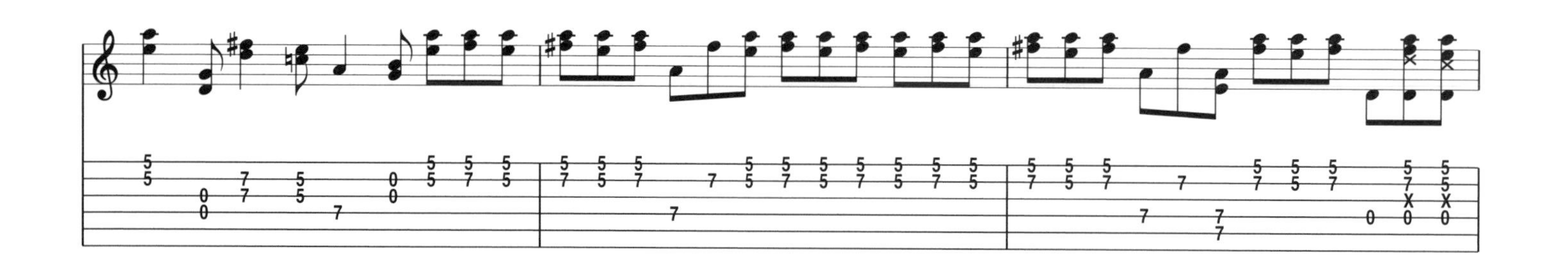
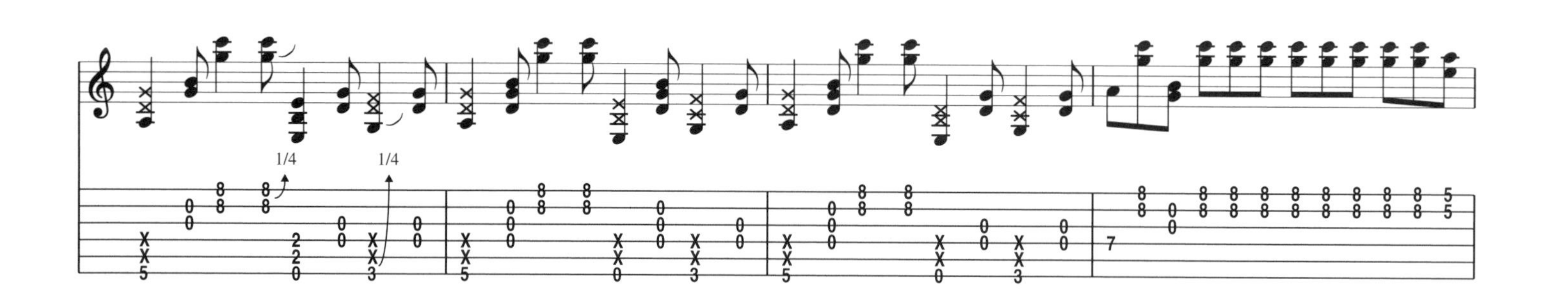
1/4
1/4
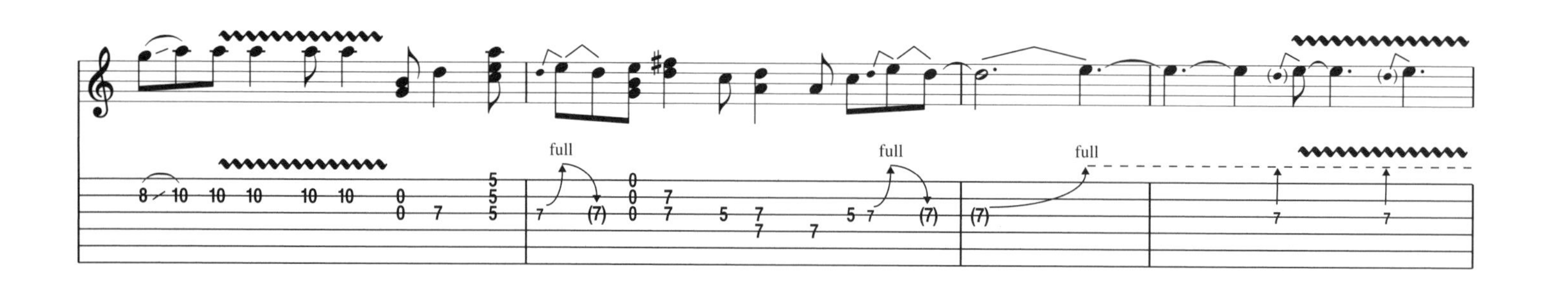
full
full
full
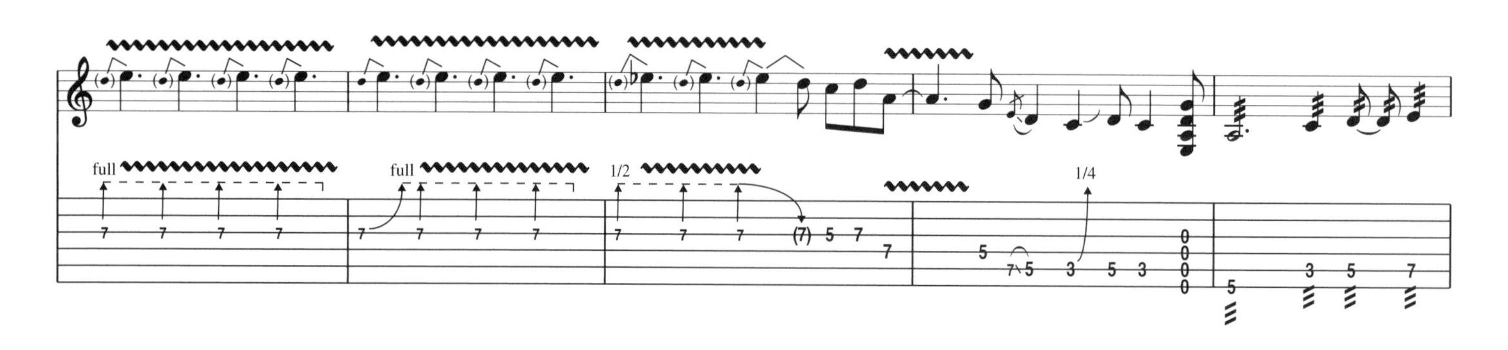
full
full
1/2
1/4

Begin Fade
full
1/2
full

Play 6 Times & Fade Out
8va
rake
let ring

Déjà Voodoo

Words and Music by Kenny Wayne Shepherd, Mark Selby and Tia Sillers

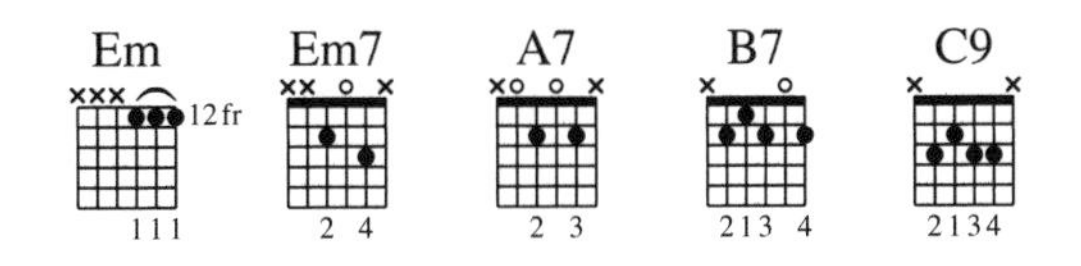

Tune Down 1/2 Step:
① = E♭ ④ = D♭
② = B♭ ⑤ = A♭
③ = G♭ ⑥ = E♭

Intro

Moderately ♩ = 102

N.C.(Em) (A7)

Em

Gtr. 2 (clean)

mp

Gtr. 1 (slight dist.)

8va loco

mf

w/ volume knob

p *mf*

full

* Key signature denotes E Dorian.

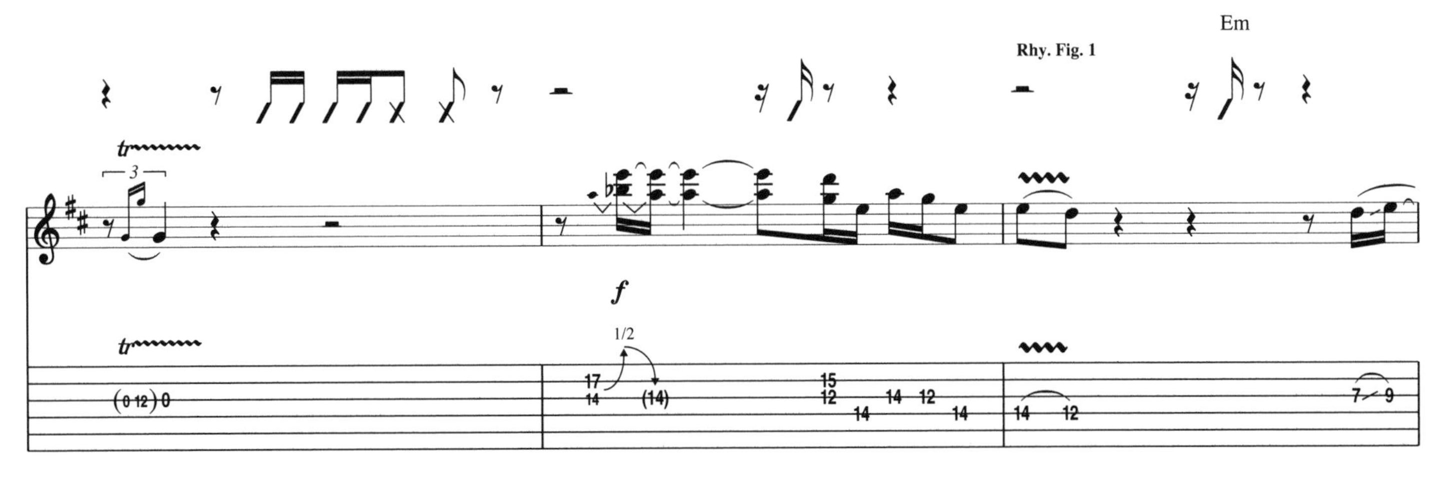

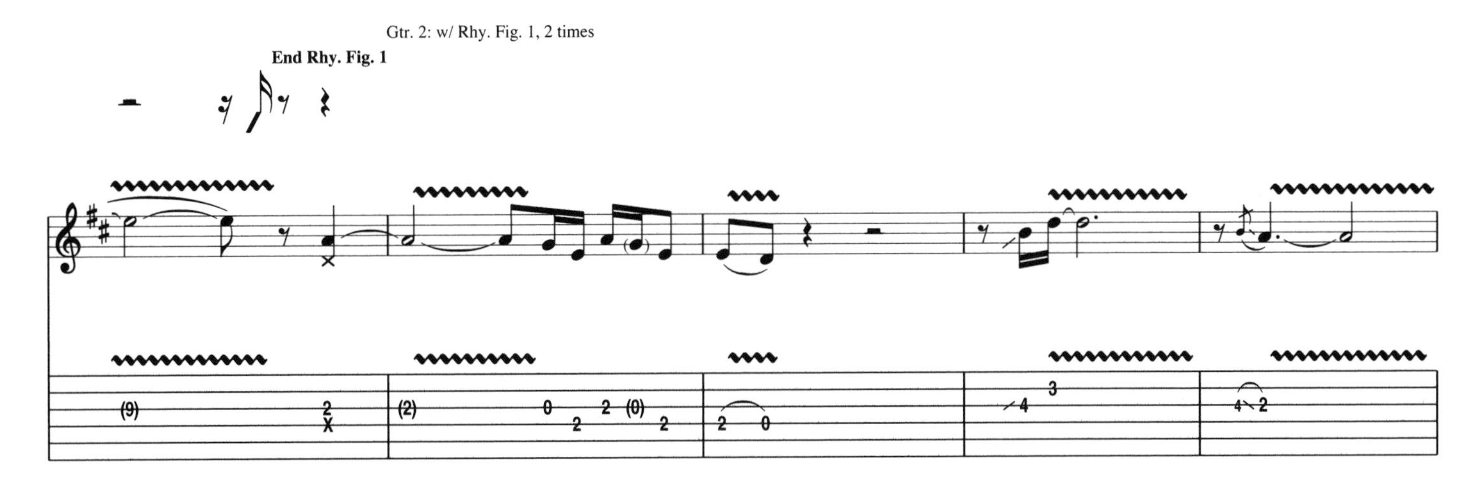

Em
G
12fr
Em
Gtr. 2
Gtr. 1
full
Gtr. 3 (clean)
8va
mp
Harm.
Harm.
Gtr. 2: w/ Rhy. Fig. 1, 9 times, simile
* Em
A7
8va
Em
A7
1/4
8va
Harm.
w/ bar
-1/2
* Chord symbols reflect overall tonality.
Em
loco
A7
Em
Gtr. 3 tacet
A7
Gtr. 1
1/4
let ring
Gtr. 3
loco
Gtr. 4
(clean)
divisi
mp

Gtr. 1
Em
A7
let ring
Gtr. 4
Gtr. 3
divisi

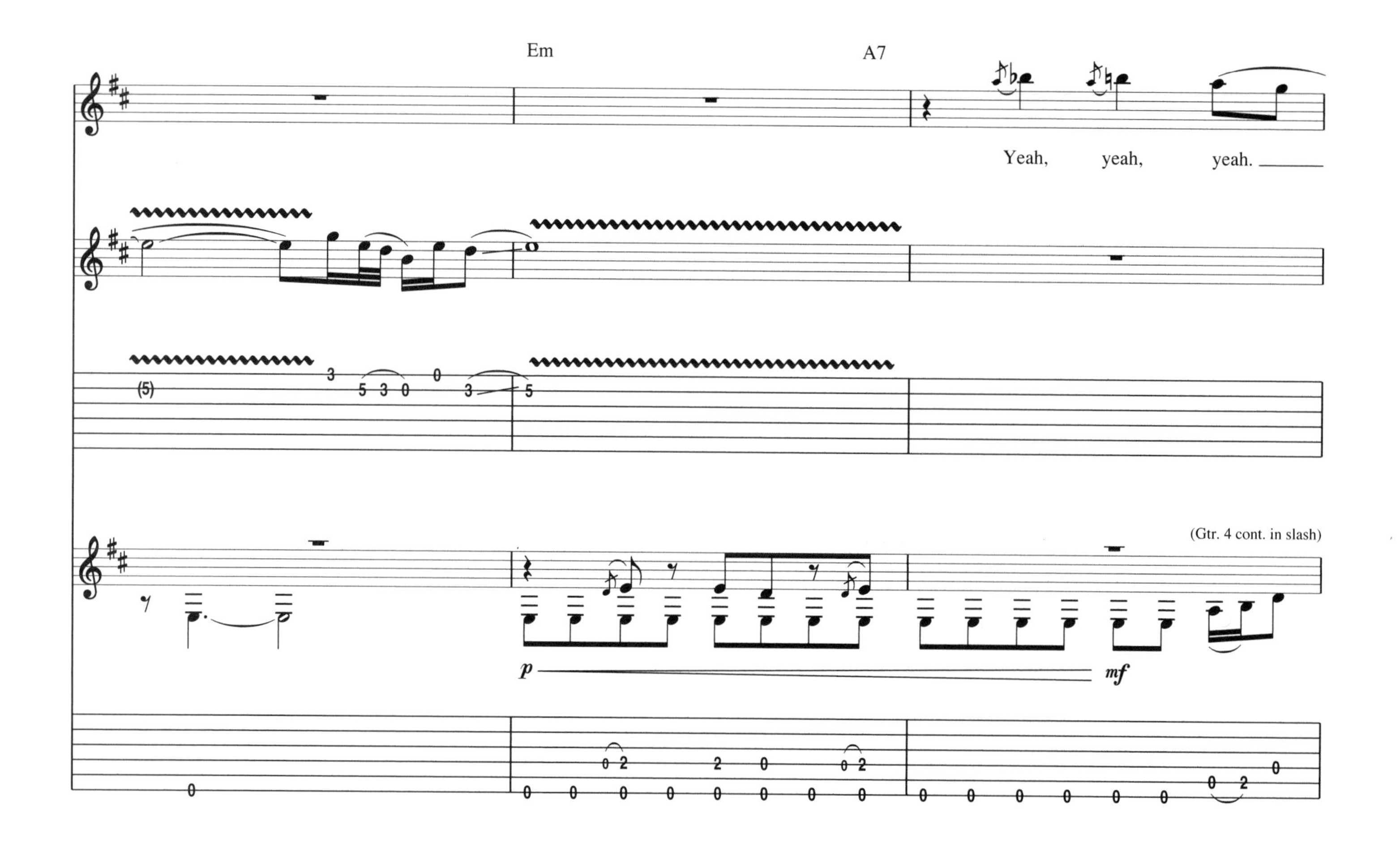
Em
A7
Yeah, yeah, yeah.
(Gtr. 4 cont. in slash)
p
mf

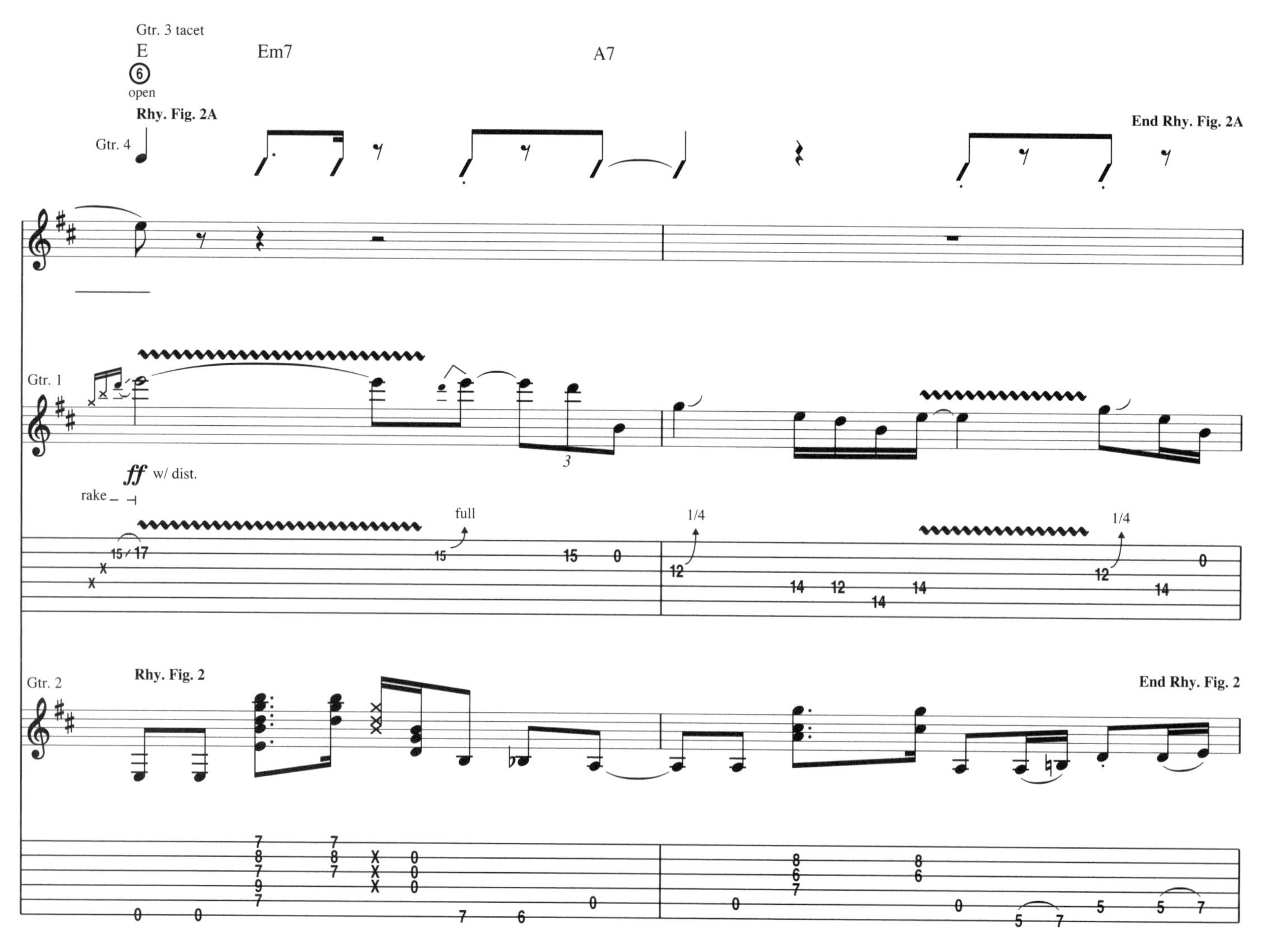
Gtr. 3 tacet
E
6
open
Em7
A7
Rhy. Fig. 2A
Gtr. 4
End Rhy. Fig. 2A
Gtr. 1
ff w/ dist.
rake
full
1/4
1/4
Gtr. 2
Rhy. Fig. 2
End Rhy. Fig. 2

Gtrs. 2 & 4: w/ Rhy. Figs. 2 & 2A, 3 times, simile
Em7
A7
Ha!
Yeah!
Gtr. 1
8va
loco
full
1/4
1/2
1. Need-les in my
Verse
Gtr. 1 tacet 1st time; w/ Fill 2, 2nd time
Gtrs. 2 & 4: w/ Rhy. Figs. 2 & 2A, 5 times
heart,
dark
and
spell on my mind.
swell on my mind.
Your pow - er - ful po - tion
gets me ev - 'ry time.
I toss and turn,
I can't sleep.
Your kiss burns
Fill 2
Gtr. 1
T
A
B

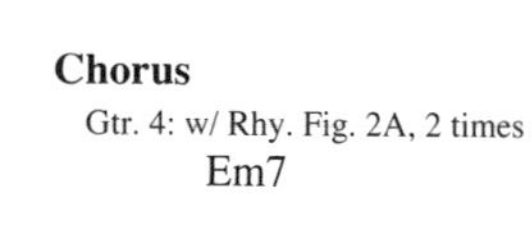
Chorus
Gtr. 4: w/ Rhy. Fig. 2A, 2 times

E
Em7
B7
C9
B7
Em7
A7
open
Rhy. Fig. A
Gtr. 4
End Rhy. Fig. 3A
through my dreams.
Here it comes a - gain.
I don't stand a
Gtr. 1
Rhy. Fig. 3
End Rhy. Fig. 3
Rhy. Fig. 4
* Gtrs. 2 & 5 (slight dist.)
1/4
* composite arrangement
chance.
Soul pos - ses - sion, got me in a trance.
Pull - in' me back, back to you.
To Coda
Interlude
Gtrs. 2 & 4: w/ Rhy. Figs. 2 & 2A, 4 times
Gtr. 5 tacet
Gtr. 3: w/ Fill 1
Dé - jà voo - doo.
Dé - jà voo - doo.
End Rhy. Fig. 4
Fill 1
Gtr. 3
w/ slight dist.
P.S.
TAB

Em7
A7
* Played behind the beat.
Verse
Gtrs. 2 & 4: w/ Rhy. Figs. 2 & 2A, 5 times
2. Fire in the dark, mm, pound-ing on my
brain, mm. Driv-en by the chant, oo call-ing out my
Gtr. 1 tacet
name, yeah. I toss and turn, I can't sleep. Your kiss burns

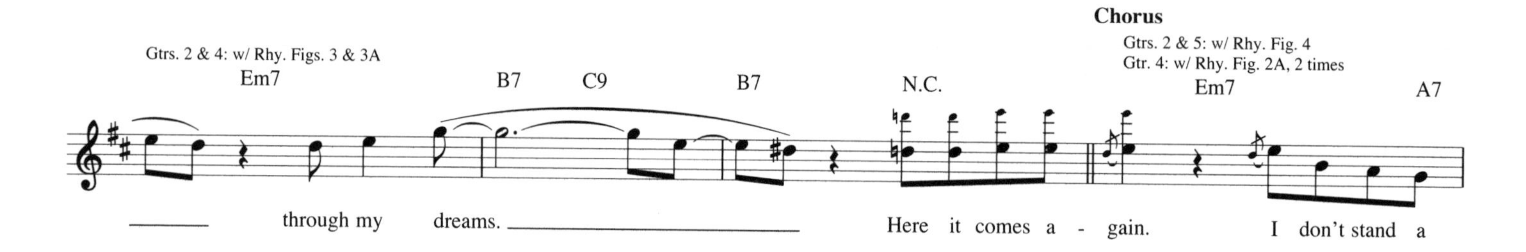
Chorus
Gtrs. 2 & 4: w/ Rhy. Figs. 3 & 3A
Gtrs. 2 & 5: w/ Rhy. Fig. 4
Gtr. 4: w/ Rhy. Fig. 2A, 2 times
Em7
B7
C9
B7
N.C.
Em7
A7
through my dreams.
Here it comes a - gain.
I don't stand a

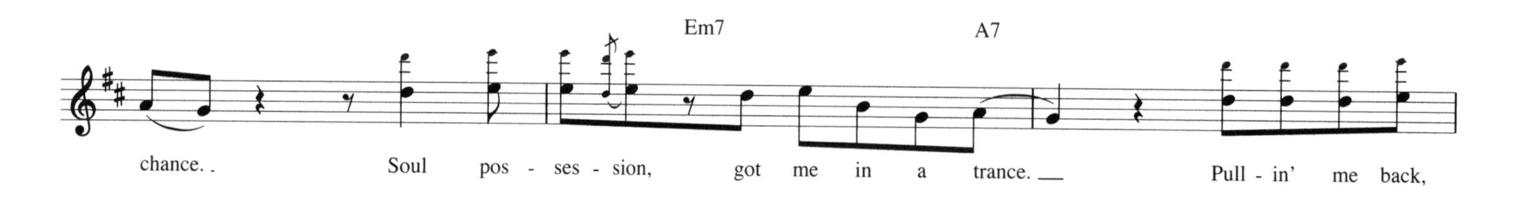
Em7
A7
chance.
Soul pos - ses - sion,
got me in a trance.
Pull - in' me back,

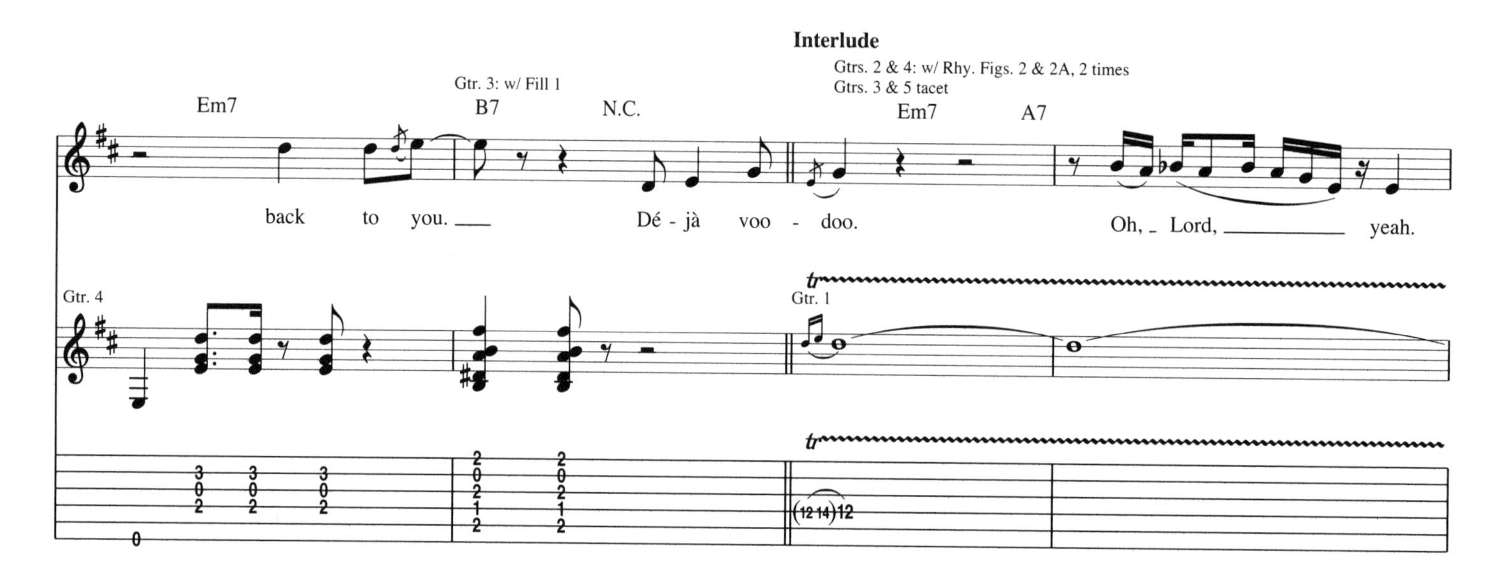
Interlude
Gtr. 3: w/ Fill 1
Gtrs. 2 & 4: w/ Rhy. Figs. 2 & 2A, 2 times
Gtrs. 3 & 5 tacet
Em7
B7
N.C.
Em7
A7
back to you.
Dé - jà voo - doo.
Oh, Lord, yeah.
Gtr. 4
Gtr. 1
tr

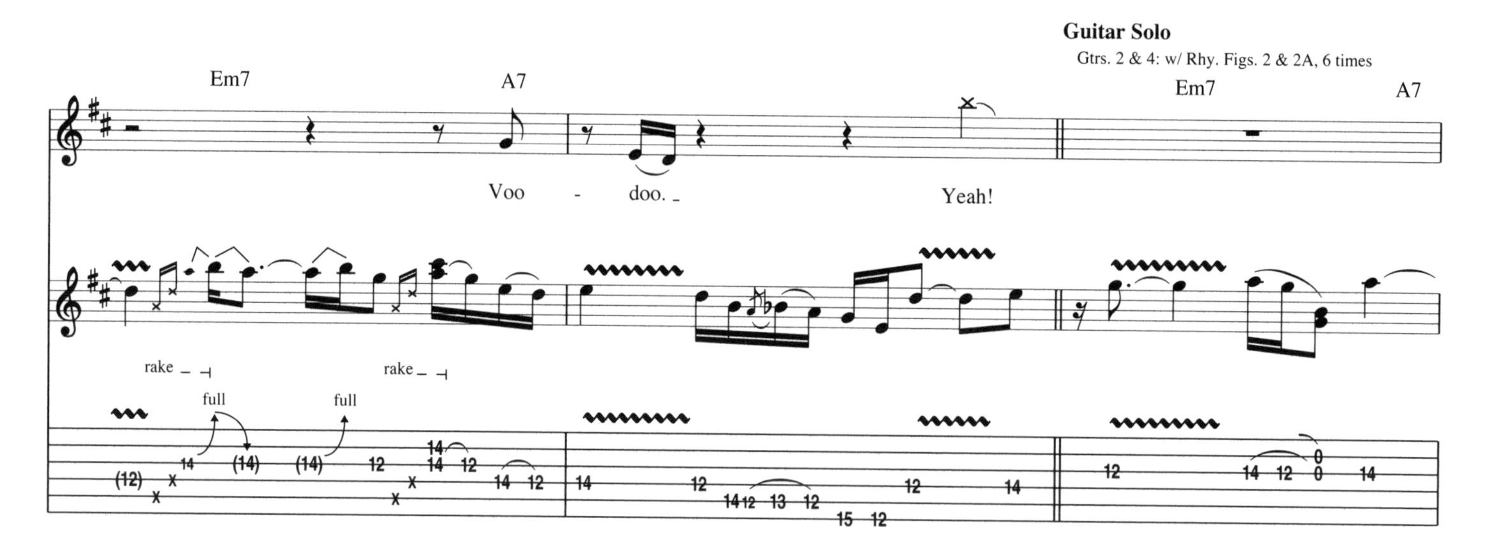
Guitar Solo
Gtrs. 2 & 4: w/ Rhy. Figs. 2 & 2A, 6 times
Em7
A7
Em7
A7
Voo - doo.
Yeah!
rake
full

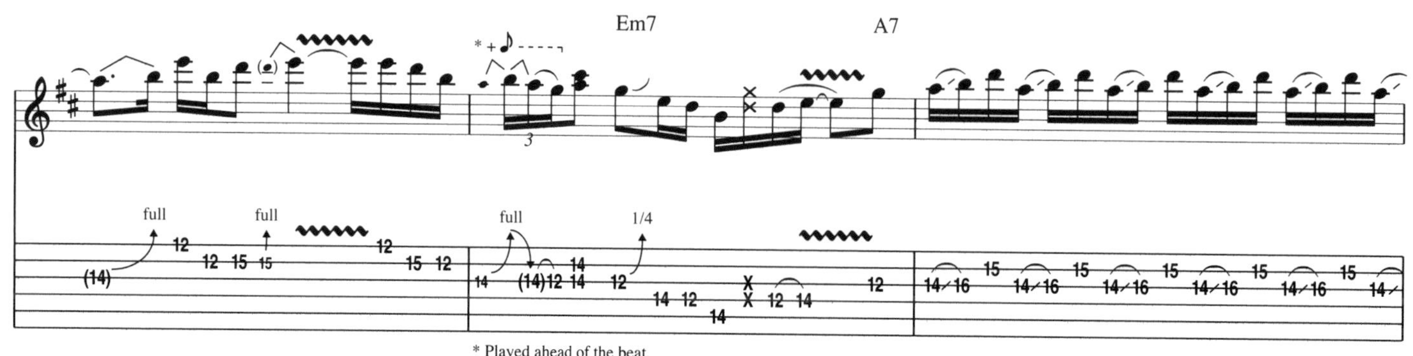
Em7
A7
full
1/4
* Played ahead of the beat.

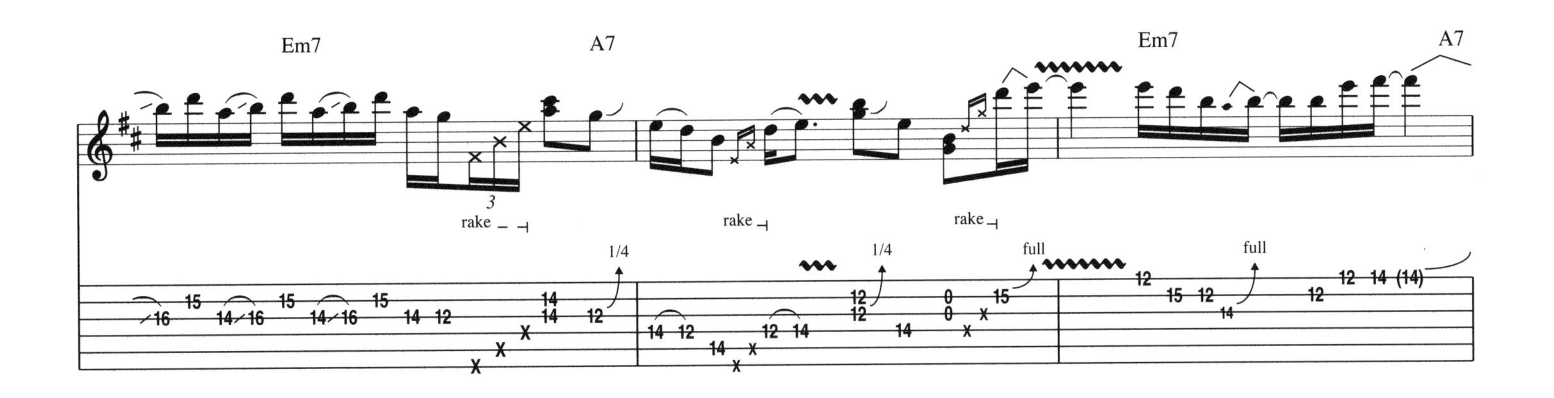
Em7
A7
Em7
A7
rake
rake
rake
1/4
1/4
full
full

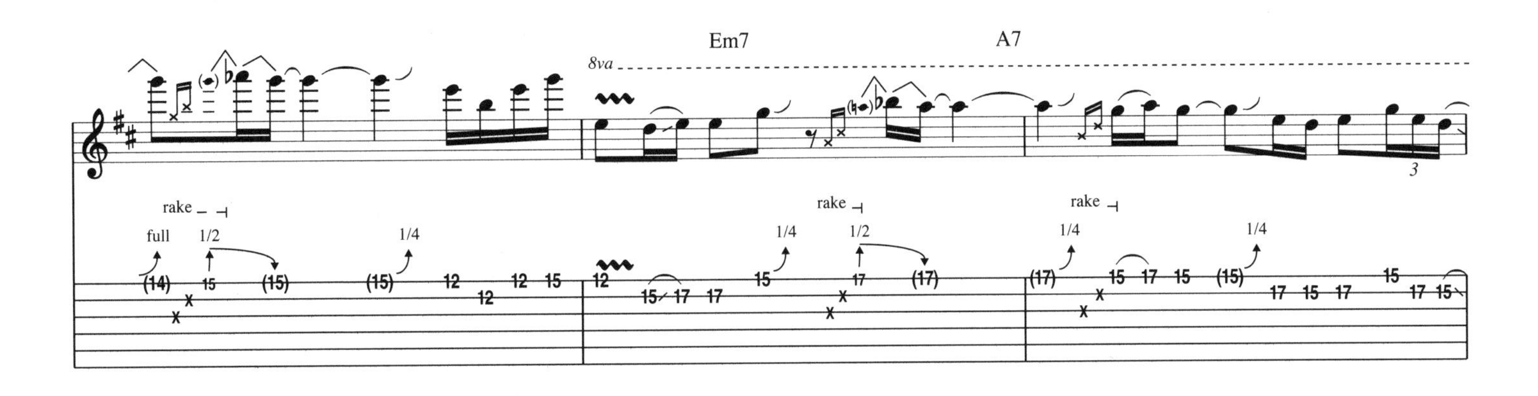
8va
Em7
A7
rake
rake
rake
full
1/2
1/4
1/4
1/2
1/4
1/4

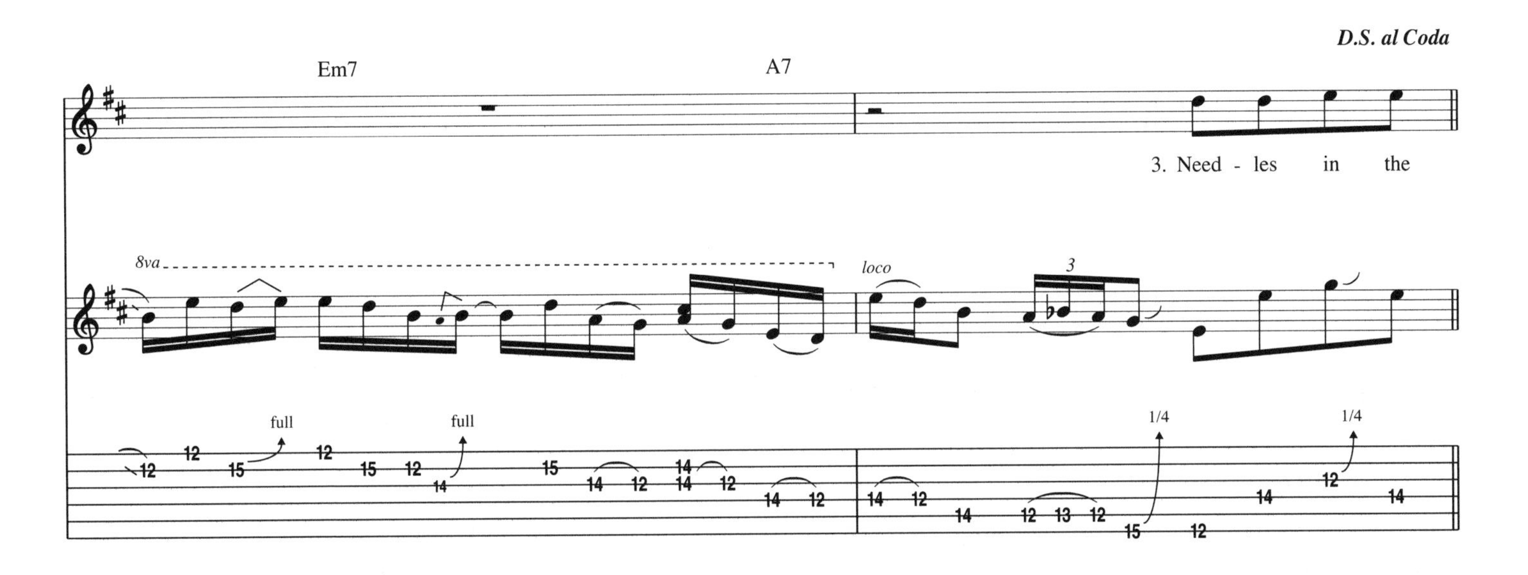
D.S. al Coda
Em7
A7
3. Need - les in the
8va
loco
full
full
1/4
1/4

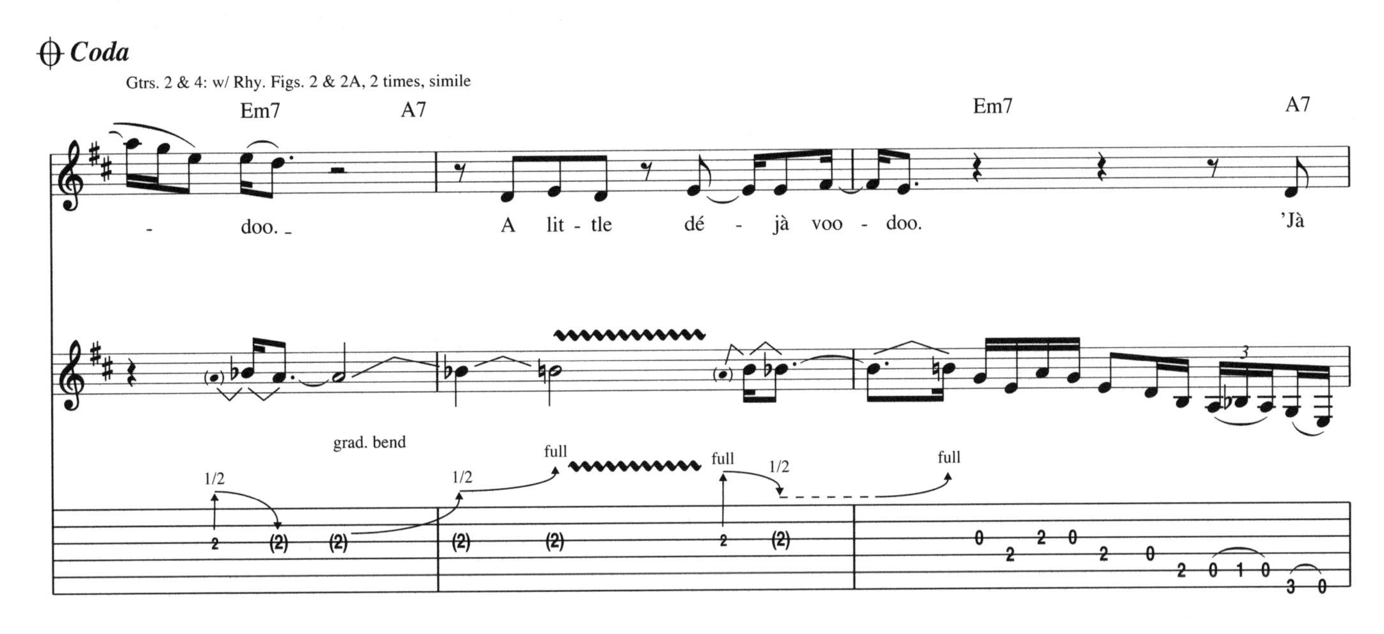
Coda
Gtrs. 2 & 4: w/ Rhy. Figs. 2 & 2A, 2 times, simile
Em7
A7
Em7
A7
- doo. A lit - tle dé - jà voo - doo. 'Jà
grad. bend
1/2
1/2
full
full
1/2
full

Guitar Solo

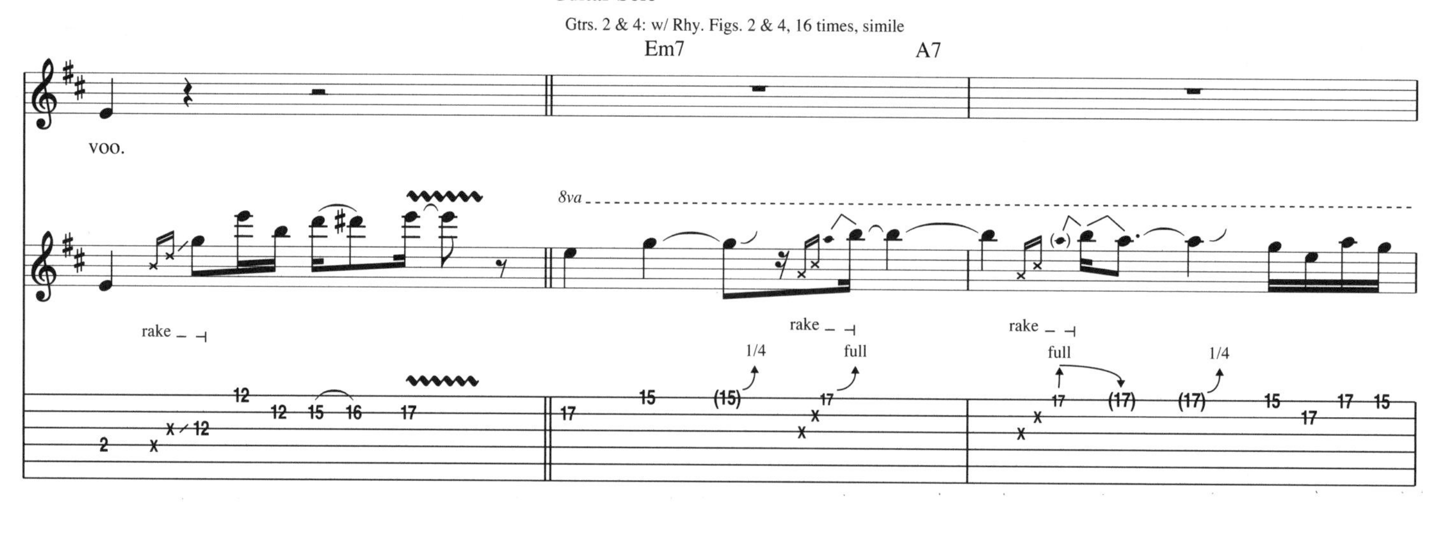
Gtrs. 2 & 4: w/ Rhy. Figs. 2 & 4, 16 times, simile
Em7
A7
voo.
8va
rake
1/4
full

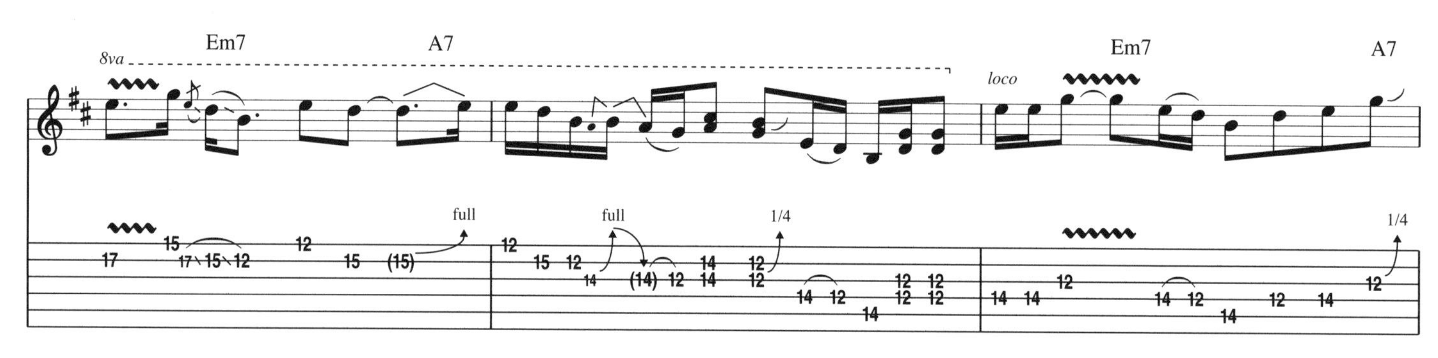
Em7
A7
8va
loco
full
1/4

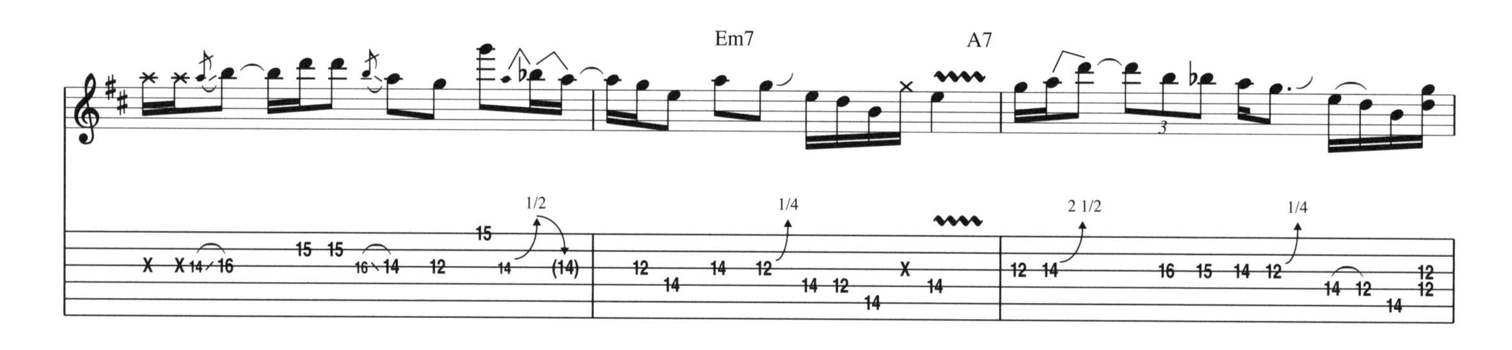
Em7
A7
1/2
1/4
2 1/2

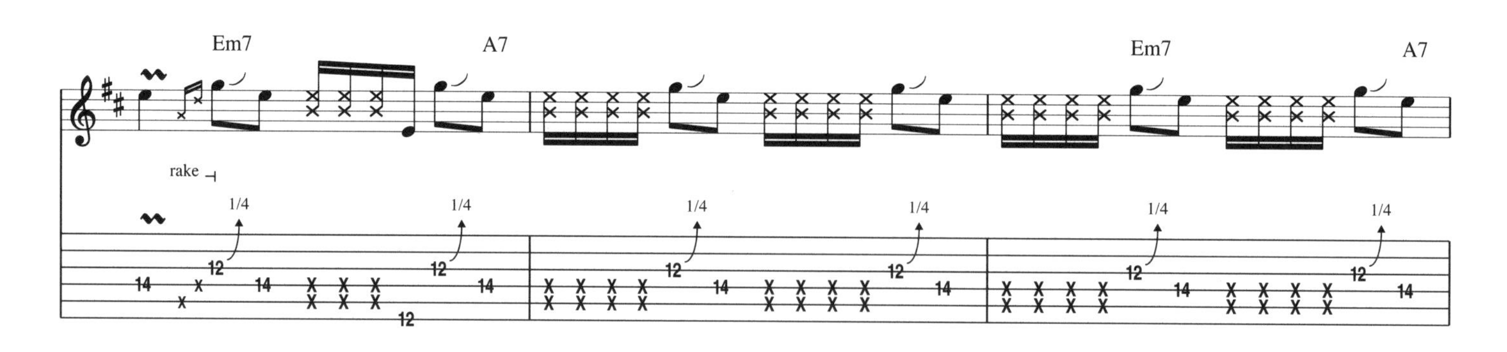
Em7
A7
rake
1/4

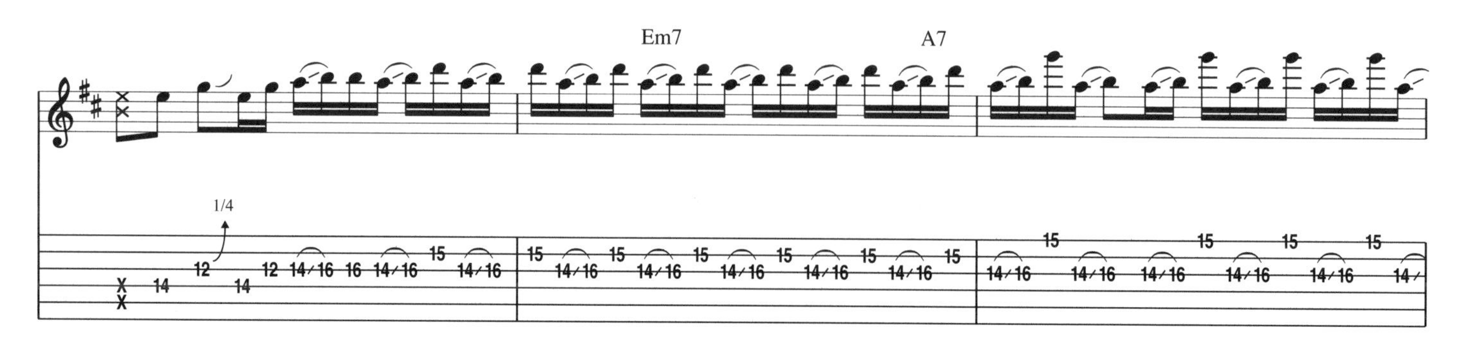
Em7
A7
1/4

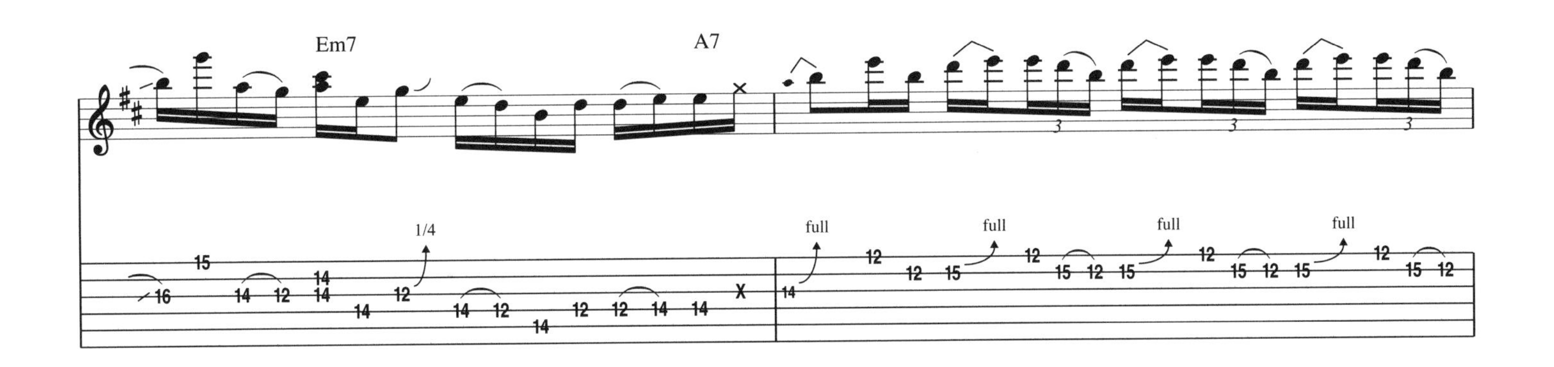
Em7
A7
full
1/4

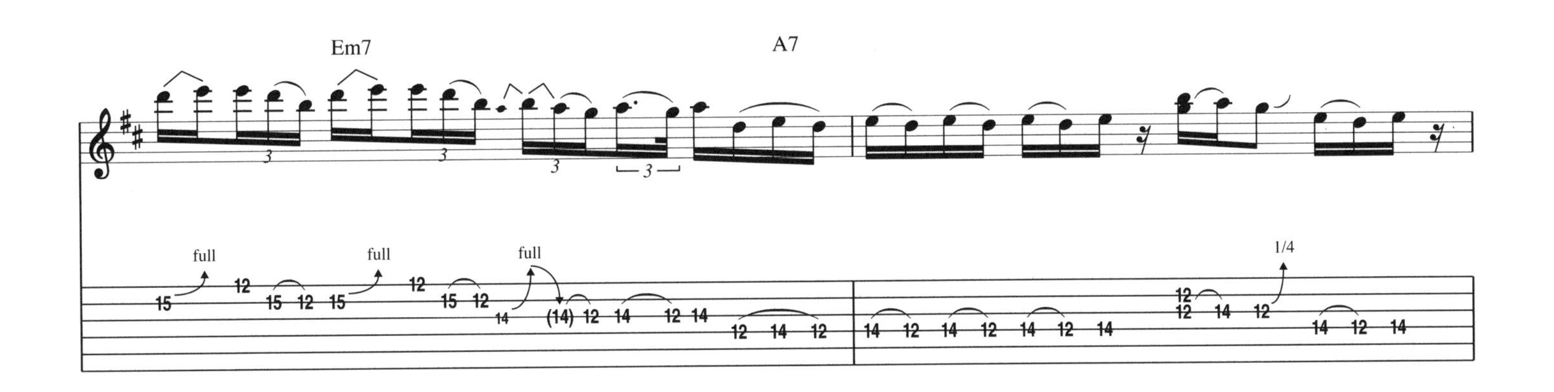
Em7
A7
full
1/4

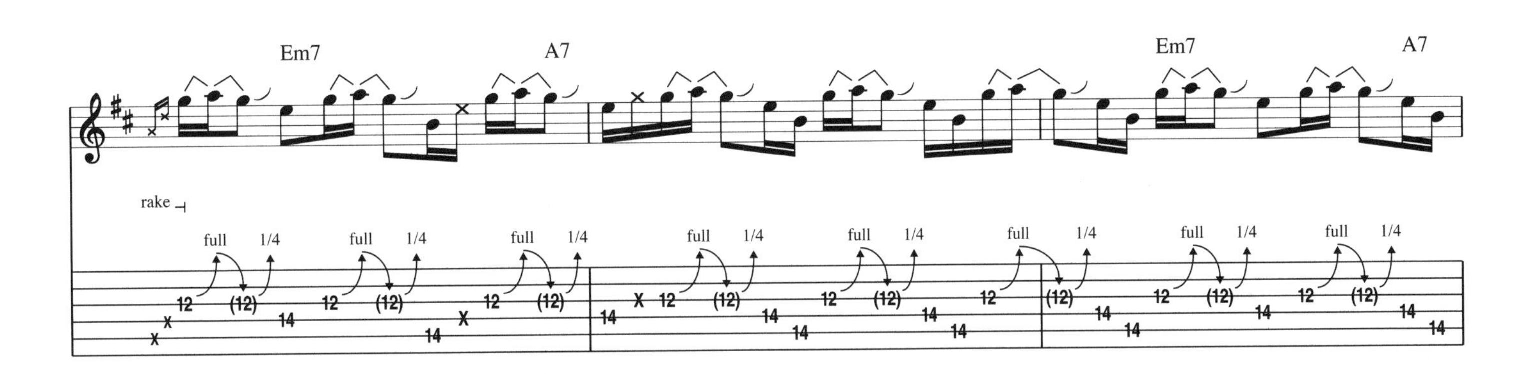
Em7
A7
Em7
A7
rake
full
1/4

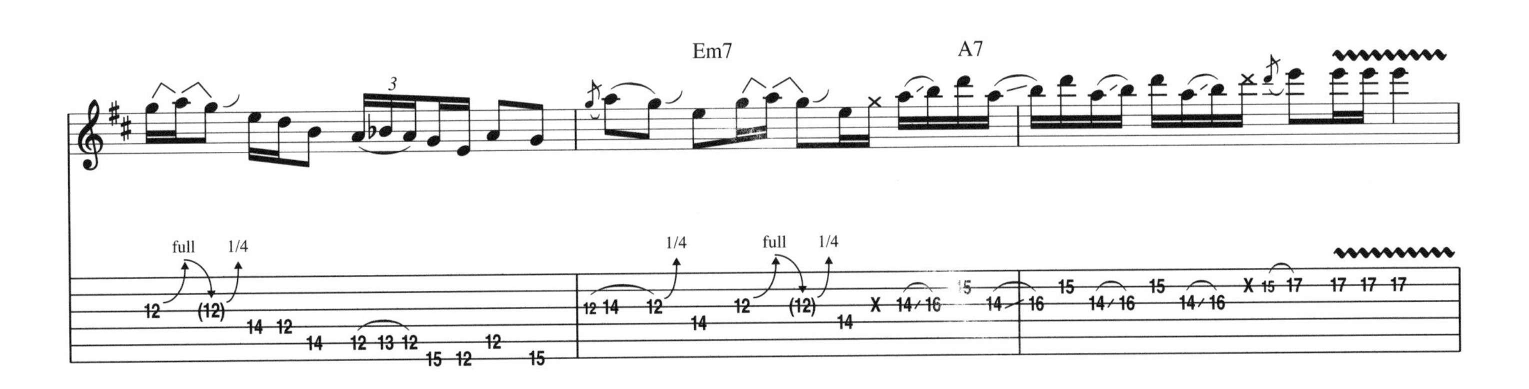
Em7
A7
full
1/4

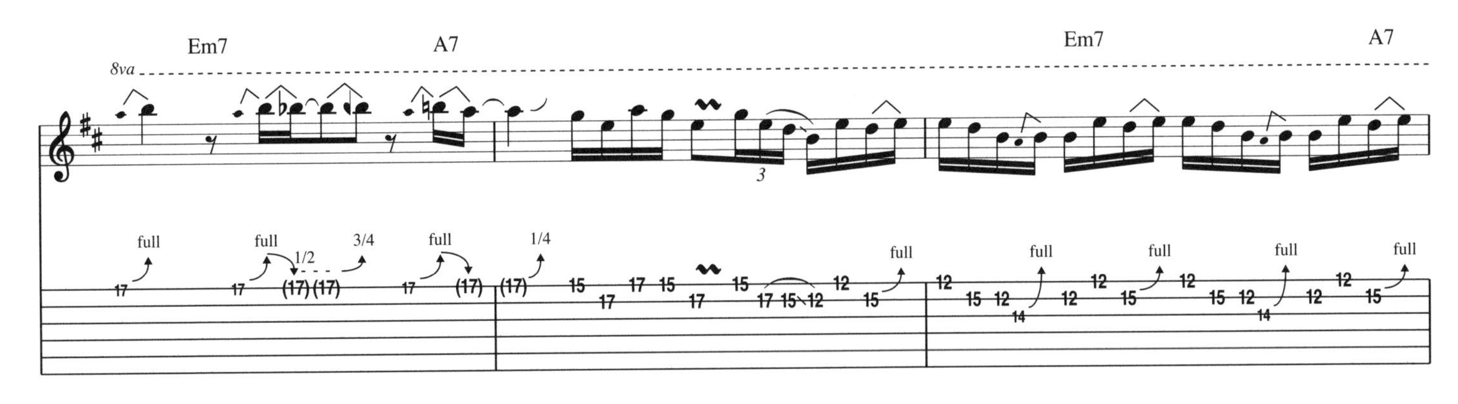
8va
Em7
A7
Em7
A7
full
1/2
3/4
1/4

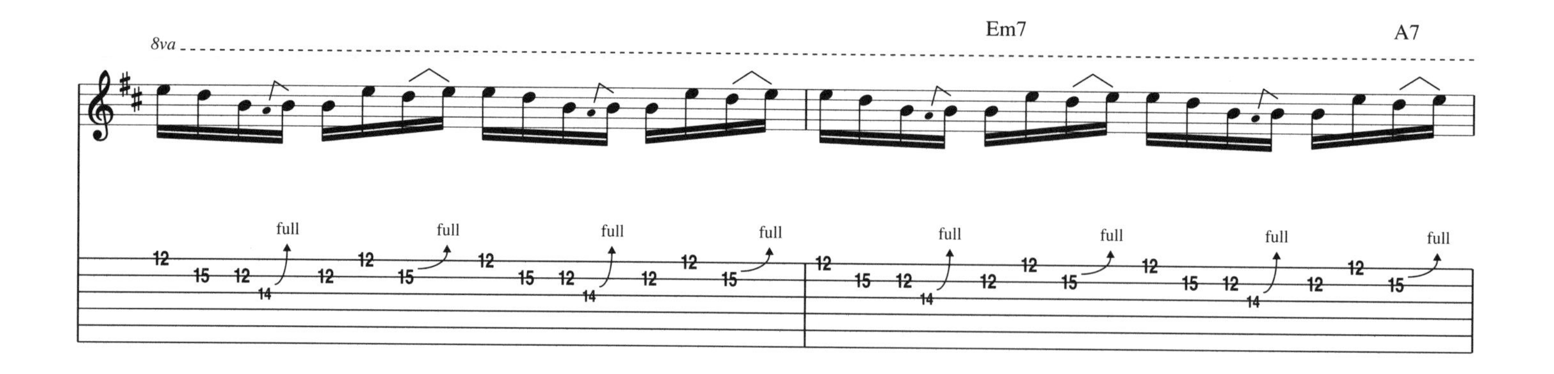
8va
Em7
A7
full

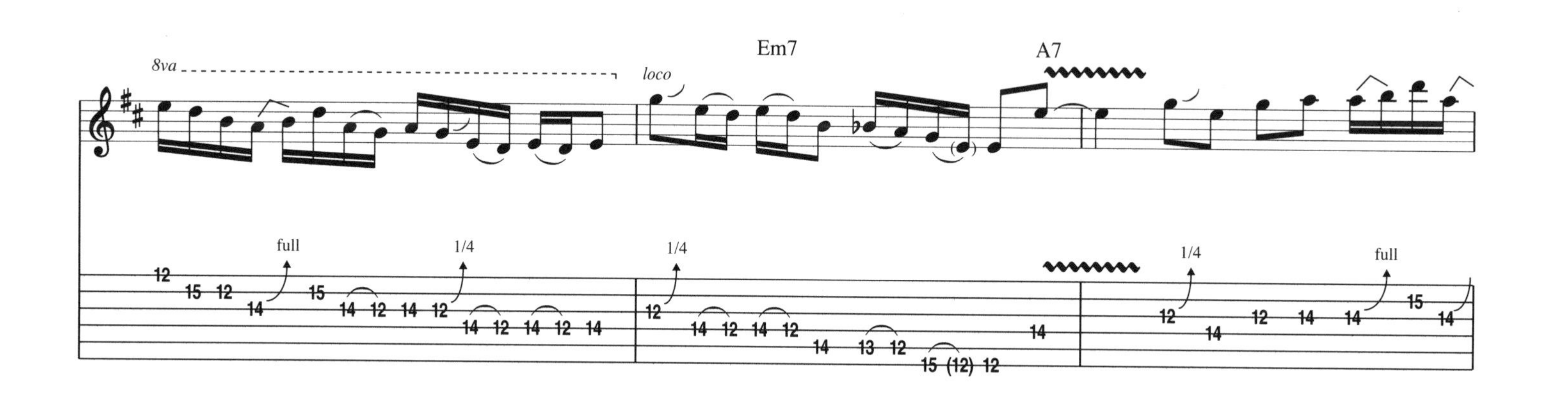
8va
loco
Em7
A7
full
1/4

Em7
A7
Gtr. 1
mp
full
Gtr. 2
Gtr. 4
let ring

Aberdeen Mississippi Blues

Words and Music by Booker T. White

Bb5
o - ver in Ab - er - deen on my
deen's my home, but they
way to New Or - leans.
just don't want me a - round.
Ab5
w/ slide
F Fsus4 F Fsus4 F Fsus4 F Fsus4 F N.C.
Well, them Ab - er-deen wom-en told me they would
Yeah, you know I'm gon-na take 'em with me, gon - na
w/o slide
w/ slide
F Fsus4 F Fsus4 F Fsus4 F Fsus4 F
give me my gas - o - line.
take them out this town.
2. Ab - er -
Yeah.
End Rhy. Fig. 1
w/o slide
Guitar Solo
Bb Ab F Fsus4 F Fsus4 F Ab5 F5 F
8va
loco
w/ slide
w/o slide
w/ slide

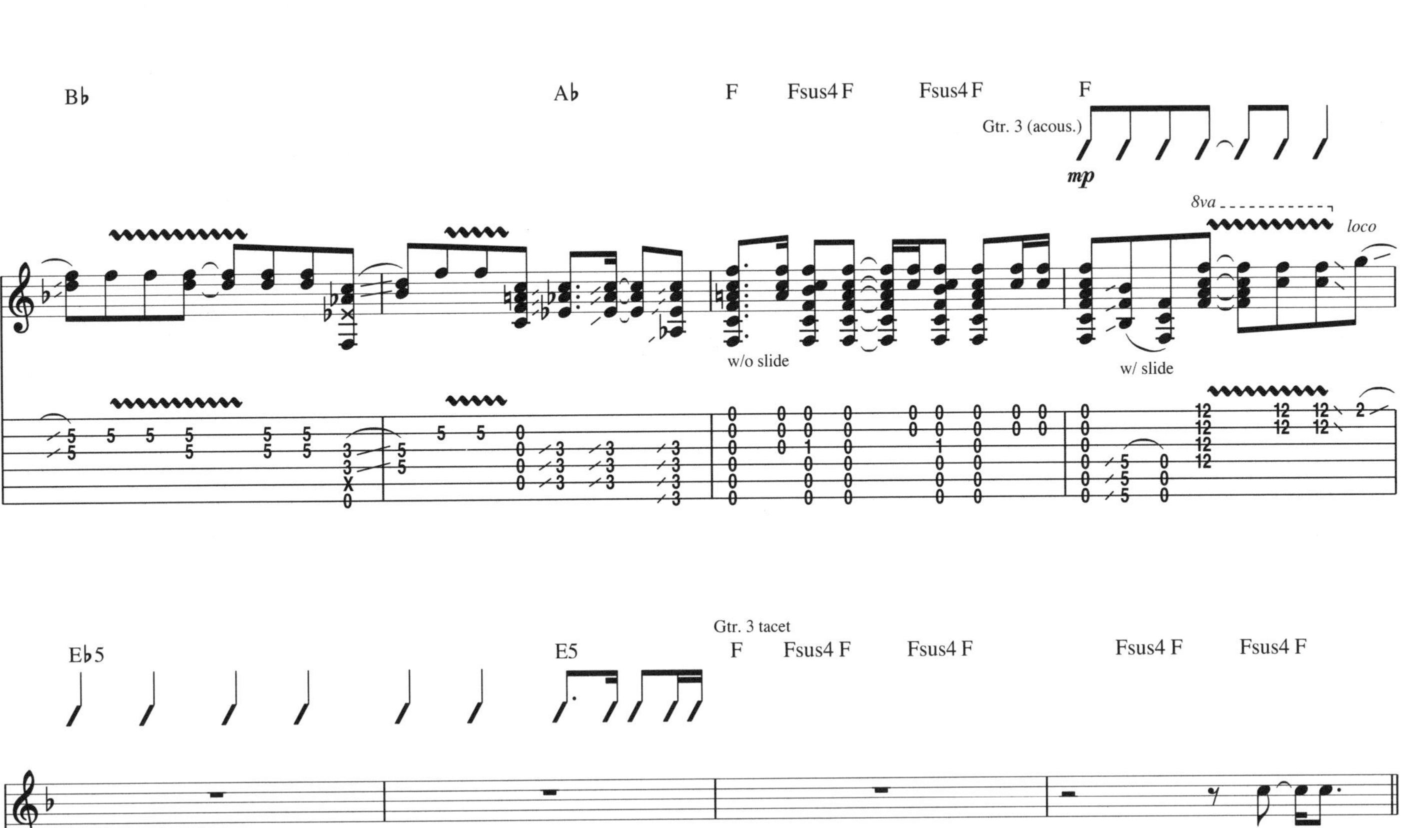
B♭
A♭
F Fsus4 F Fsus4 F
F
Gtr. 3 (acous.)
mp
8va
loco
w/o slide
w/ slide

E♭5
E5
Gtr. 3 tacet
F Fsus4 F Fsus4 F
Fsus4 F Fsus4 F
3. Well, just
w/o slide

Verse
Gtrs. 1 & 2: w/ Rhy. Fig. 1
B♭5
A♭5
F Fsus4 F Fsus4 F
look o - ver yon - der, com - ing down the road.

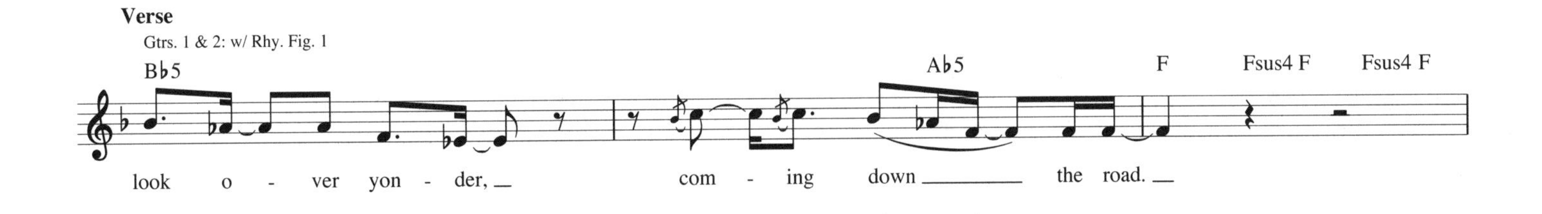
Fsus4 F Fsus4 F
B♭5
A♭5
Yeah, just look o - ver yon - der, com - ing down the road.

F Fsus4 F Fsus4 F
Fsus4 F Fsus4 F
N.C.
That must be my ba - by com - ing, tell me she don't want me no more.

Gtr. 2 tacet
F Fsus4 F Fsus4 F Fsus4 F Fsus4 F
Verse
Bb5
4. Well, there's too man - y wom - en
stand - in 'round cry - in' with my
* Gtrs. 1 & 4 (elec.)**
Rhy. Fig. 2
f w/ slide
let ring throughout
w/ slide
simile on repeat
* composite arrangement
** w/ dist.
Ab5 F Bb5 F5 F
I ain't nev - er seen. Well, there's
heart right in my hand. Mm, well I was
8va
Bb5 Ab5 F
too man-y wom - en, yeah, I ain't nev-er seen.
stand - in' 'round cry - in' with my heart right in my hand.
loco
Bb5 F5 F Eb5 E5
Well, I bring too man - y wom - en back from New - Or - leans.
I was look - in' for that wom - an, one ain't got no man.
8va
loco

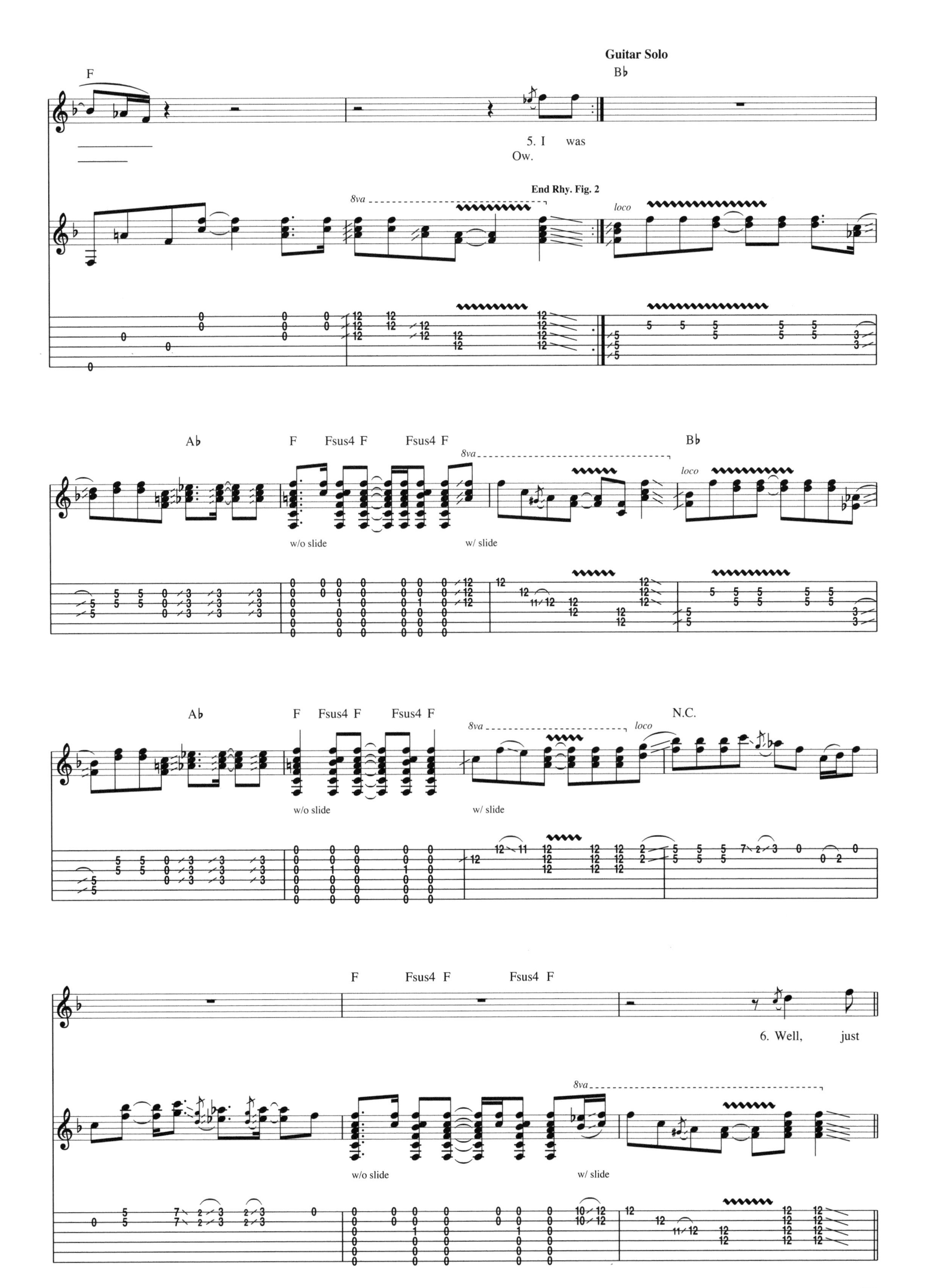
Guitar Solo
F
B♭
5. I was
Ow.
End Rhy. Fig. 2
8va
loco
A♭
F Fsus4 F Fsus4 F
w/o slide
w/ slide
N.C.
6. Well, just

Verse
Gtrs. 1 & 4: w/ Rhy. Fig. 2, 1st 10 meas., simile
Bb5
Ab5
F
Bb5 F5 F
look o - ver yon - der,
where we used to live.
Well, just
Bb5
Ab5
F
look o - ver yon - der,
where we used to live.
Bb5 F5 F
Eb5
E5
Don't you know it's kill-ing me, ba-by, how we
can't live there no more.
F Fsus4 F Fsus4 F
Bb5 F
Guitar Solo
Bb
Ab
Ow.
8va
Gtr. 2
Gtr. 4
w/ slide
Gtr. 4
Gtr. 1
w/ slide
F
Bb5 F5 F
Bb5
8va
loco

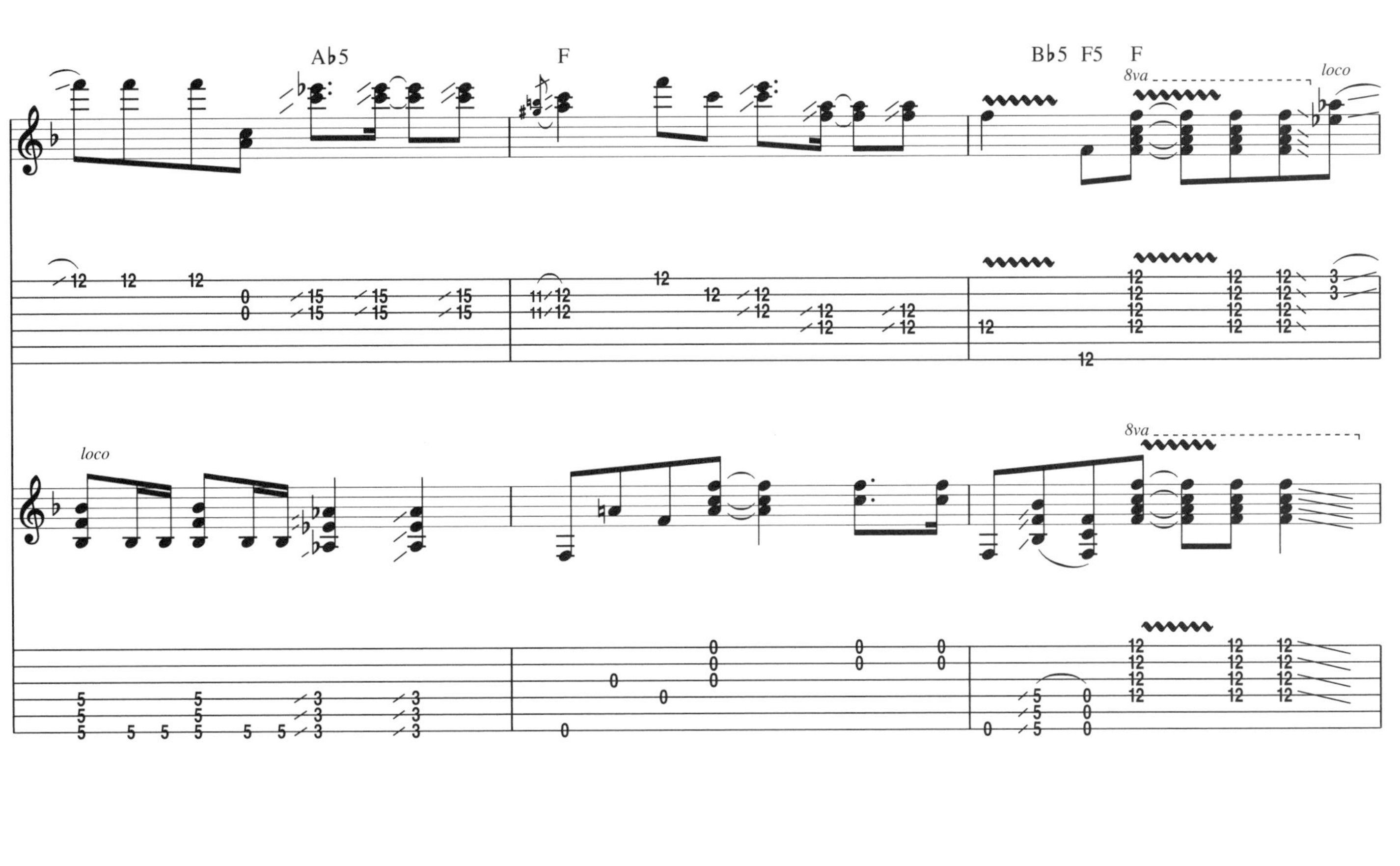
Ab5
F
Bb5 F5 F
8va
loco
8va
loco

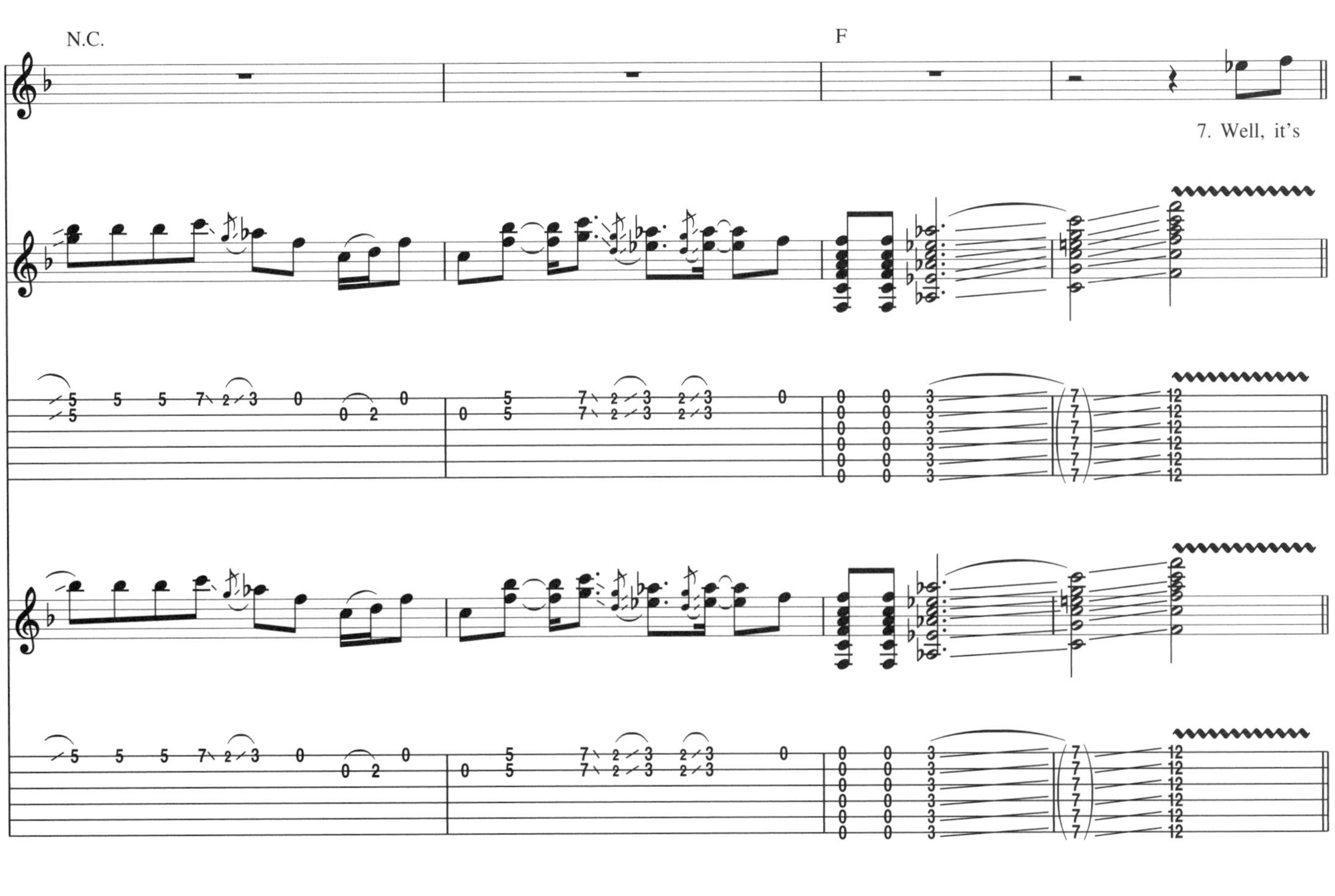
N.C.
F
7. Well, it's

Verse

Gtrs. 1 & 4: w/ Rhy. Fig. 2, 1st 4 meas.
Bb5
Ab5
F
Bb5 F5 F
good-bye, ba-by, if I'm nev-er gon-na see you no more.
Yeah, it's

B♭5
A♭5
rit.
Free Time
F
good - bye, ba - by.
Nev-er gon - na see you no more.
Gtrs. 1 & 4
rit.

Outro
Moderately Slow ♩ = 83
N.C.
I'm gon - na tell ev - 'ry - bod - y you've been still knock - in' at my door.
Gtr. 1
mp
Gtr. 4
mp

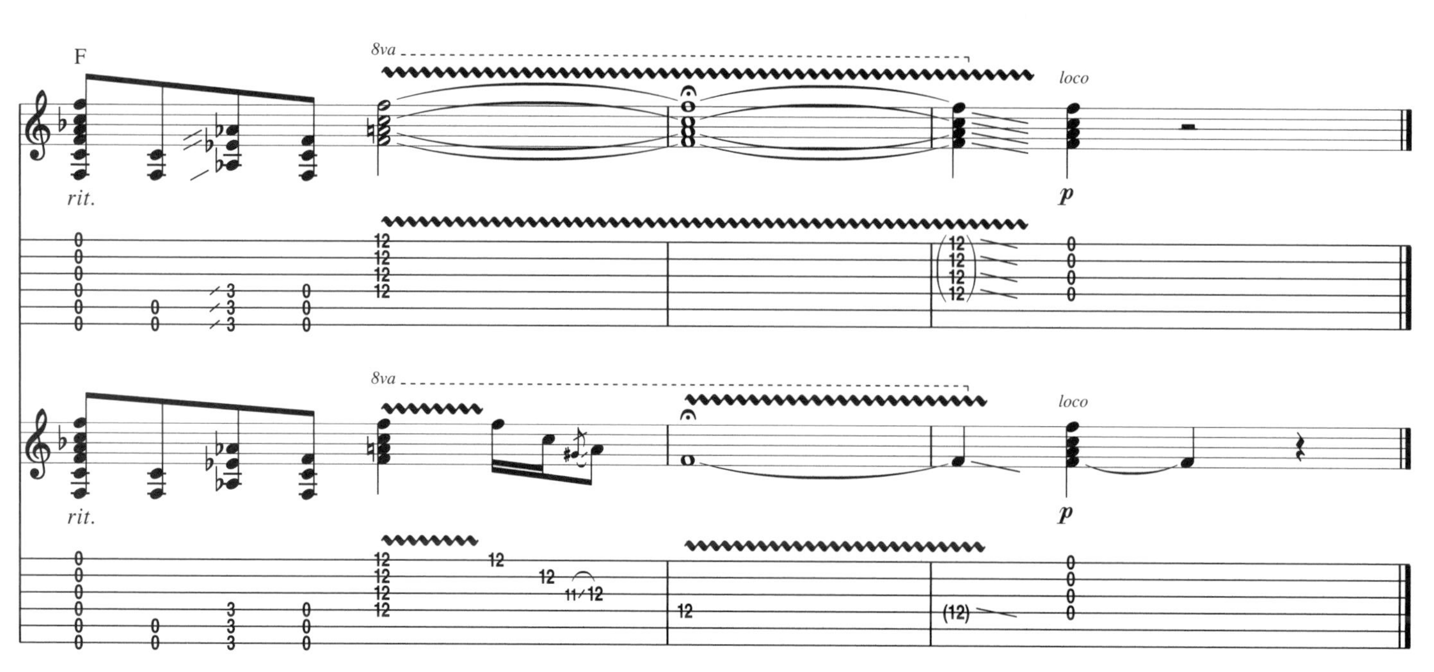
F
rit.
8va
loco
p
rit.
8va
loco
p

Shame, Shame, Shame

Words and Music by Kenny Wayne Shepherd and Joe Nadeau

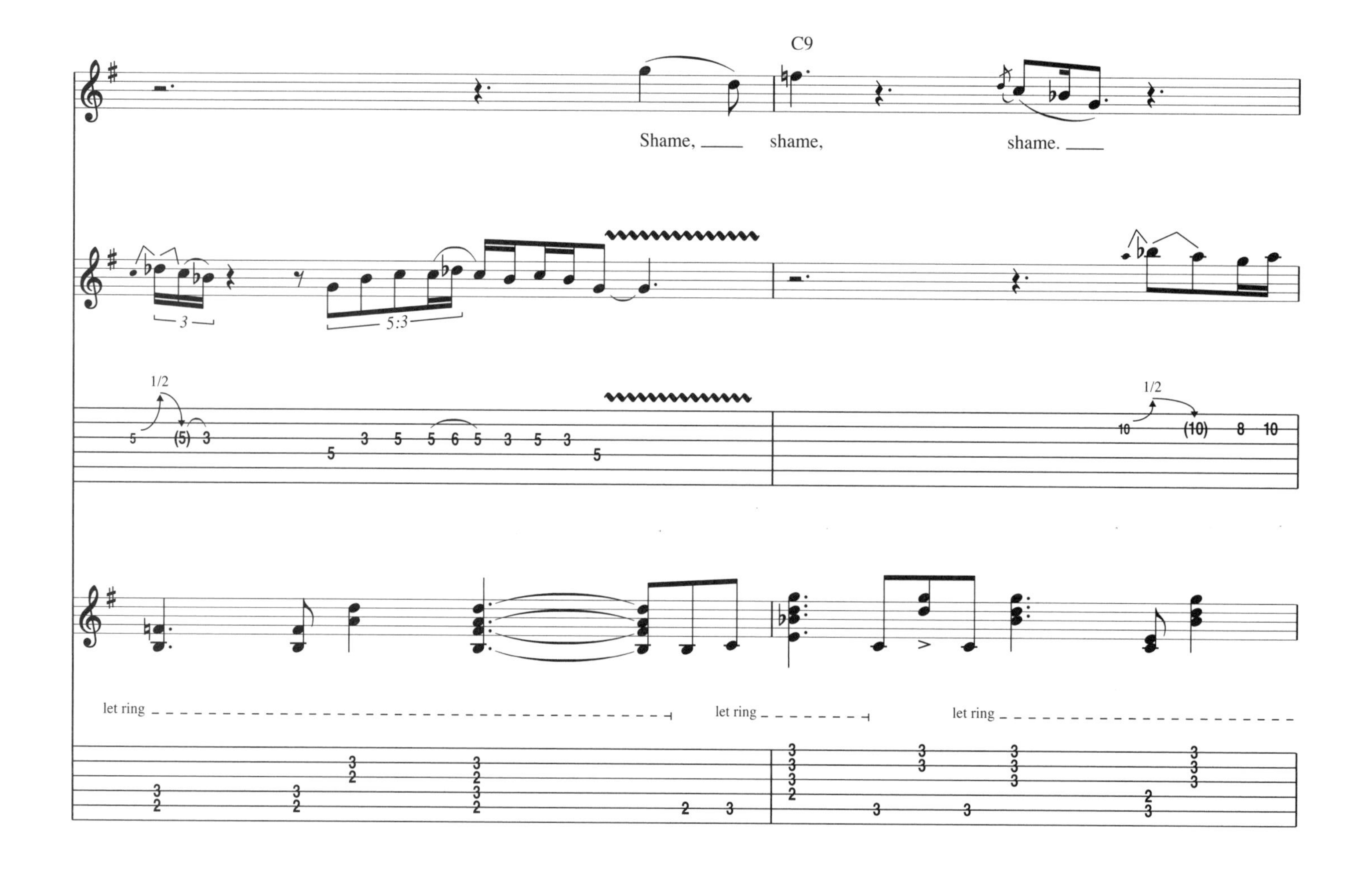
C9
Shame, shame, shame.
1/2
1/2
let ring
let ring
let ring

G9
Ha, shame on me for ev-er lov - in' you, babe.
let ring
let ring

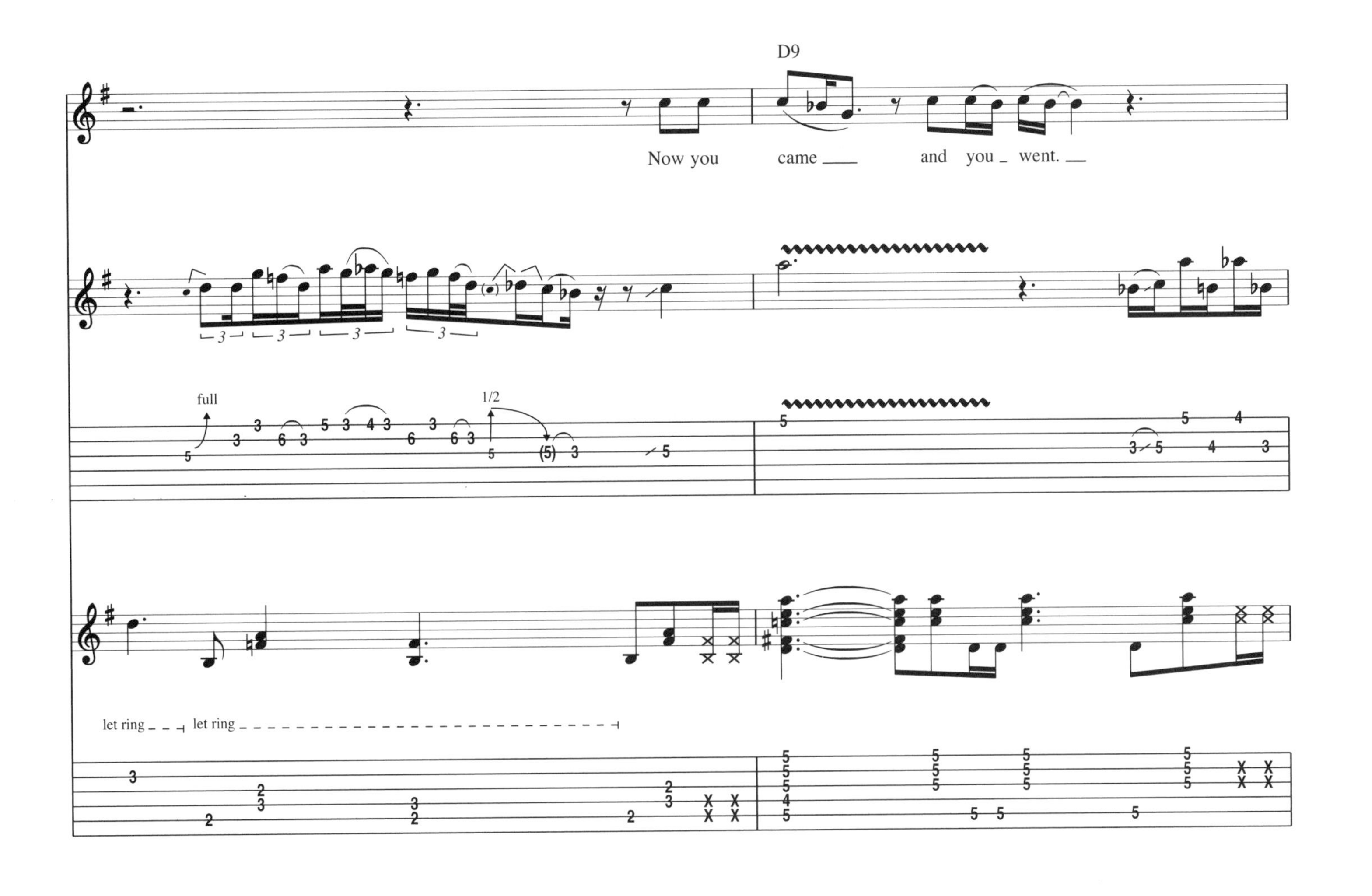
D9
Now you came and you went.
full
1/2
let ring
let ring

C9
G9
C9
G9
D9
What's this poor boy to do?
Oo, yeah.
2. Lord,
1/2
1/4
let ring
End Rhy. Fig. 1
let ring

Verse
Gtr. 2: w/ Rhy. Fig. 1, simile
G9
C9
Lord I tried,
but you took, you took ev - 'ry-thing that I
Gtr. 1
owned,
which was-n't much.
And Lord,
Lord I tried,
done took ev - 'ry-thing that
* Sung behind the beat.
G9
D9
I owned.
Oh, hey now lit-tle girl, I won-der,

C9
G9
D9
was your love to me on loan?
Least I think it was.
Piano Solo
Gtr. 2: w/ Rhy. Fig. 1, simile
Gtr. 3 (dist.)
Gtr. 1

Guitar Solo

Gtr. 1 tacet
Gtr. 2: w/ Rhy. Fig. 1, 3 times, simile

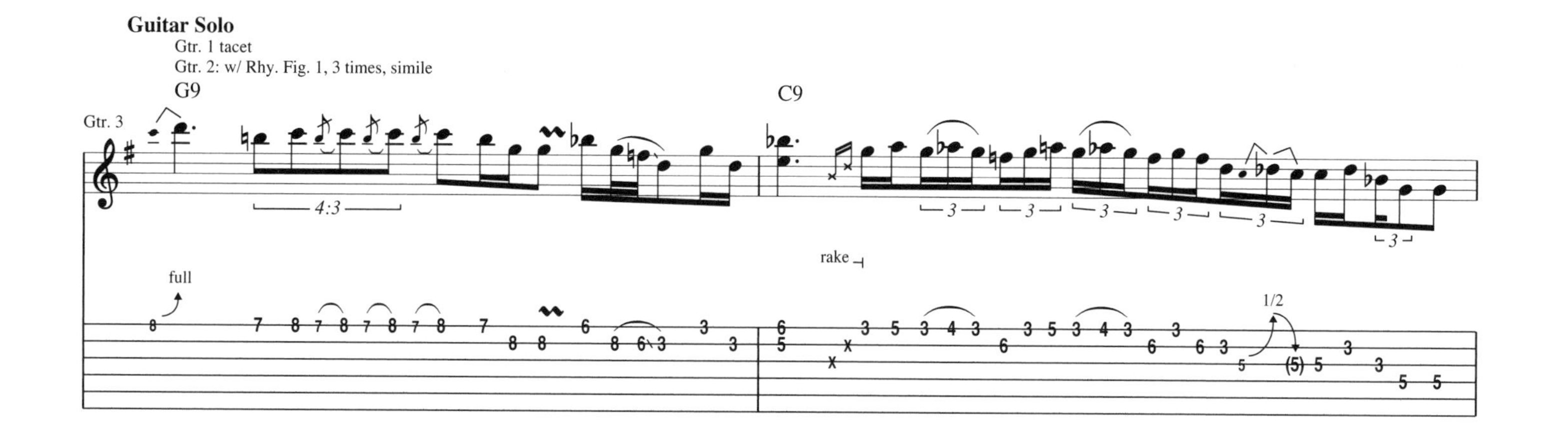

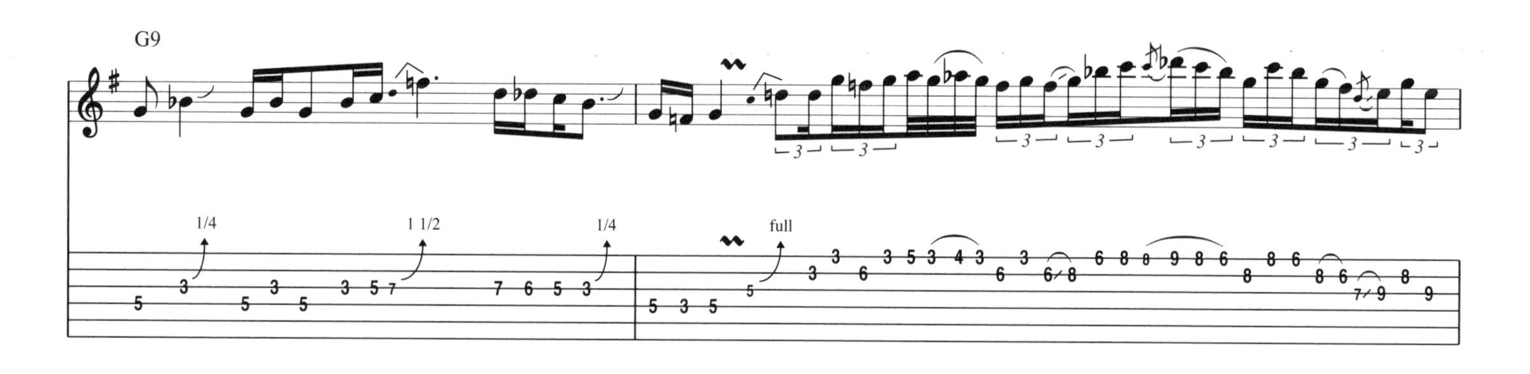

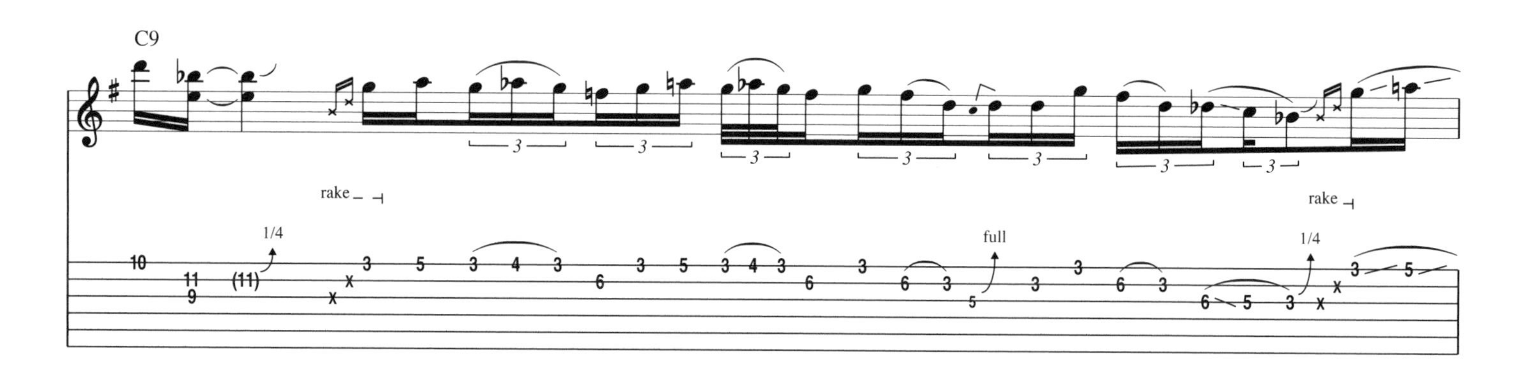

D9
4:3
4:3
1/2
full

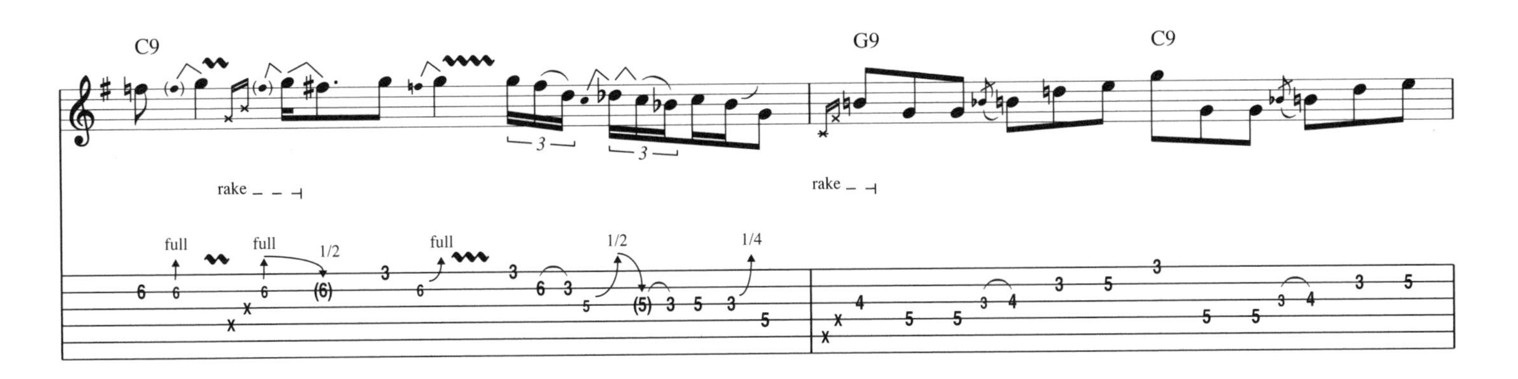
C9
G9
C9
rake
rake
full
full
1/2
full
1/2
1/4

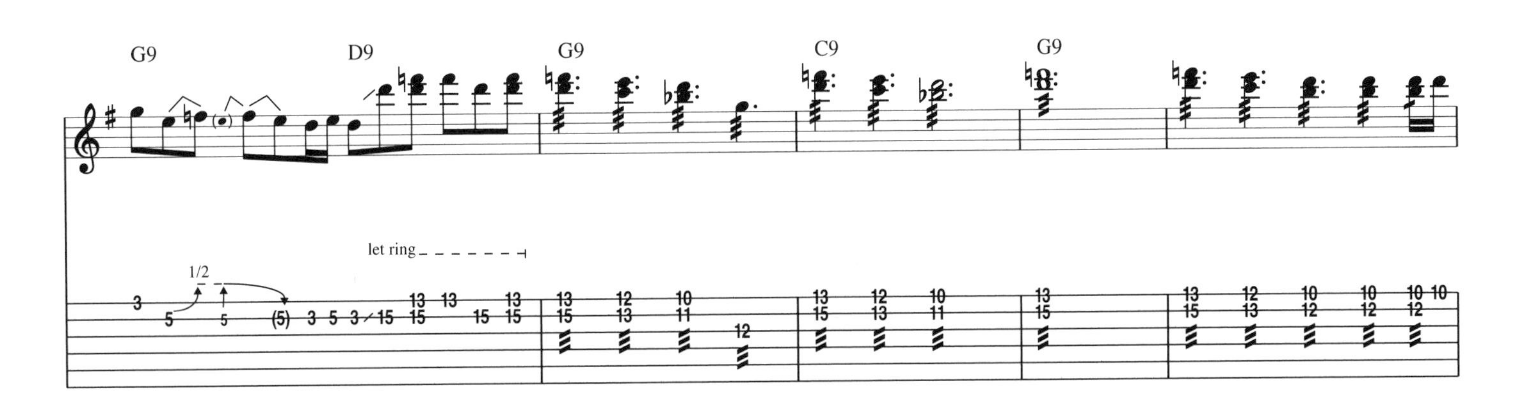
G9
D9
G9
C9
G9
let ring
1/2

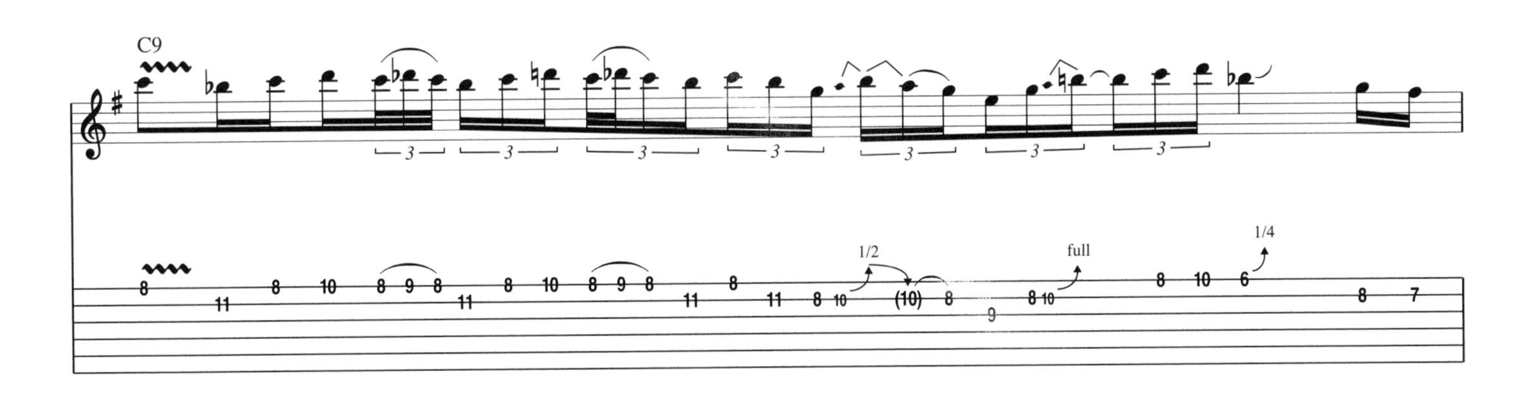
C9
1/2
full
1/4

full
full
full

G9
rake
full
rake
full
D9
rake
full
rake
1/4
C9
rake
rake
1/4
1/4
G9
C9
1/4
G9
D9
8va
G9
8va
rake
1/2
1/2
1/2
C9
full
full
1/2
1/2
G9
8va
1/2
full
full
full
full
C9
8va
full

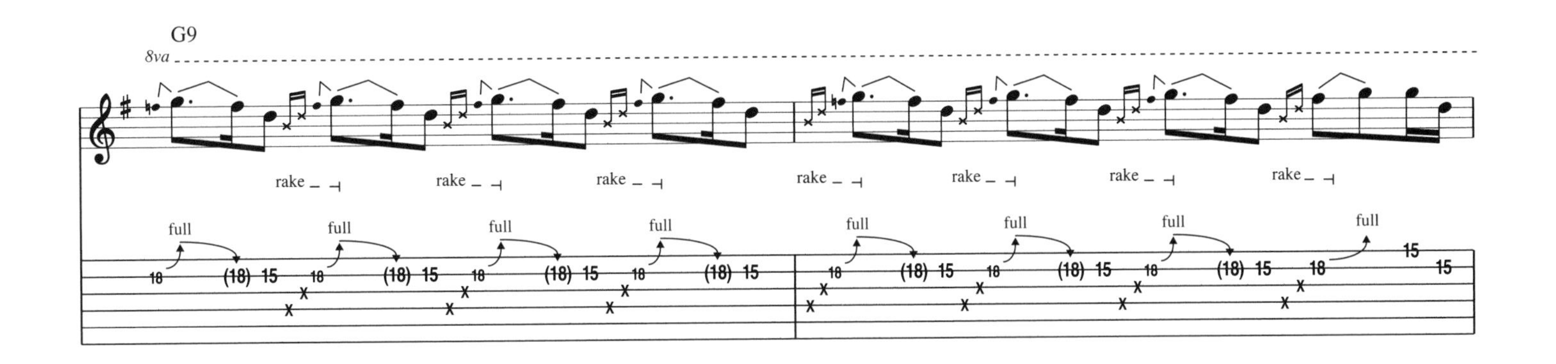
G9
8va
rake
full

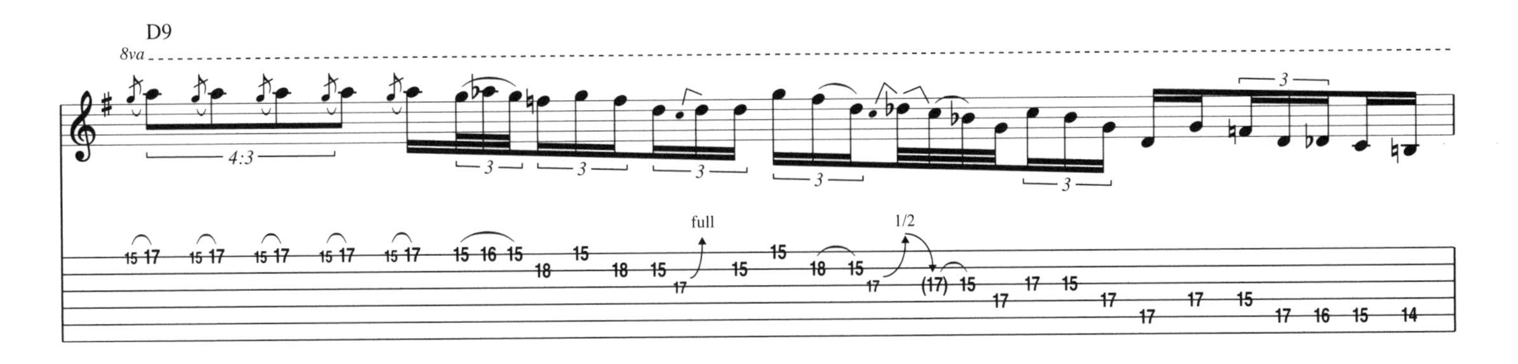
D9
8va
4:3
full
1/2

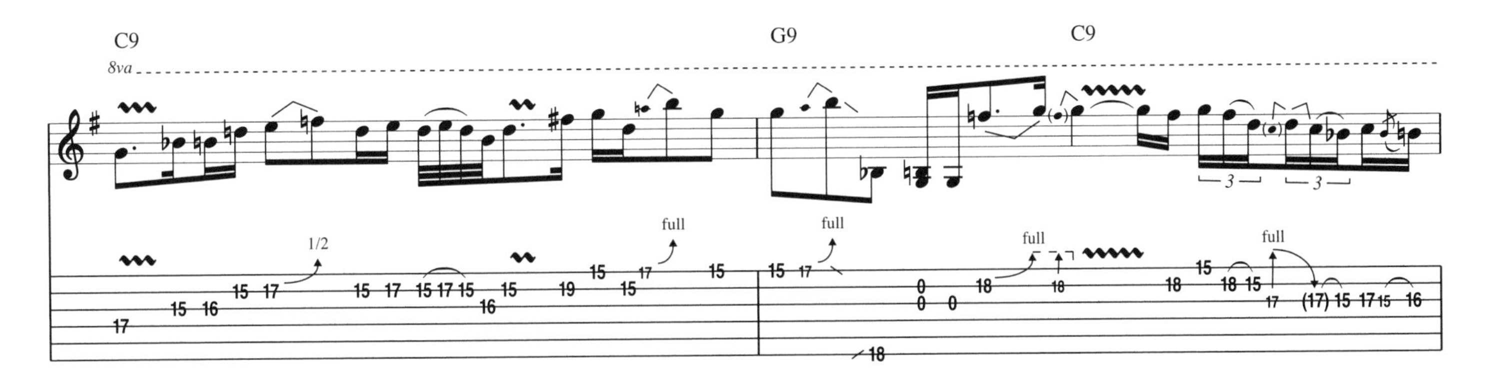
C9
G9
8va
full
1/2

G9
D9
Verse
G9/B (no root)
Gtr. 2
3. Shame, shame,
Gtr. 1
Gtr. 3
8va
loco
rake
let ring

Gtr. 3 tacet
Gtr. 2: w/ Rhy. Fig. 2, 2nd through 9th meas., simile
C9
G9
shame. Yeah, oh, shame on me for ev - er lov - in' you,
Gtr. 1
rake
girl. Shame, shame, shame. Yeah,
shame on me for lov-in' you.
D9
Now you came and you went,
full
P.H.
pitch: F E

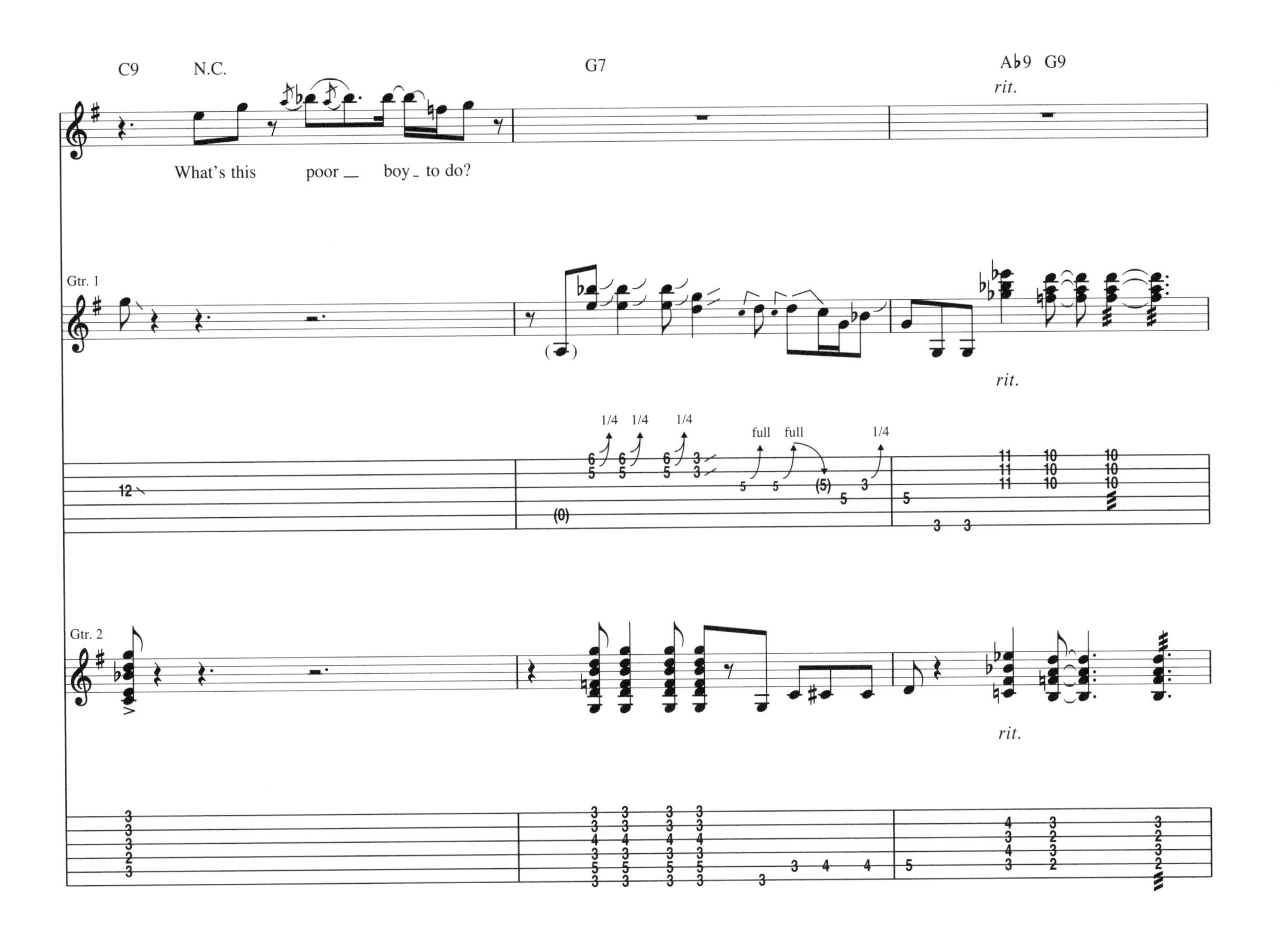
C9
N.C.
G7
A♭9 G9
rit.
What's this poor boy to do?
Gtr. 1
rit.
Gtr. 2
rit.

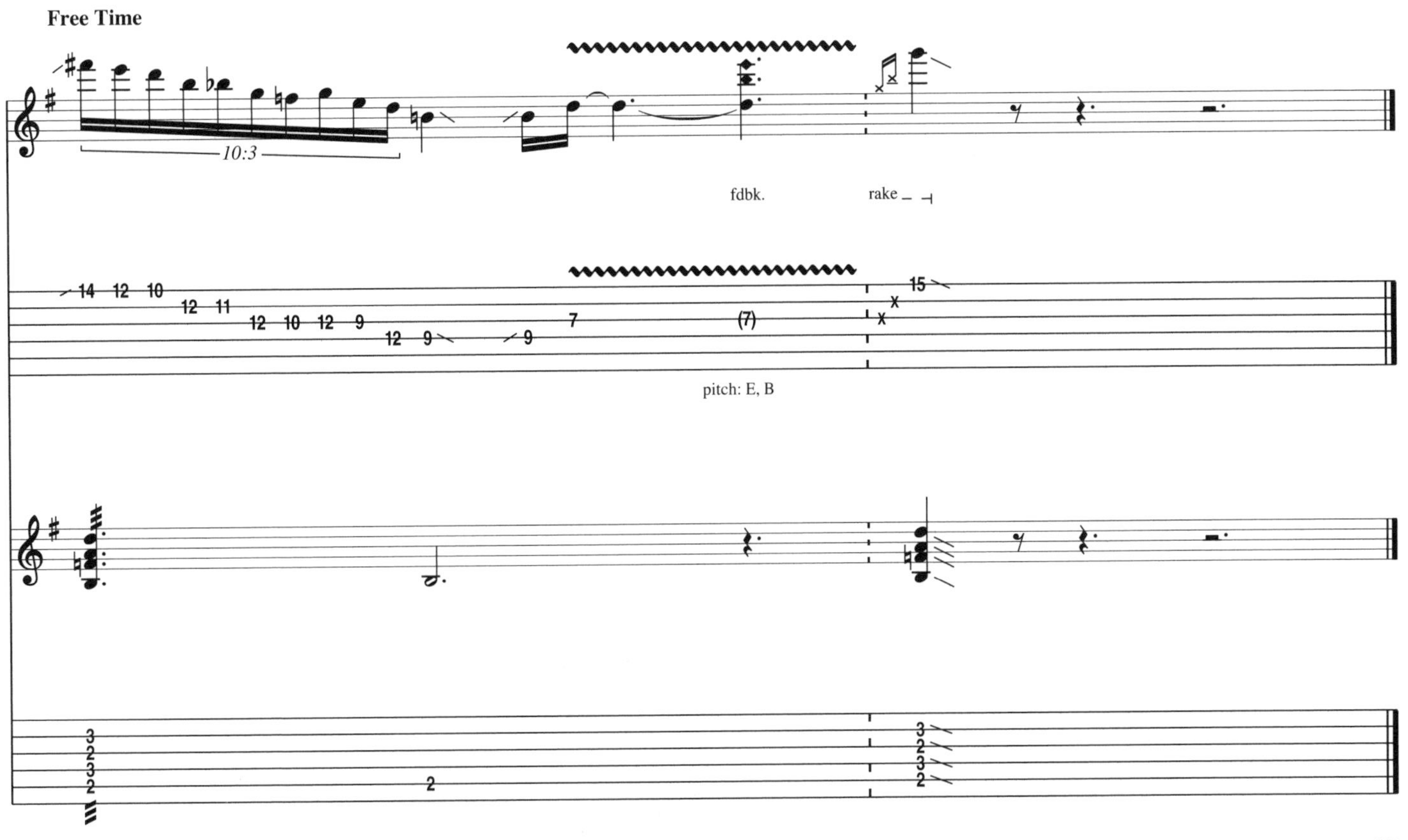
Free Time
10:3
fdbk.
rake
pitch: E, B

One Foot on the Path

Words and Music by Kenny Wayne Shepherd and Mark Selby

* Chord symbols reflect implied harmony.

Verse
A7
"Come o - ver, ba - by. Uh, come talk to me." Then you
I love you, ba - by. Don't get me wrong. This
Rhy. Fig. 2
Gtr. 1
simile on repeat
Gtr. 2
Riff A
simile on repeat
1/4
1/4

drive me so cra - zy, and I can't hard - ly see. (If)
heart of mine may not be that strong. You
1/4
1/4

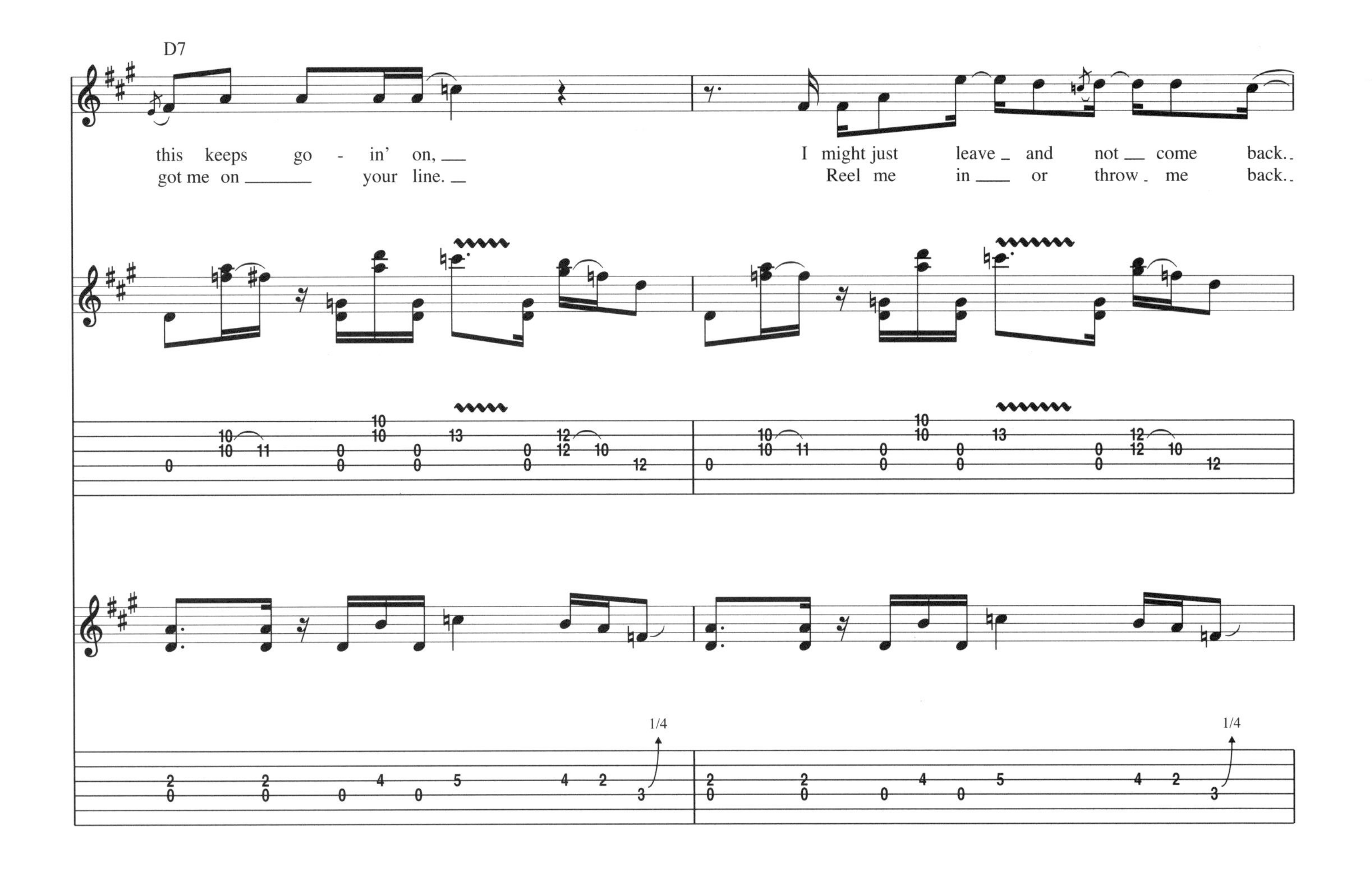
D7
this keeps go - in' on,
got me on your line.
I might just leave and not come back.
Reel me in or throw me back.
1/4
1/4

A7
I got

* Played behind the beat.

E7
D7
one foot in your door - way, ba - by.
I got one foot on the path.
1/4
A7
2. Well, you
4. Now, well,
End Rhy. Fig. 2
End Riff A
1/4
Verse
Gtrs. 1 & 2: w/ Rhy. Fig. 2 & Riff A, simile
A7
beg me to stay, then you or - der me to go. All this up and down is
think a - bout it, ba - by, but don't take too long. If we can't get it right now, ba - by,
tear - in' on my soul. Well, I'm won - der - in' if our fu - ture
just be mov - in' on. Well, I can't wait for - ev - er,
D7

A7
is gon - na look just like our past.
to get this thing. back on its track.
On track.
I got
To Coda
E7
D7
A7
one foot in your door - way, ba - by.
I got one foot on the path.
(On the path.)
Guitar Solo
Gtrs. 1 & 2 tacet
* A7
It's in the path.
Gtr. 3 (dist.)
rake
full
1/4
* Chord symbols reflect overall tonality.
1/2
D7
A7
E7
1 1/2

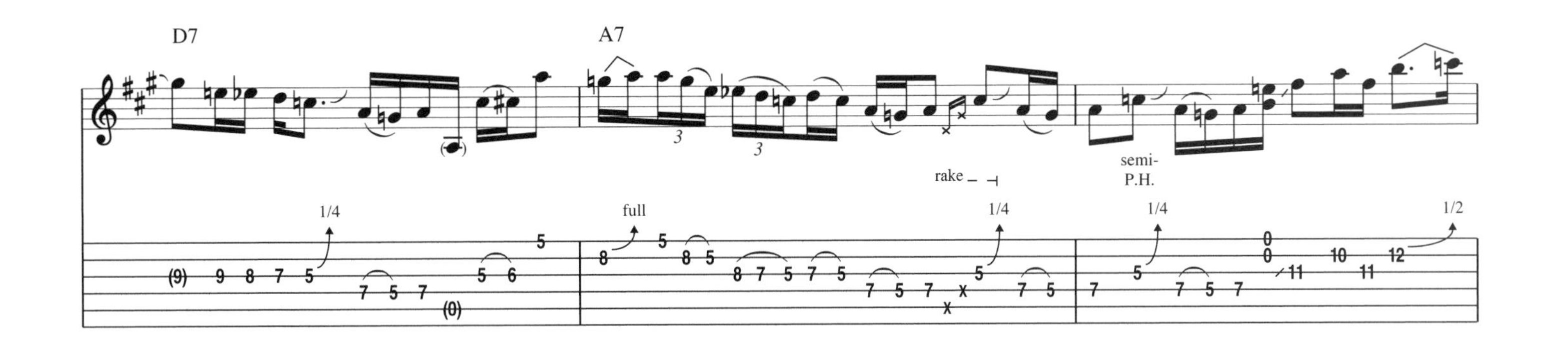
D7
A7
rake
semi-
P.H.
1/4
full
1/4
1/4
1/2

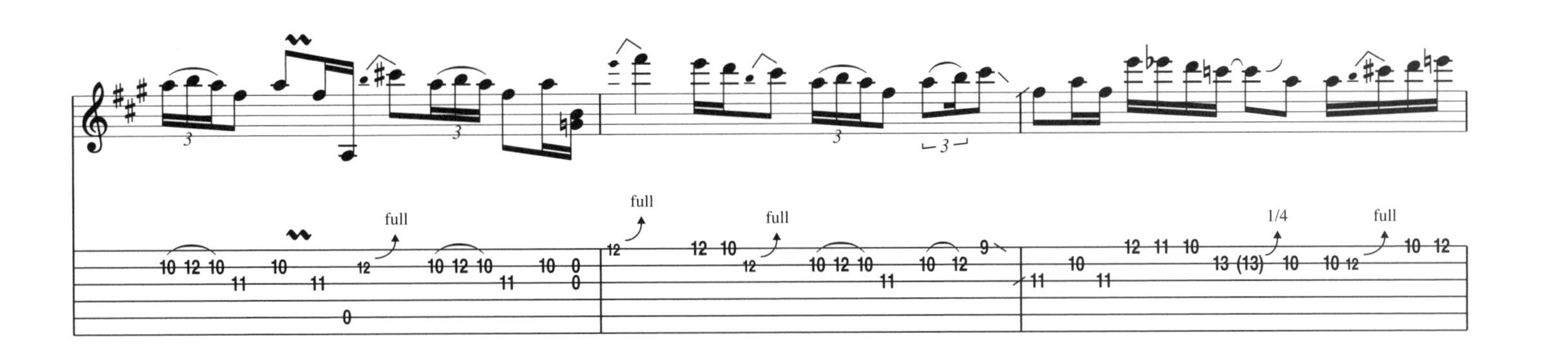
full
full
full
1/4
full

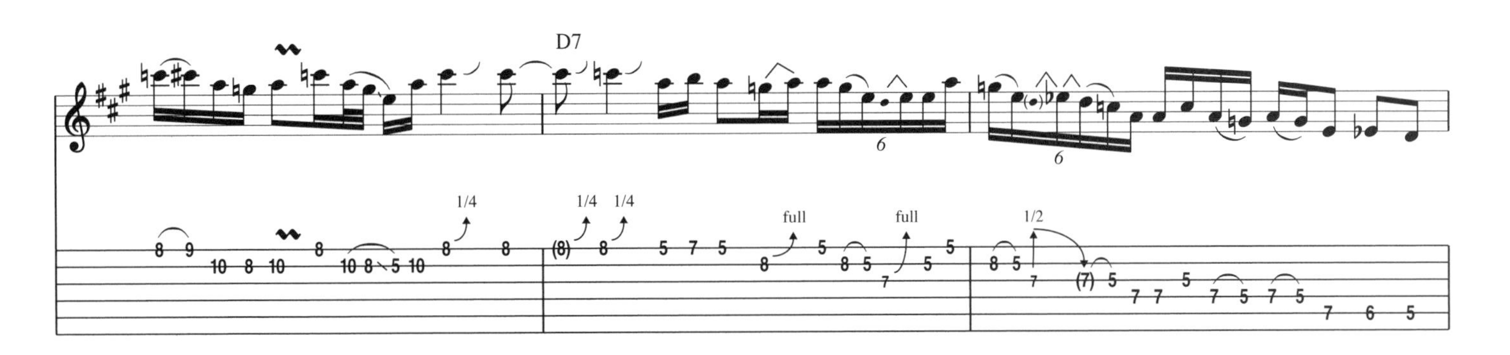
D7
1/4
1/4
1/4
full
full
1/2

A7
E7
rake
1/2
full
full
1/2

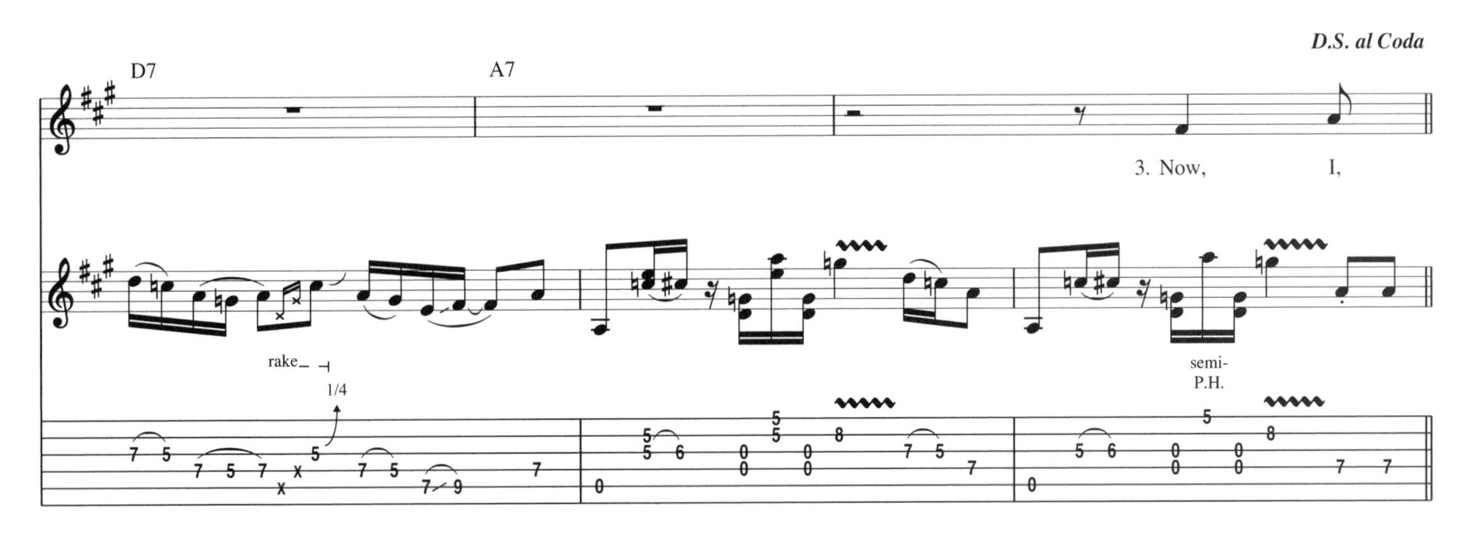
D.S. al Coda
D7
A7
3. Now,
I,
rake
semi-
P.H.
1/4

Coda
D7
A7
I got one foot on the path.
I got
(Got
Gtr. 1
Gtr. 2
1/4
1/4

Outro
E7
D7
A7
one foot in your door - way, ba - by,
and one foot on the path.
one foot in your door - way,
one foot on the path.)
1/4
1/4

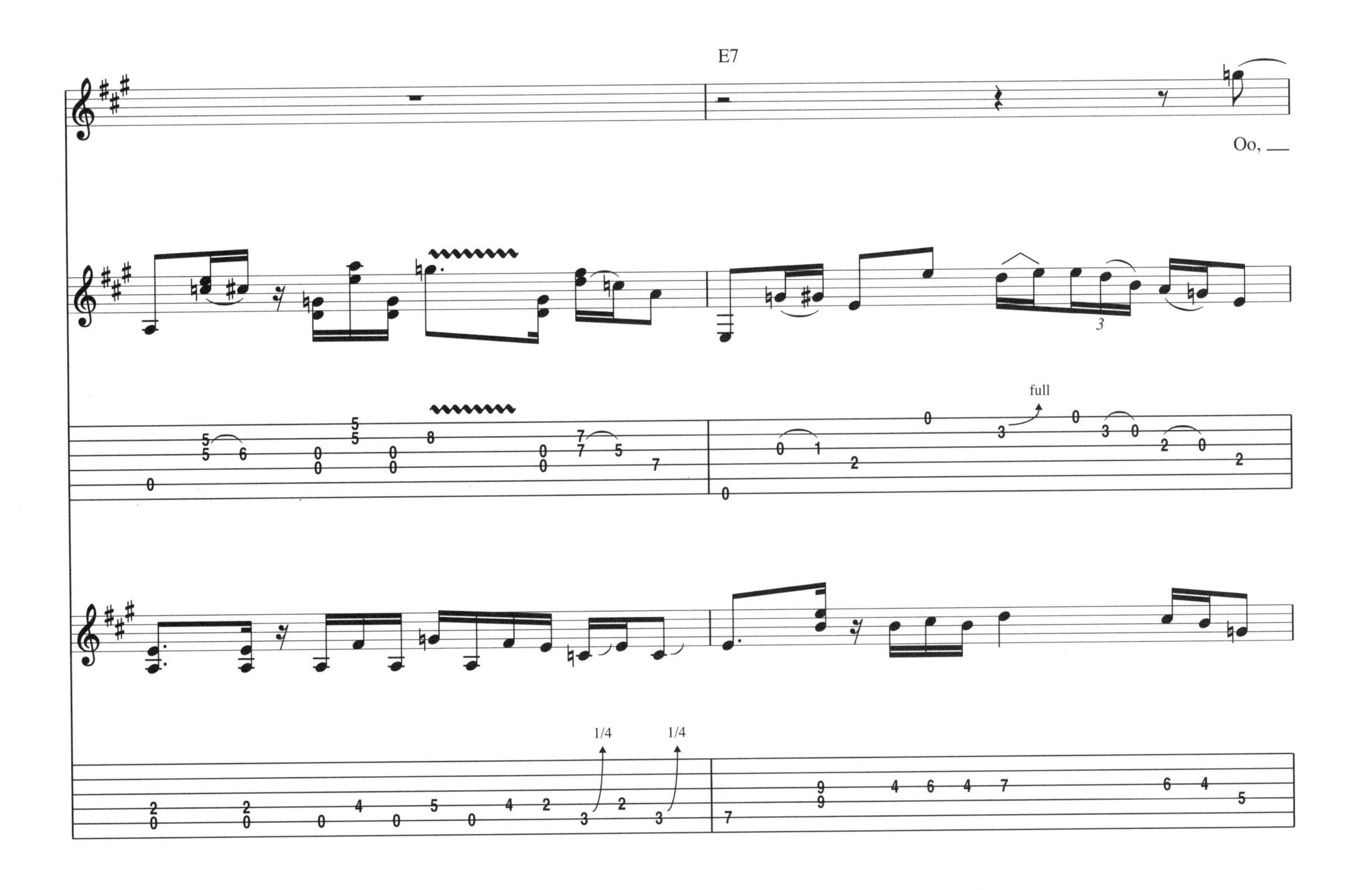
E7
Oo,
full
1/4
1/4

D7
A7
A
ah, and one foot on the path.
1/4
1/4

Everybody Gets the Blues

Words and Music by Angel Michael

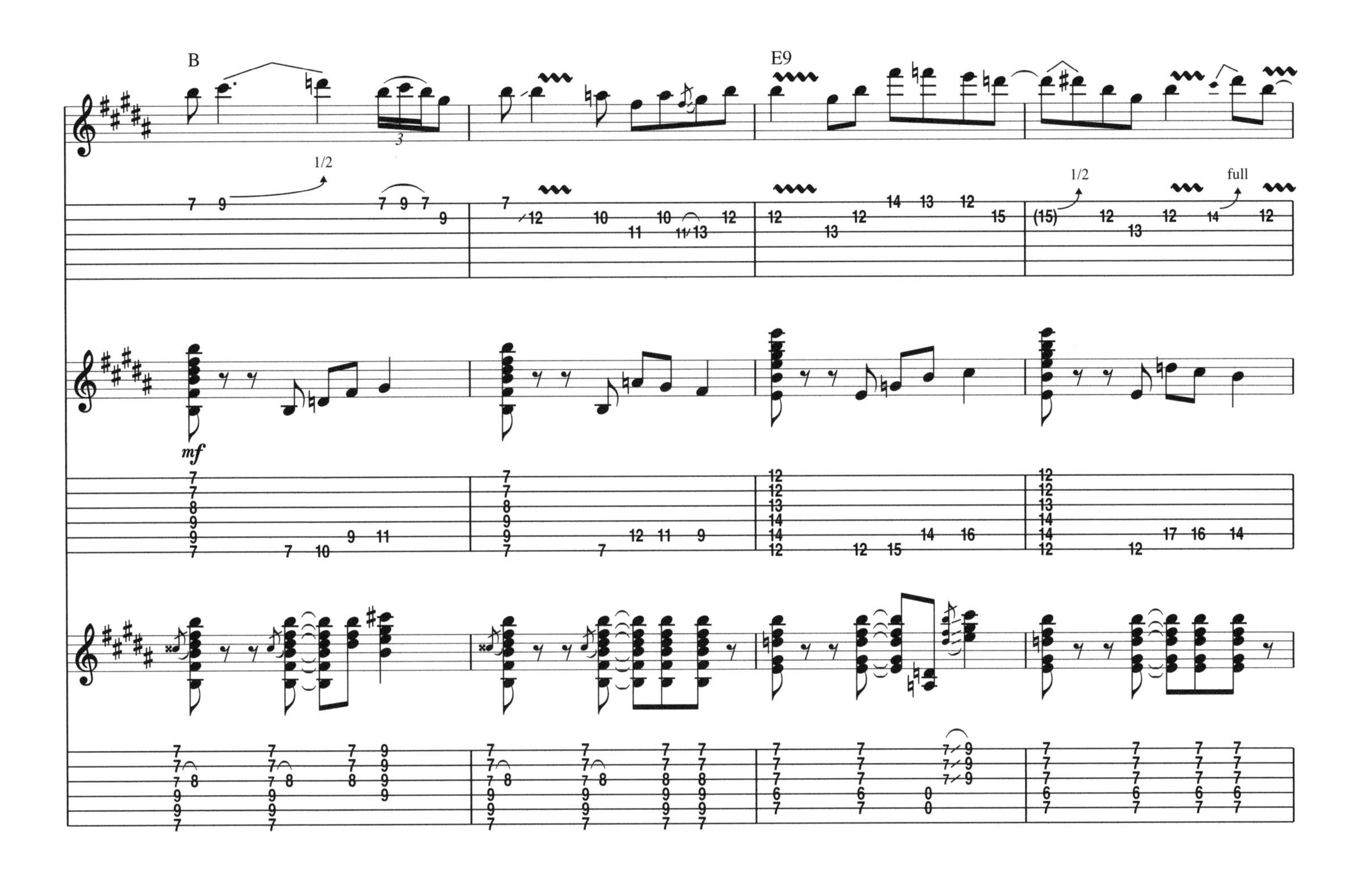
B
E9
1/2
1/2
full
mf

B
F#
B
N.C.
1. It does-n't mat-ter if you're
1/4
End Rhy. Fig. 1
End Rhy. Fig. 1A

Verse
Gtr. 1 tacet
Gtrs. 2 & 3: w/ Rhy. Figs. 1 & 1A, simile
B
Gtr. 1: w/ Fill 1, 2nd time
E9
rich. Don't make no dif - 'rence if you're poor.
wom - an that it is for a man.
B
The sim - ple things in life can make me mad to the
Ev - 'ry - bod - y goes danc - ing, ev - 'ry - bod - y pays the
F#9
Gtr. 1: w/ Fill 2, 2nd time
B
core. Does - n't mat - ter if you're young.
band. Ev - 'ry - bod - y got to take, oh,
E9
Don't make no dif - 'rence if you're old. You got to stand a lit - tle
ev - 'ry - bod - y got to give. Ev - 'ry - bod - y got to
B
F#9
B
N.C.
rain be - fore you reach a pot of gold.
eat, ev - 'ry - bod - y got to live.
Ev - 'ry - bod - y gets the
Gtr. 1
1/2
Chorus
Gtrs. 2 & 3: w/ Rhy. Figs. 1 & 1A, simile
B
E9
blues. Ev - 'ry - bod - y got to cry. You take the good with the
B
F#9
bad. You take the lows and the highs.
Fill 1
Gtr. 1
1/4
Fill 2
Gtr. 1
full
1/4
6

Gtr. 1: w/ Fill 3, 3rd time
B
E9
Well, you work and you wor - ry.
And spend your life pay - ing dues.
To Coda
B
F#9
Ev - 'ry - bod - y has a hard time some - time.
Ev - 'ry - bod - y gets the
1.
B
N.C.
blues.
2. It ain't no dif - 'rent for a
2.
B
N.C.
blues.
Huh! Yeah! Ha!
Gtr. 1
Gtr. 1
1/2
Guitar Solo
Gtrs. 2 & 3: w/ Rhy. Figs. 1 & 1A, 2 times, simile
B
E9
B
full
1 1/4
full
*Played behind the beat.
F#9
B
8va
1/2
1 1/2

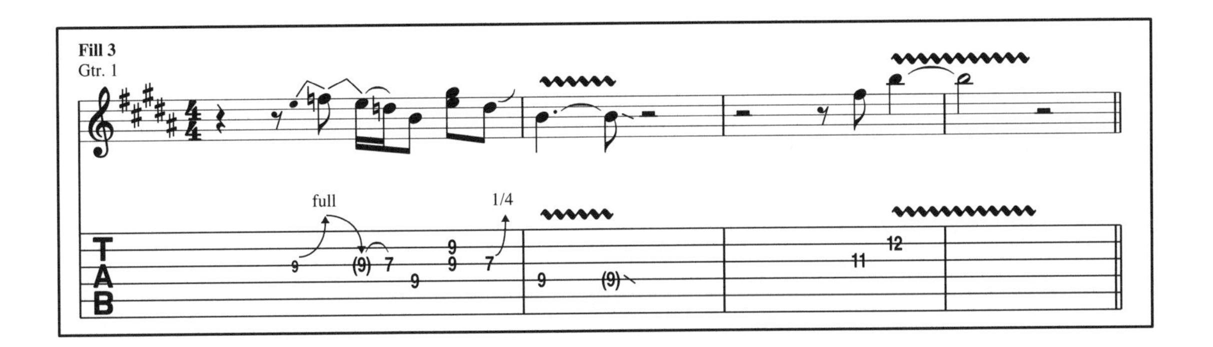
Fill 3
Gtr. 1
full
1/4
T
A
B

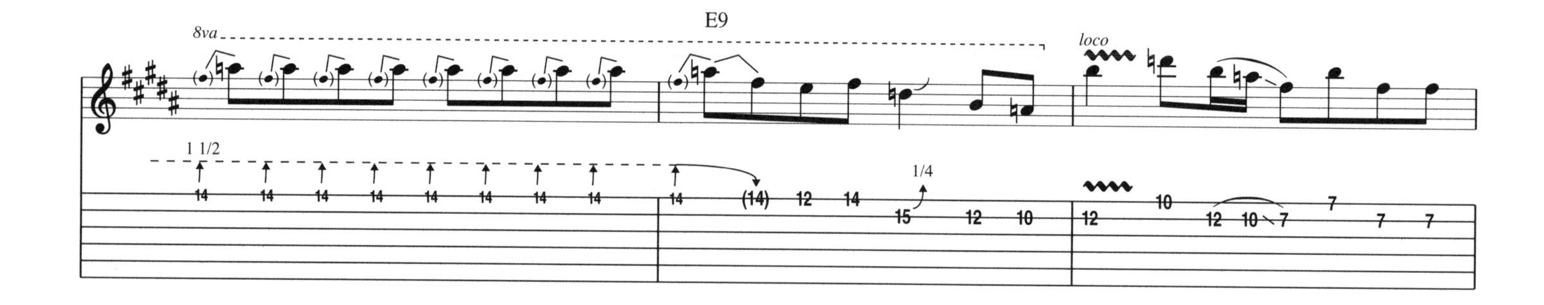
E9
8va
loco
1 1/2
1/4

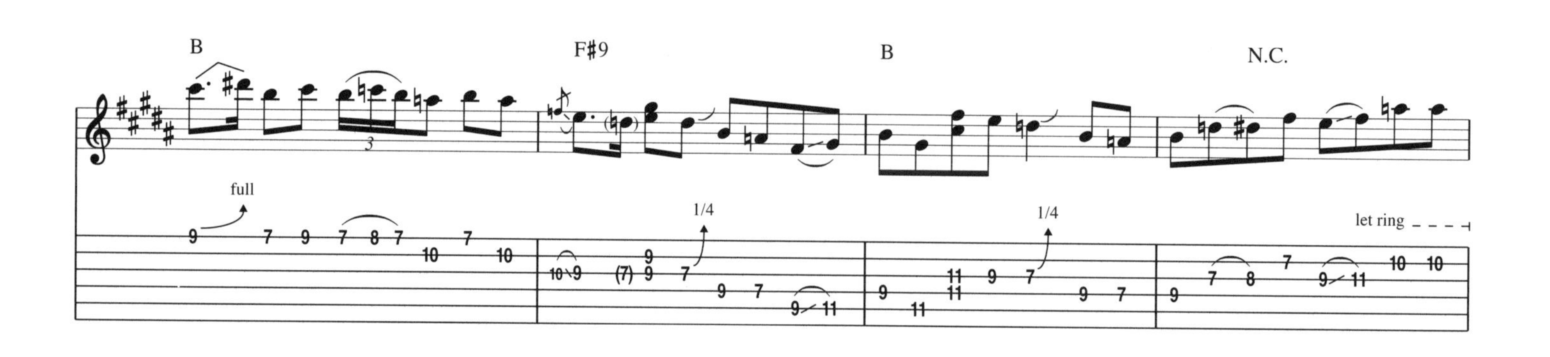
B
F#9
B
N.C.
full
1/4
1/4
let ring

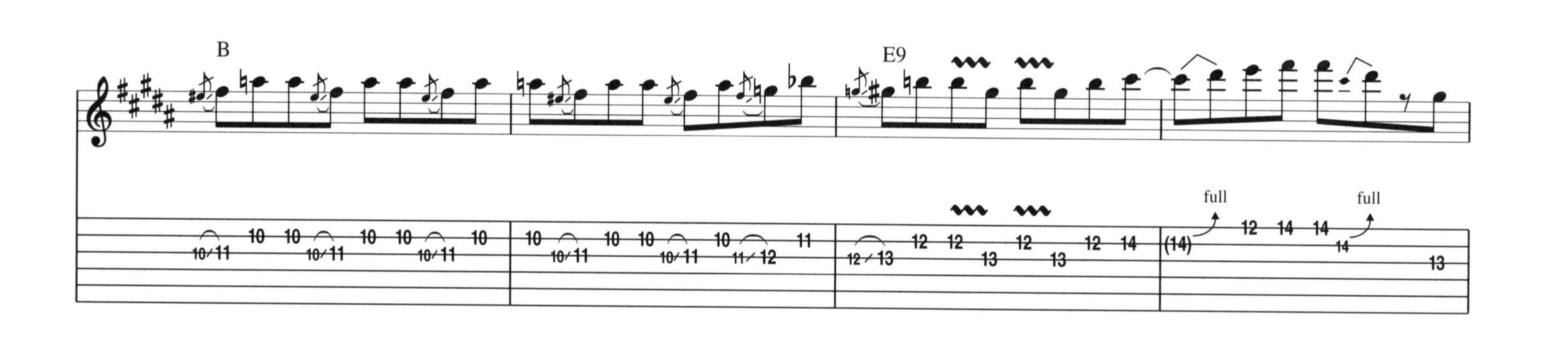
B
E9
full
full

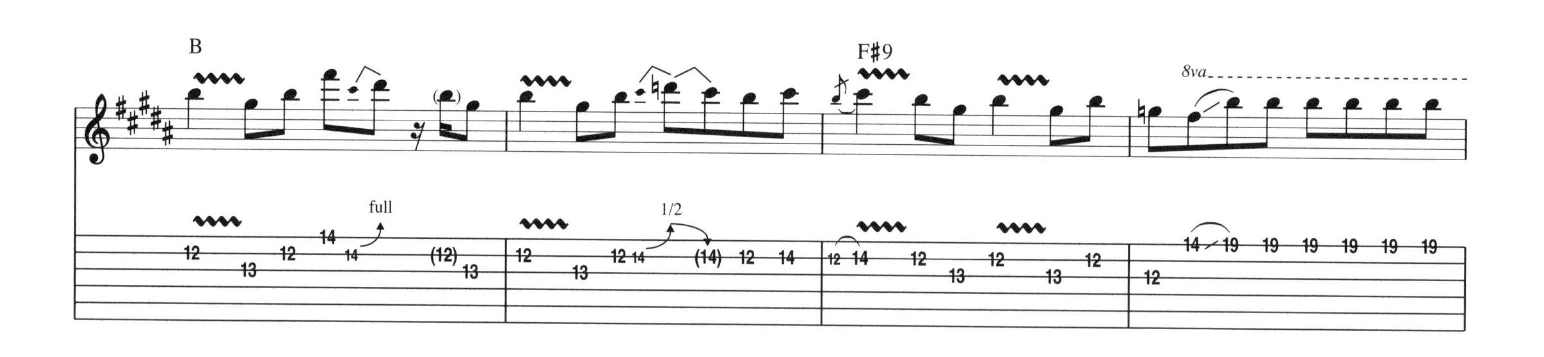
B
F#9
8va
full
1/2

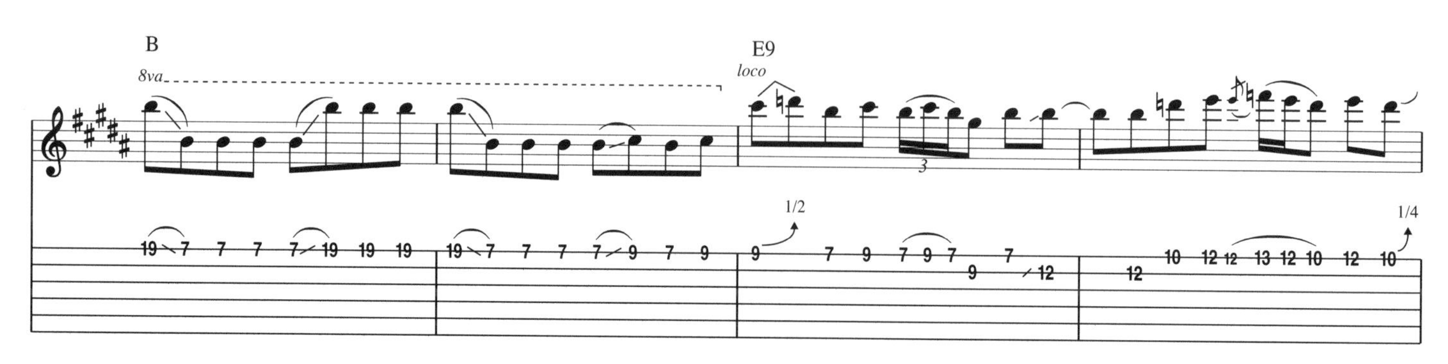
B
8va
E9
loco
1/2
1/4

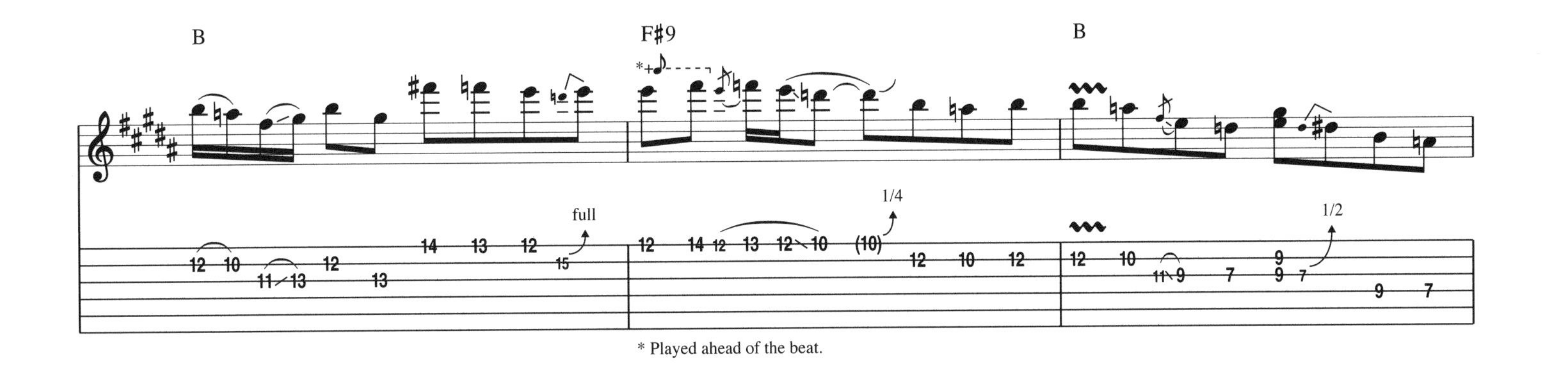

* Played ahead of the beat.

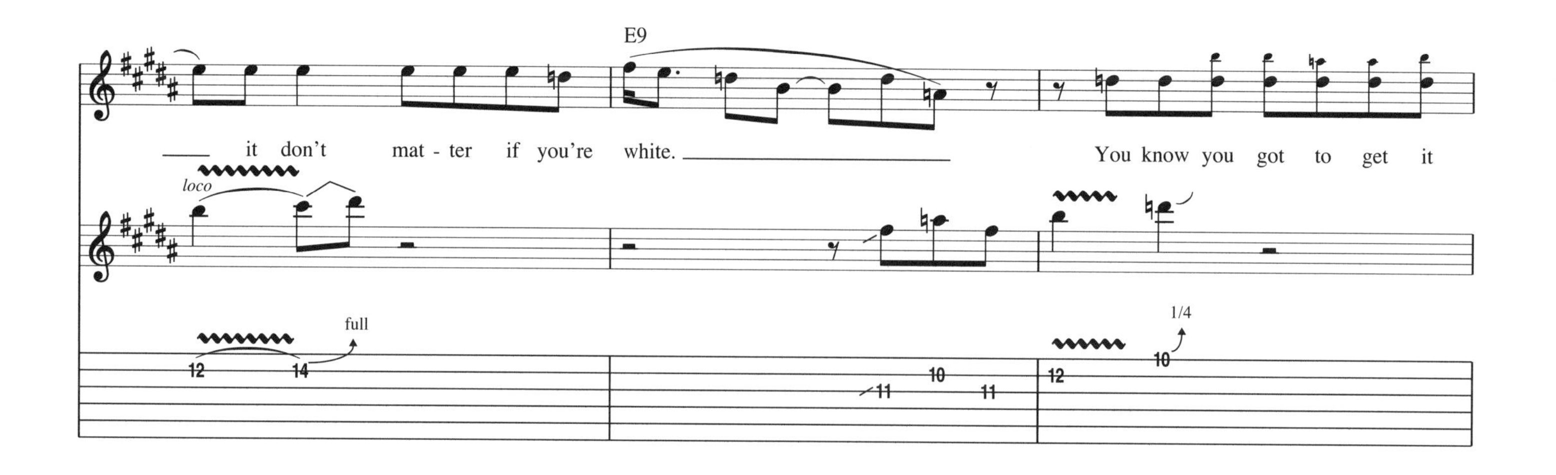
E9
it don't mat - ter if you're white.
You know you got to get it
loco
full
1/4

D.S. al Coda
B
F♯9
B
N.C.
wrong
to have a chance to make it right.
Ev - 'ry - bod - y gets the

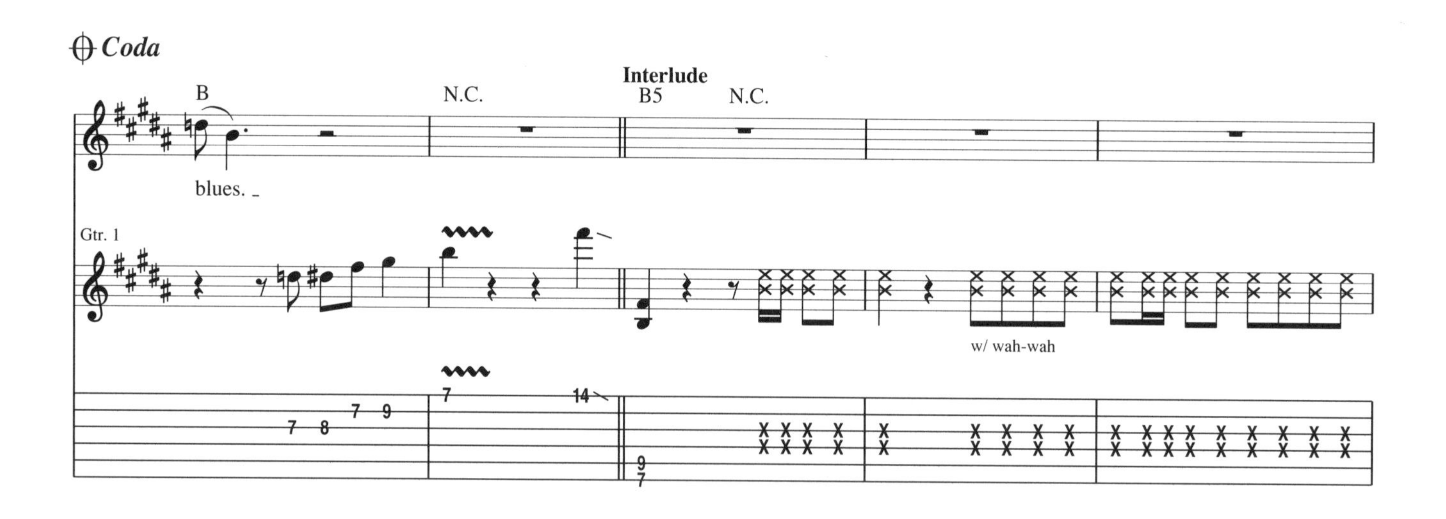
Coda
Interlude
B
N.C.
B5
N.C.
blues.
Gtr. 1
w/ wah-wah

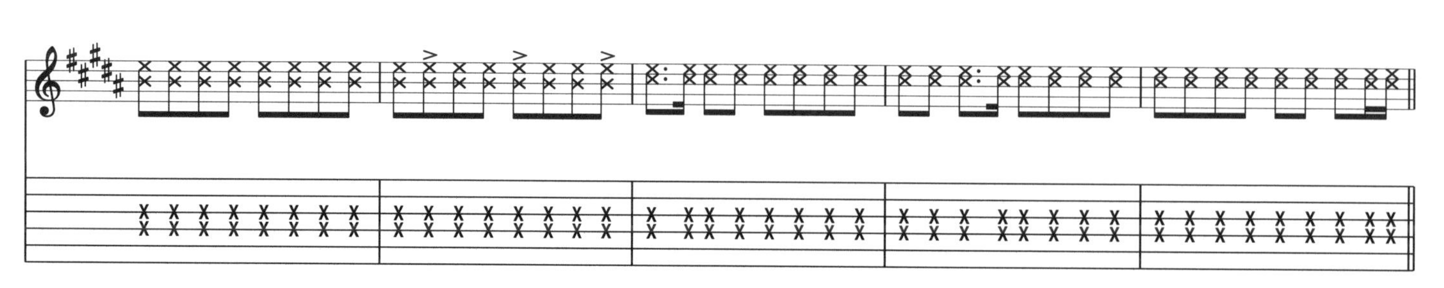

Piano Solo
B
E9
Gtrs. 2 & 3
Gtr. 1
F#9
8va
Outro-Guitar Solo
Gtrs. 2 & 3: w/ Rhy. Figs. 1 & 1A, 2 times, simile
loco
full
1/4
1/2
1 1/2
rake
let ring

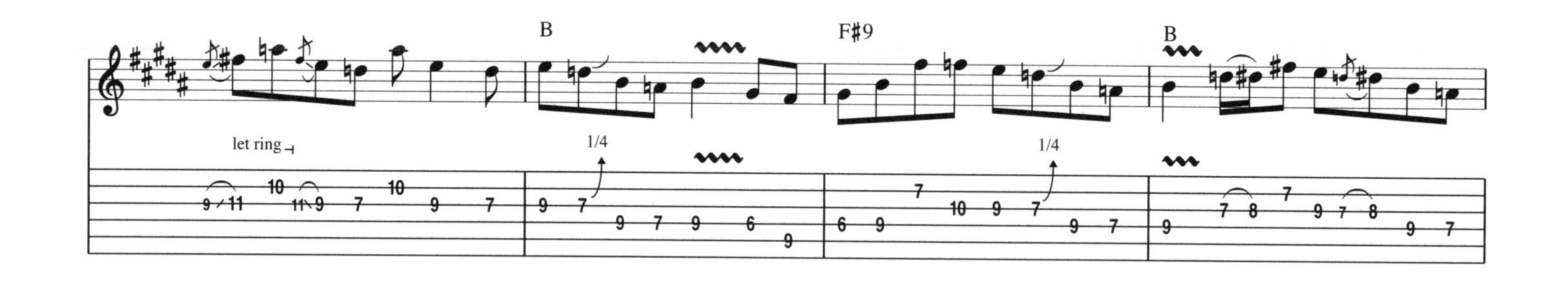
B
F#9
B
let ring

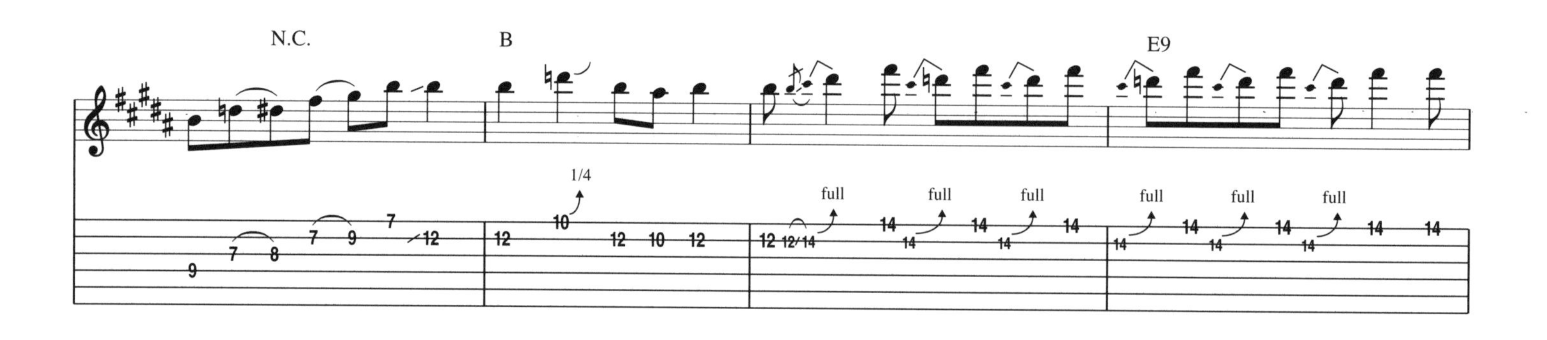
N.C.
B
E9

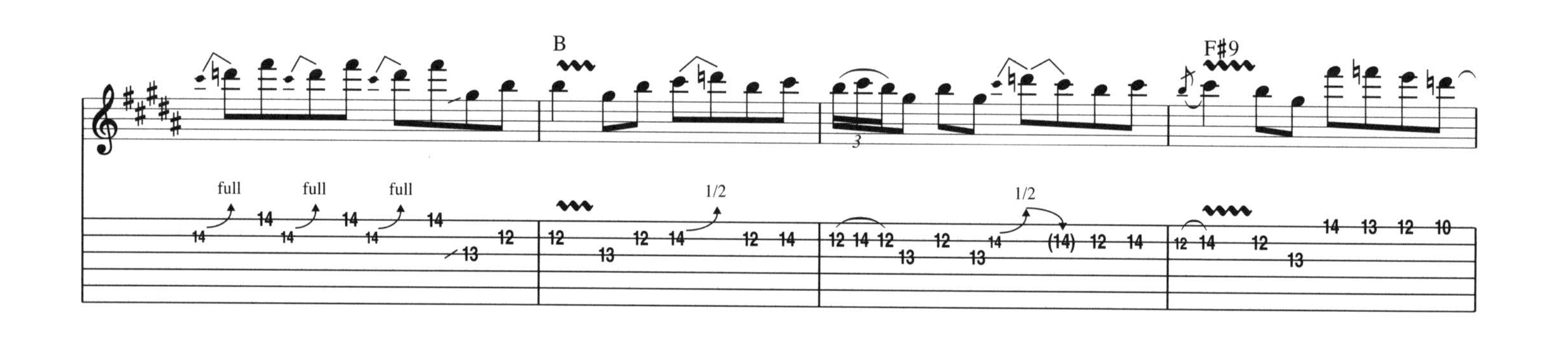
B
F#9

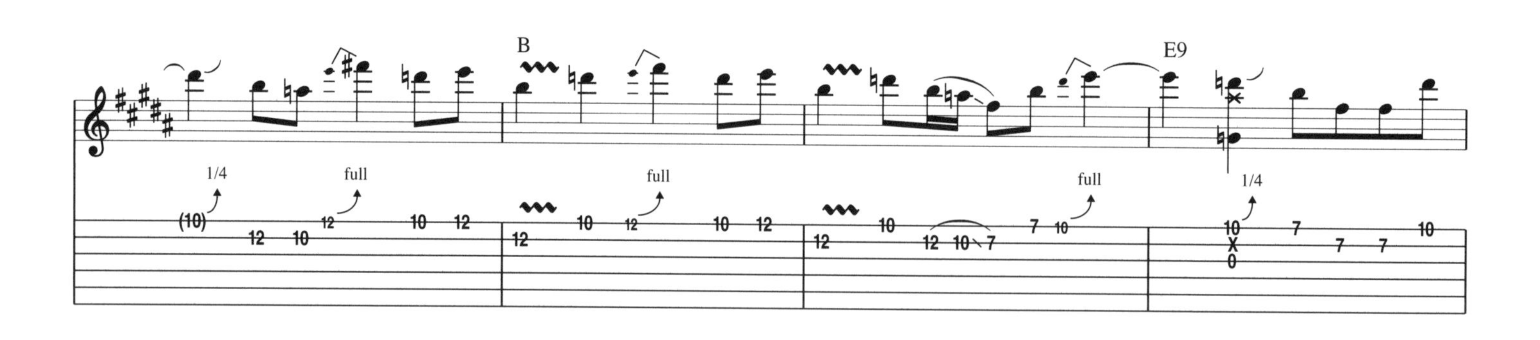
B
E9

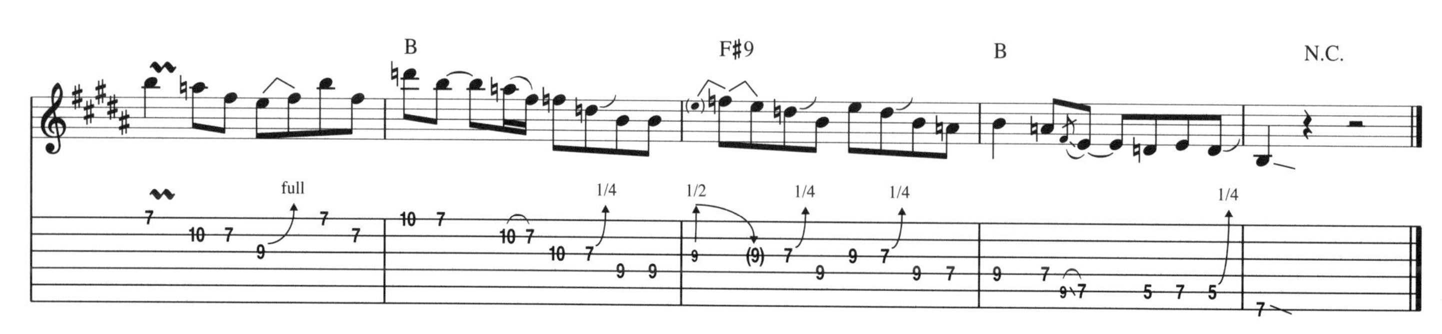
B
F#9
B
N.C.

While We Cry

By Kenny Wayne Shepherd

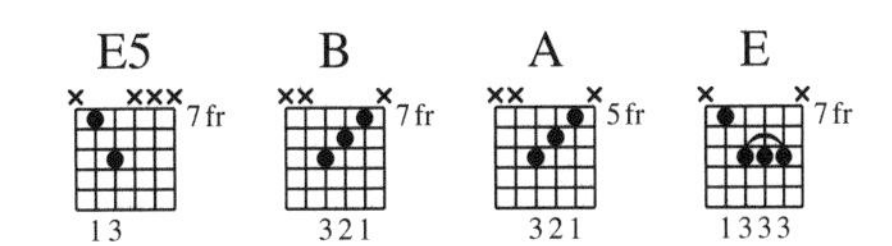

Tune Down 1/2 Step:
① = E♭ ④ = D♭
② = B♭ ⑤ = A♭
③ = G♭ ⑥ = E♭

A Intro
Slowly ♩ = 61

* E
Riff A
Gtr. 1 (slight dist.)
Bsus4
B

mp
simile on repeat
let ring throughout

** T

* Chord symbols reflect implied tonality.

** T = Thumb on ⑥

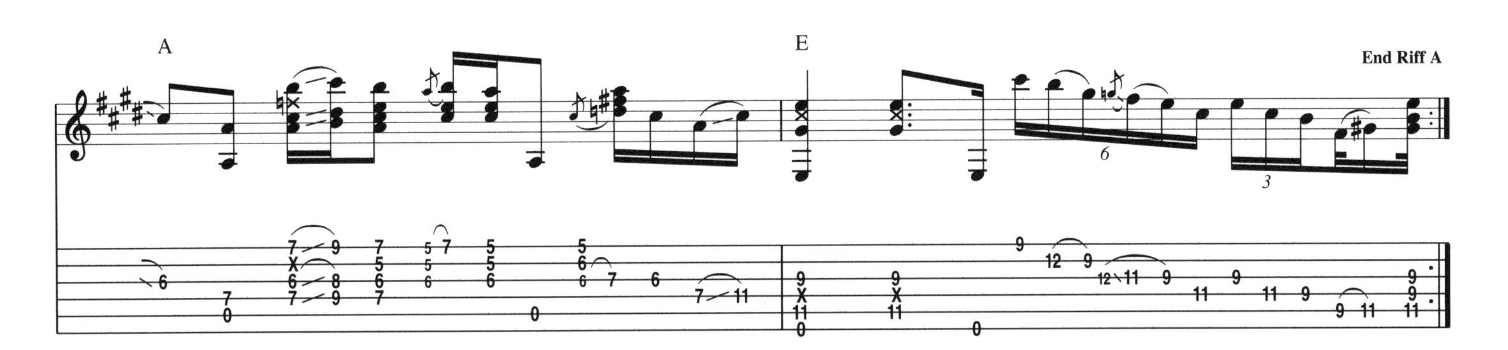

B Theme

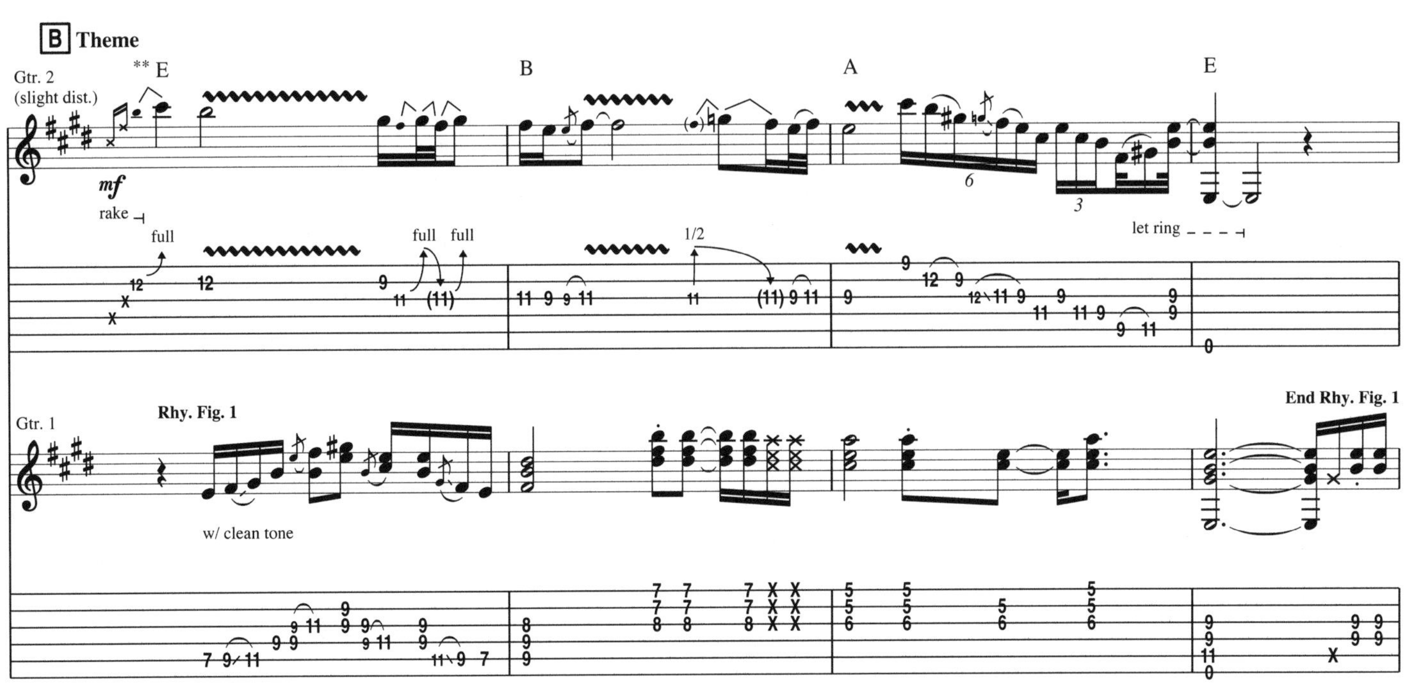

** Chord symbols reflect overall tonality.

B
A
rake
full
let ring
* Played ahead of the beat.
C Guitar Solo
E
Rhy. Fig. 2
8va
loco
Harm.
End Rhy. Fig. 2

Gtr. 1: w/ Rhy. Fig. 2, simile
Gtr. 2
B
rake
full
1/2
A
E
8va
B
loco
w/ pick & middle finger
D Theme
Gtr. 1: w/ Rhy. Fig. 2, simile
Gtr. 1: w/ Rhy. Fig. 1, simile
E Guitar Solo
open
Gtr. 1
Gtr. 2
mp

Gtr. 1 tacet
B
A
Gtr. 2
8va
rake
1/2
E
loco
full
w/ pick & middle finger
1/4

F Theme
Gtr. 1: w/ Rhy. Fig. 1, simile
E
E
B
w/ dist.
rake
full
full
1/2
* vol. swell
A
E
rake
let ring
G Guitar Solo
E
B
Gtr. 2
8va
full
1 1/4
Gtr. 1
A
E5
E
E5
1/2
(cont. in slash)

E5
Rhy. Fig. 3
Gtr. 1
B
8va
Gtr. 2
1 1/2
full
A
E
open
E5
End Rhy. Fig. 3
loco
rake
1/2
Gtr. 1: w/ Rhy. Fig. 3, simile
H Theme
mf w/ slight dist.
tr

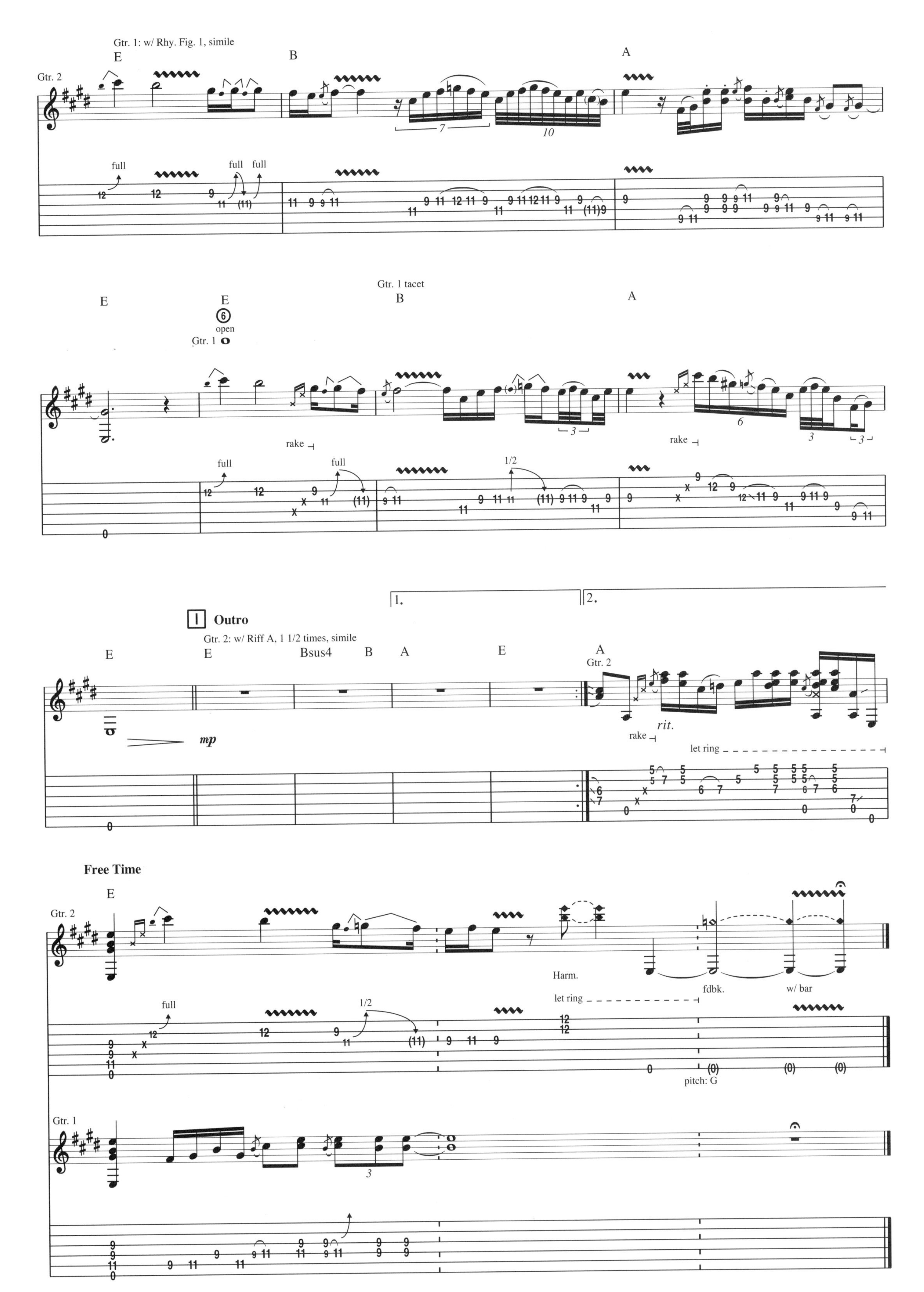

Gtr. 1: w/ Rhy. Fig. 1, simile
E
B
A
Gtr. 2
full
full full
Gtr. 1 tacet
open
Gtr. 1
rake
1/2
Outro
Gtr. 2: w/ Riff A, 1 1/2 times, simile
Bsus4
1.
2.
mp
rit.
let ring
Free Time
Harm.
fdbk.
w/ bar
pitch: G

I'm Leavin' You (Commit a Crime)

Words and Music by Chester Burnett

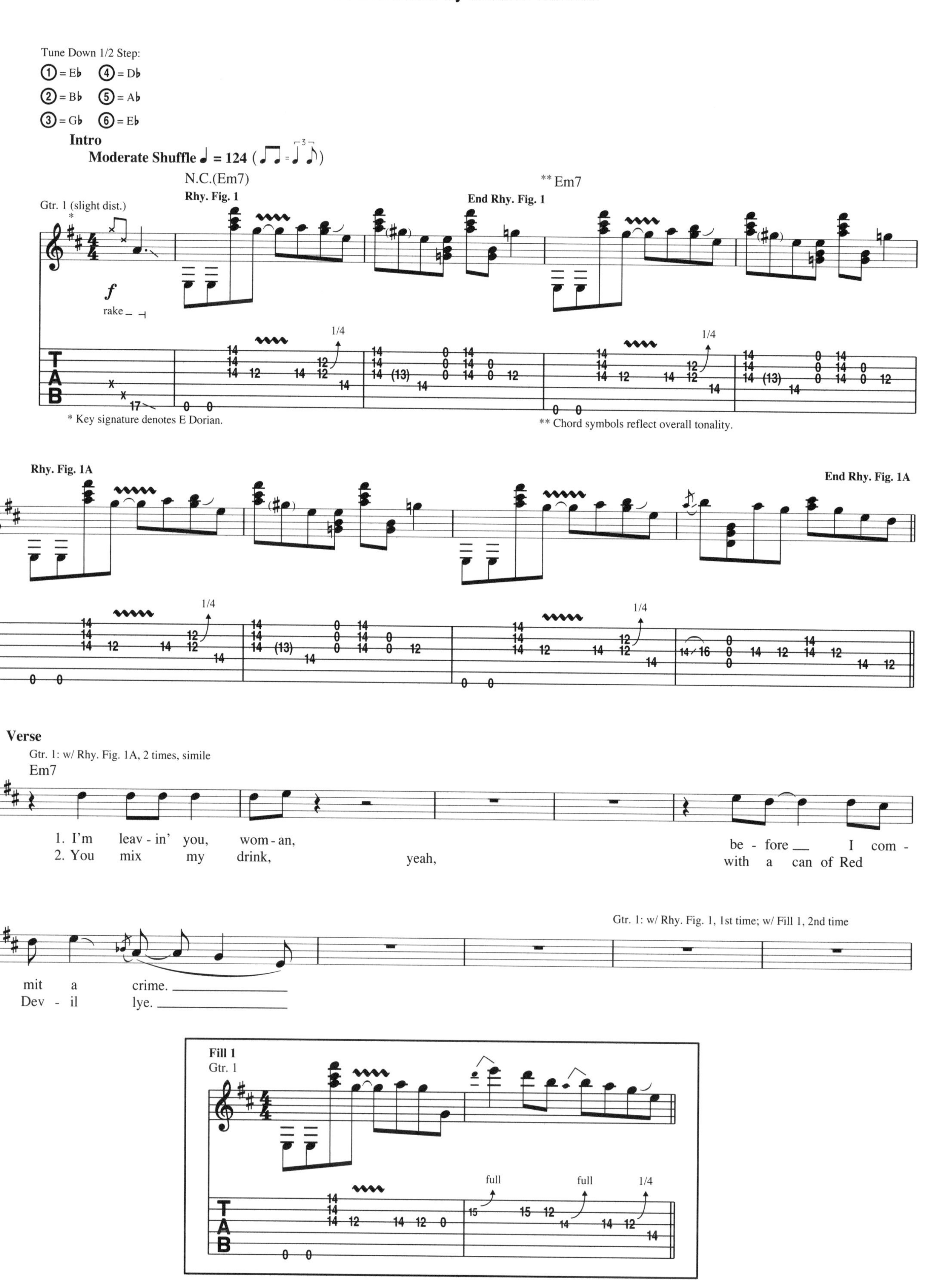

Gtr. 1: w/ Rhy. Fig. 1A, 2 times, simile, 1st time; w/ Rhy. Fig. 1, 2nd time
Gtr. 1: w/ Fill 2, 2nd time
Gtr. 1: w/ Rhy. Fig. 1, 2 times, 2nd time
I'm leav - in' you, wom - an, yeah, be - fore I com - mit a crime.
You mix my drink, ba - by, with a can of Red Dev - il lye.
Gtr. 1: w/ Rhy. Fig. 1, simile
Gtr. 1: w/ Rhy. Fig. 1A, simile, 1st time; w/ Fill 3, 2nd time
Gtr. 1: w/ Rhy. Fig. 1, 2 times, simile, 2nd time
Gtr. 1: w/ Rhy. Fig. 1, 3 times, simile
You tried so hard to kill me. Ba - by, it was not my time.
Then you sat right down watch-in' me, hop - in' I might die.
To Coda
Yeah, yeah!
Guitar Solo
Em7
Gtr. 1
Fill 2
Fill 3
Gtr. 1

full
1/2
8va
2 1/2
1/4
loco
3rd time, D.S. al Coda
play 3 times
simile on repeats

Coda
Outro-Guitar Solo
Em7
Hey!
Gtr. 1
full
Well,
yeah.
rake

Begin Fade
Fade Out

(Let Me Up) I've Had Enough

Words and Music by Kenny Wayne Shepherd, Mark Selby and Joe Nadeau

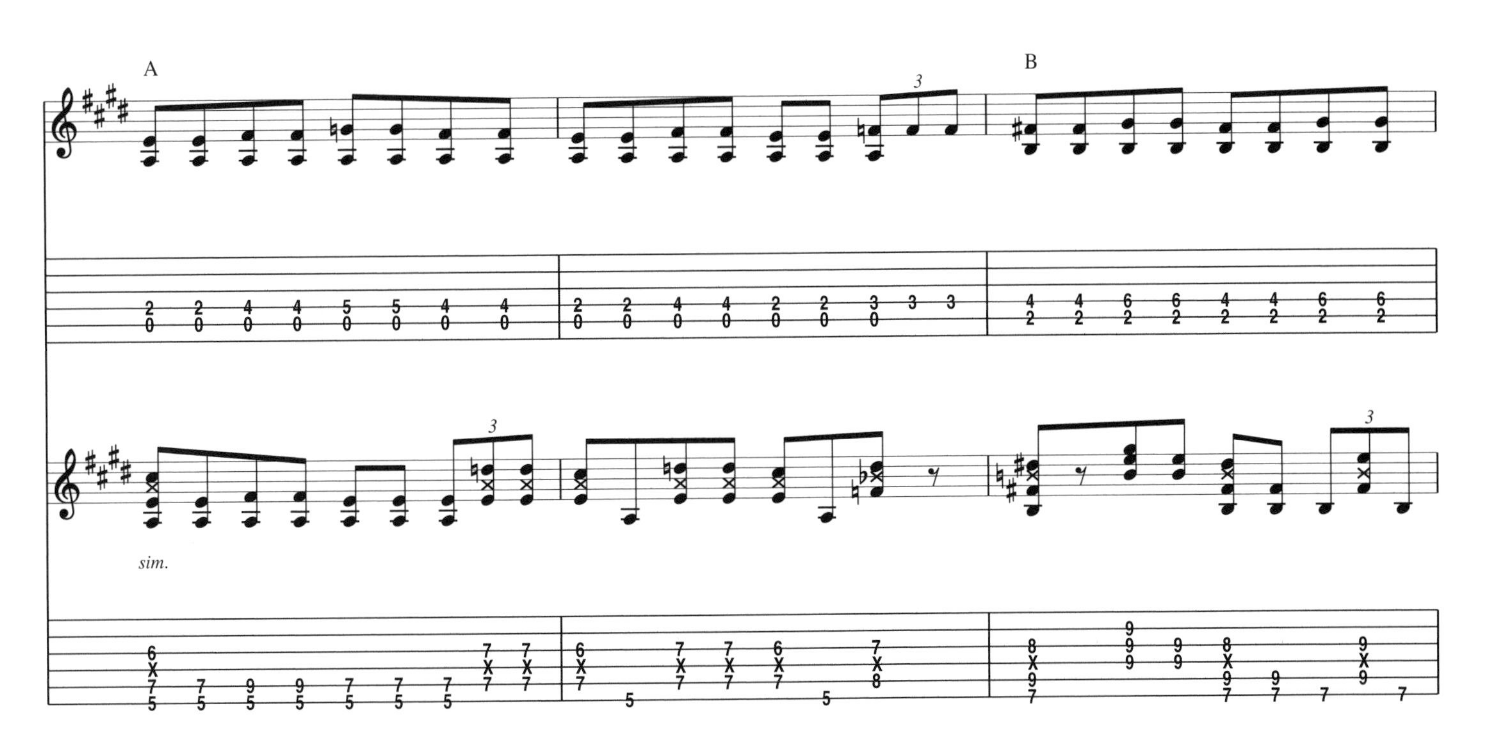

E
B7
1. Uh, when I
End Rhy. Fig. 1
End Rhy. Fig. 1A
let ring
Verse
Gtrs. 1 & 2: w/ Rhy. Fig. 1, simile
Gtr. 3: w/ Rhy. Fig. 1A, simile
E
A
fell for you, ba - by, I real - ly met my match. You use me, a - buse me, but
B
I keep com - in' back. Let me up, ba - by, I've had e - nough.
E
B7
2. Well, it
Verse
Gtrs. 1 & 2: w/ Rhy. Fig. 1, 1st 6 meas., simile
Gtr. 3: w/ Rhy. Fig. 1A, 1st 7 meas., simile
E
does - n't seem to mat - ter a
A
what we fight a - bout. Well, I'm the one who winds up down
B
for the count. Let me up now, ba - by, I've had e - nough.

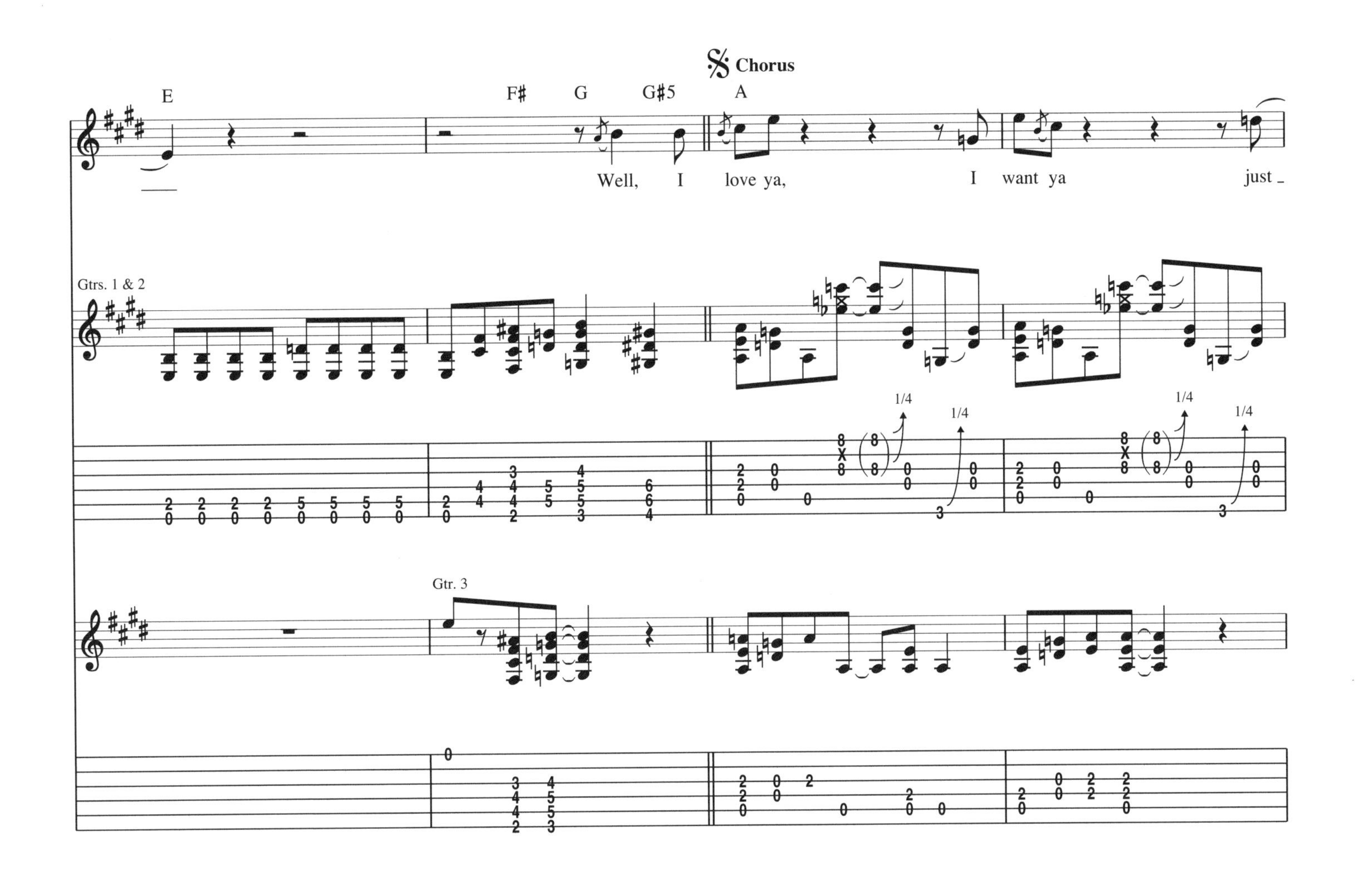
Chorus
E
F#
G
G#5
A
Well, I love ya, I want ya just
Gtrs. 1 & 2
1/4
Gtr. 3

E
A
like I did before.
I need ya, but if I
1/4

B7
Gtr. 2
leave ya it's 'cause I just can't take no more, no, no. 3. Well, some-
4. When I
Gtr. 1
(Gtr. 2 cont. in slash)
1/4
1/4
Gtr. 3
Verse
Gtrs. 1 & 2: w/ Rhy. Fig. 1, 1st 5 meas.
Gtr. 3: w/ Rhy. Fig. 1A, 1st 5 meas.
E
how you re - mem - ber ev - 'ry lit - tle thing I've done, but
fell for you, ba - by, I real - ly met my match. You
A
ba - by, I sur - ren - der. I've lost and you've won.
use me, a - buse me, but I keep com - in' back.
Let me up now, ba -
B
To Coda
E
- by, I've had e - nough.
B
Hey!
Gtrs. 1 & 2
Gtr. 1
Gtr. 2
divisi
1/2
Gtr. 3
let ring

Gtr. 2 tacet
Gtr. 3: w/ Rhy. Fig. 1A, 1 7/8 times, simile

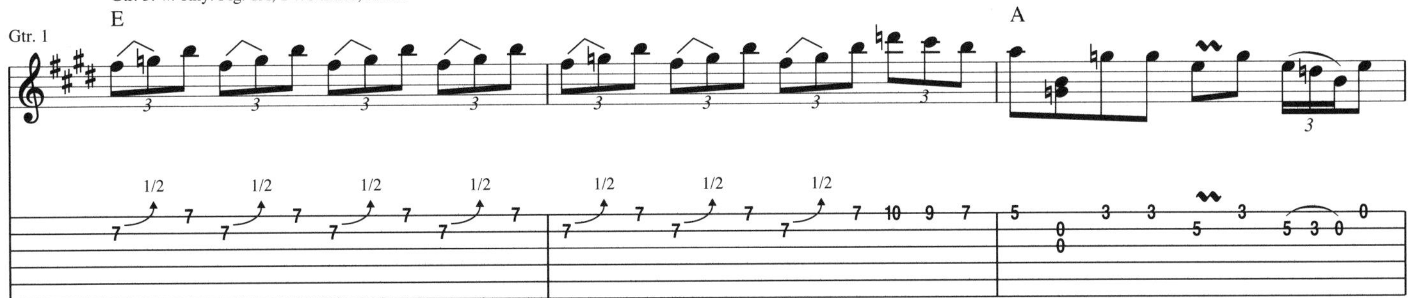

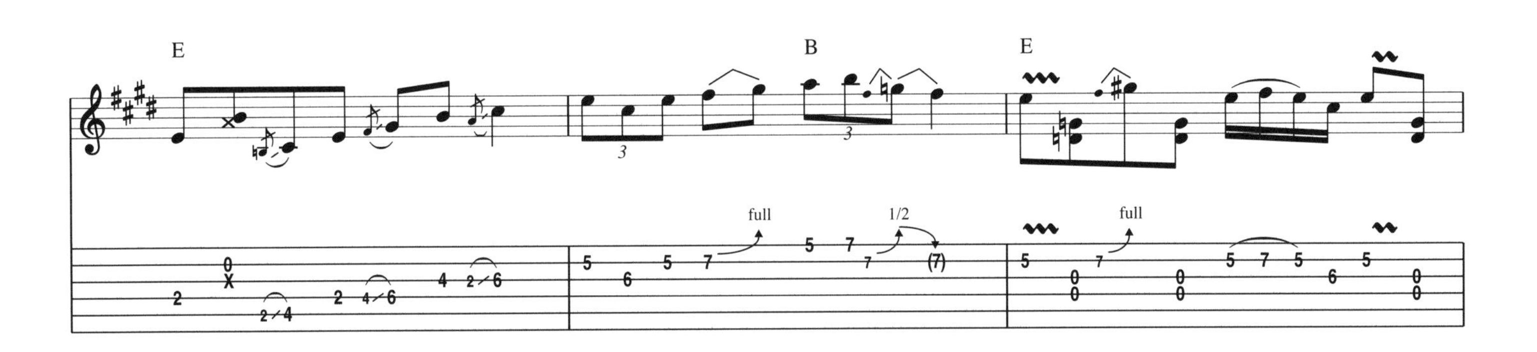

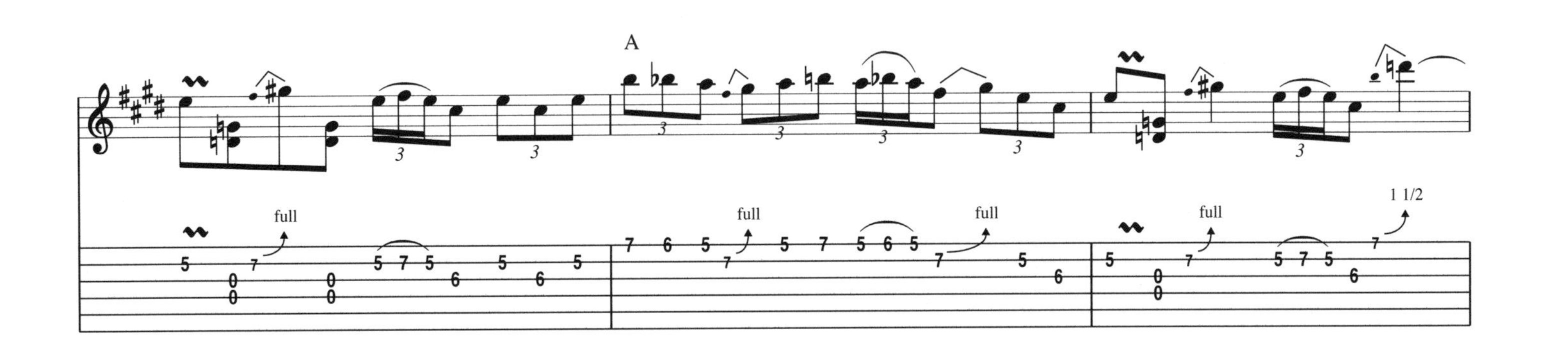

D.S. al Coda
Coda
F♯
G
G♯
E
Gtr. 2
Well, I
Uh, let me
Gtr. 1
Gtrs. 1 & 2
Gtr. 3
B
1.
up,
ba - by, I've had e - nough.

2.
B7
N.C.
E7(♯9)
- by, I've had e - nough.
Gtr. 1
Gtr. 2
Gtr. 3
1/4
Free Time

Riverside

Words and Music by Kevin Bowe

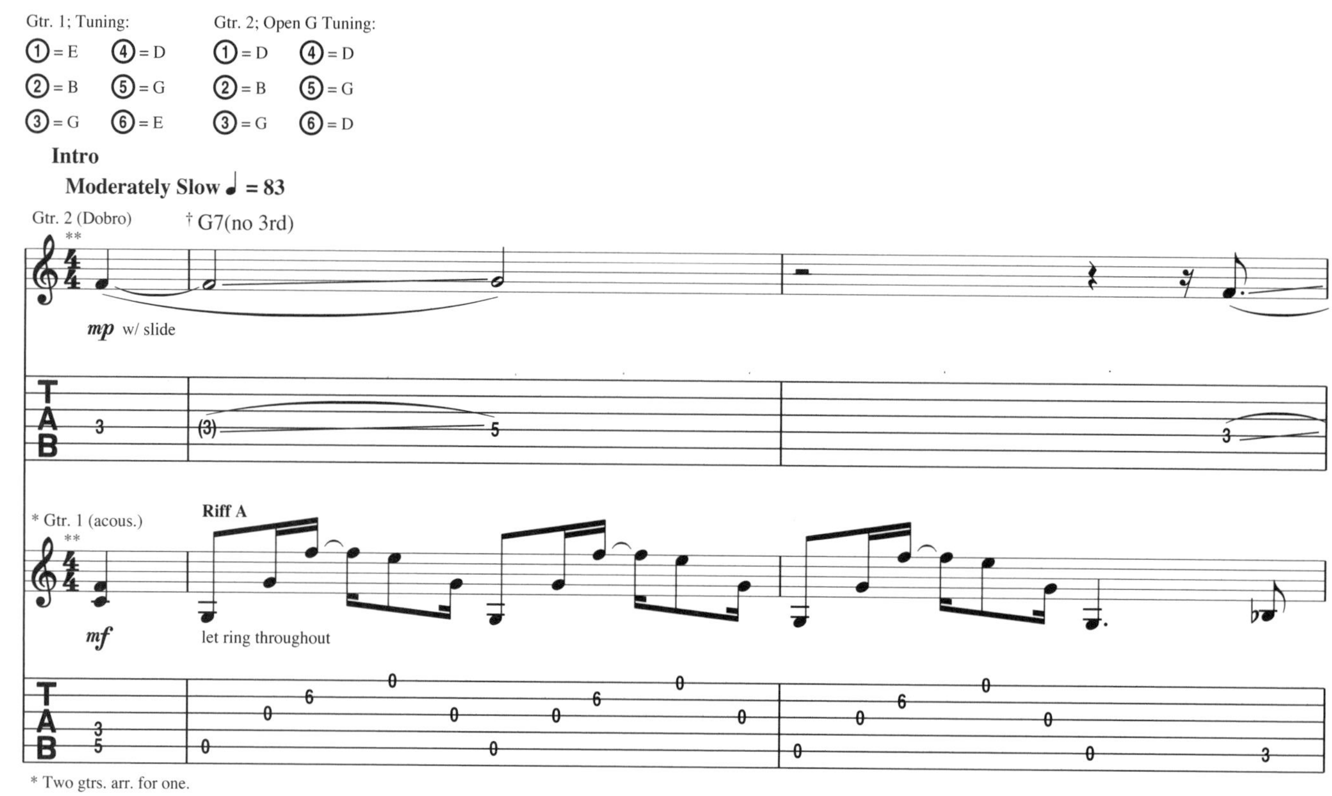

* Two gtrs. arr. for one.

** Key signature denotes G Mixolydian.

† Chord symbols reflect implied tonality.

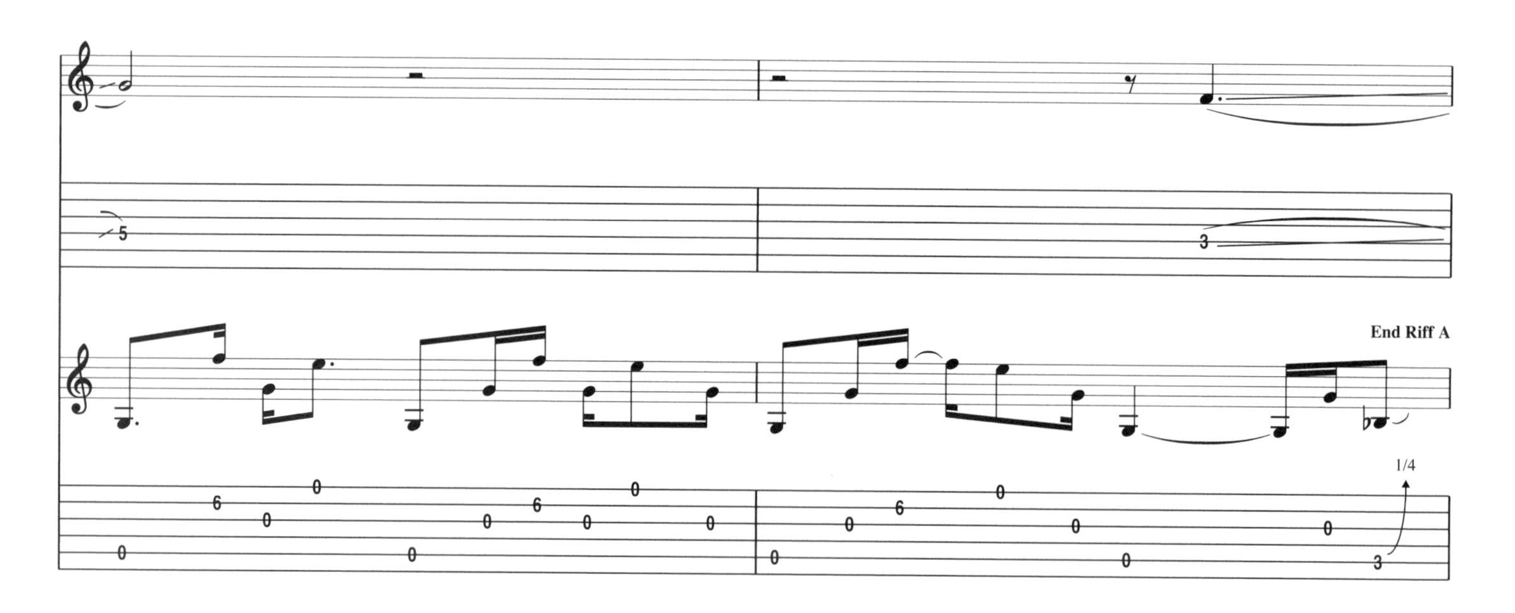

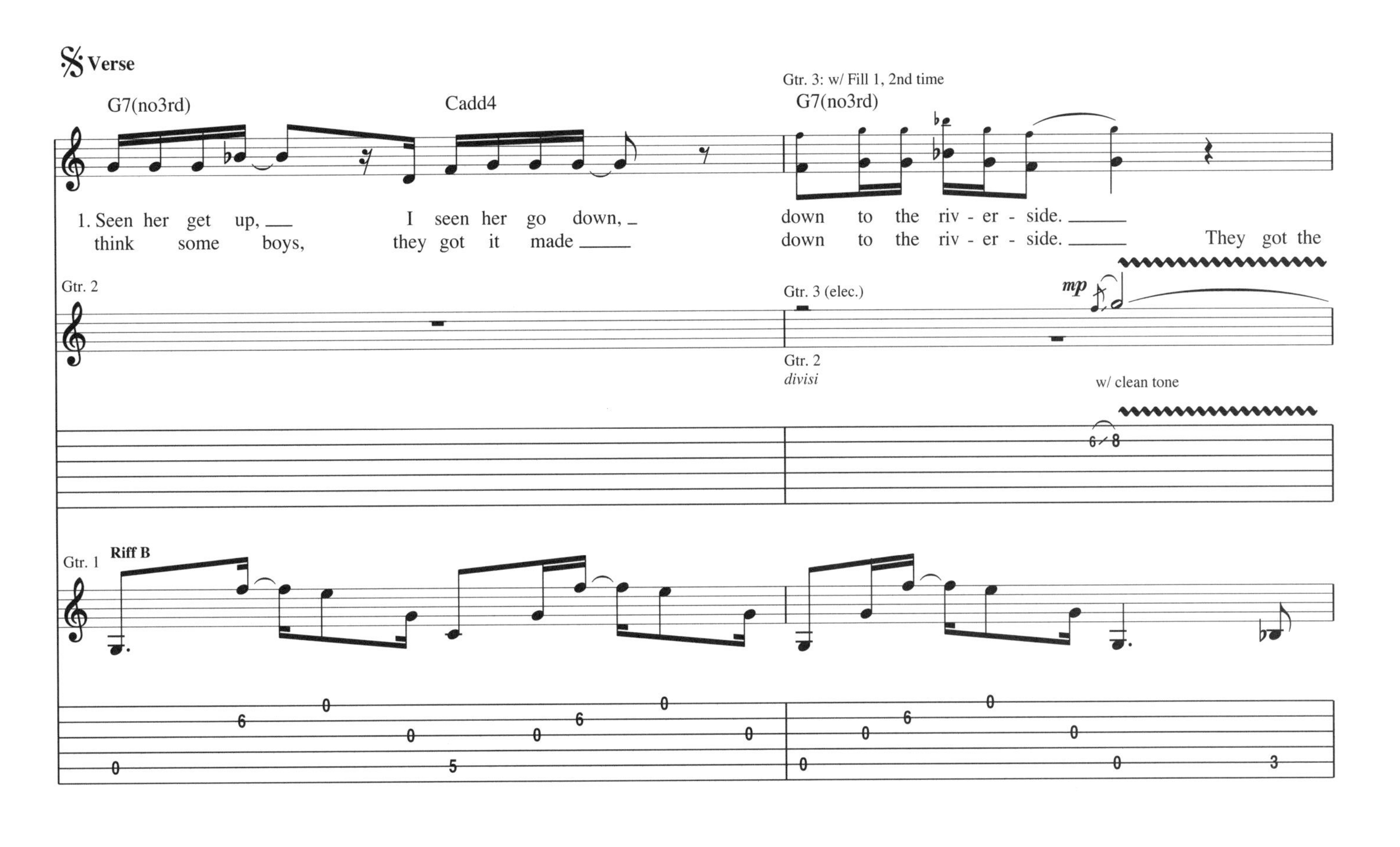
Verse
G7(no3rd)
Cadd4
Gtr. 3: w/ Fill 1, 2nd time
G7(no3rd)
1. Seen her get up,
I seen her go down,
down to the riv - er - side.
think some boys,
they got it made
down to the riv - er - side.
They got the
Gtr. 2
Gtr. 3 (elec.)
mp
Gtr. 2
divisi
w/ clean tone
Gtr. 1
Riff B

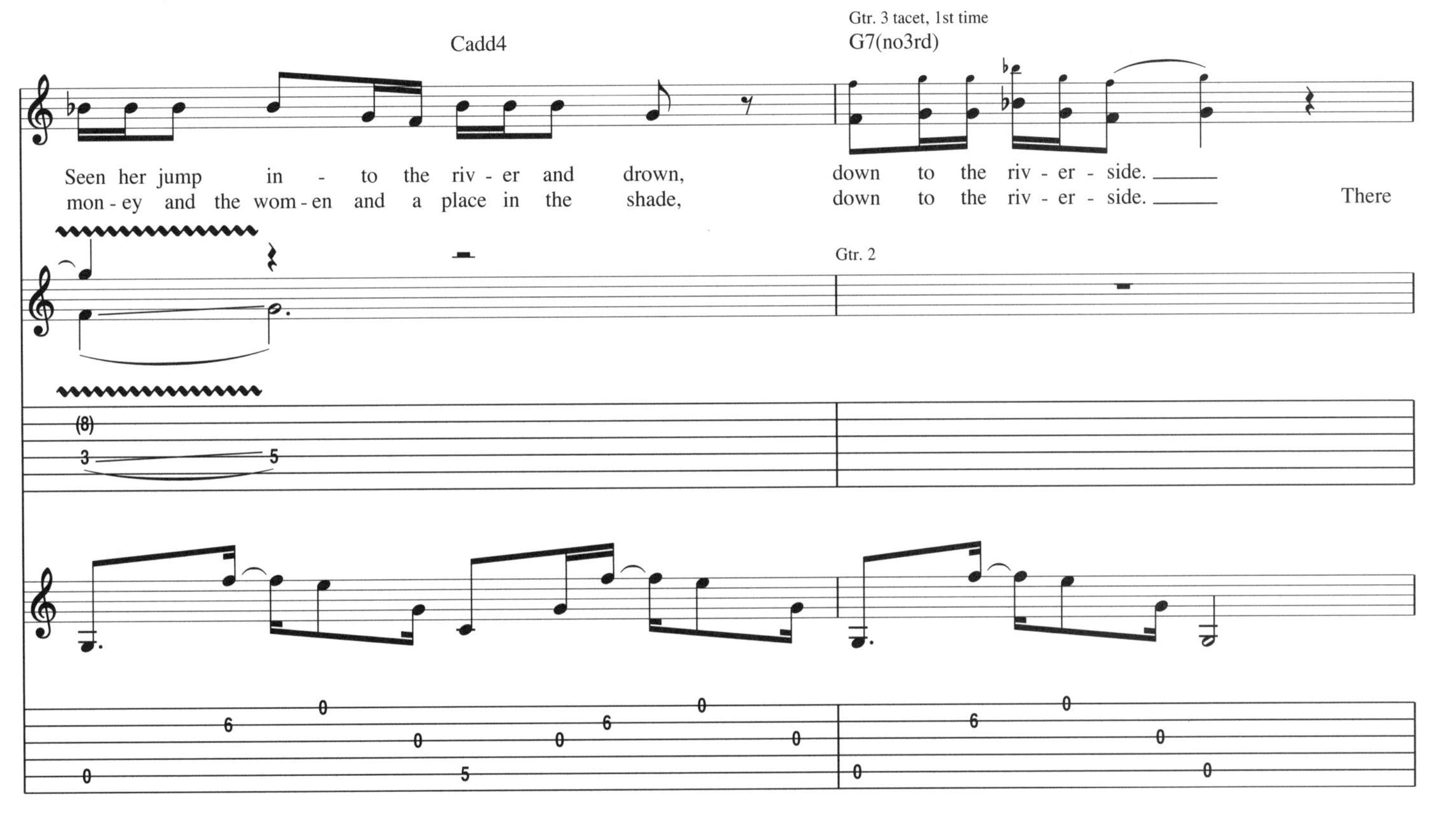
Cadd4
Gtr. 3 tacet, 1st time
G7(no3rd)
Seen her jump in - to the riv - er and drown,
down to the riv - er - side.
mon - ey and the wom - en and a place in the shade,
down to the riv - er - side.
There
Gtr. 2

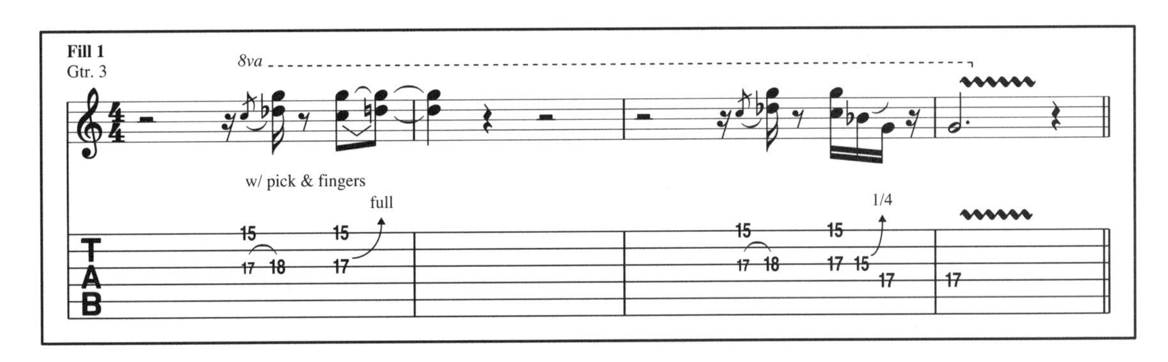
Fill 1
Gtr. 3
8va
w/ pick & fingers
full
1/4

Cadd4
Dm7
G7(no3rd)
C5
Peo - ple do just what they will. Don't mat - ter to the riv - er, it's a run - nin' still. Sing,
ain't no way to ease your pain, you can't lis - ten to the riv - er when it calls your name. Sing - in'
Riff C

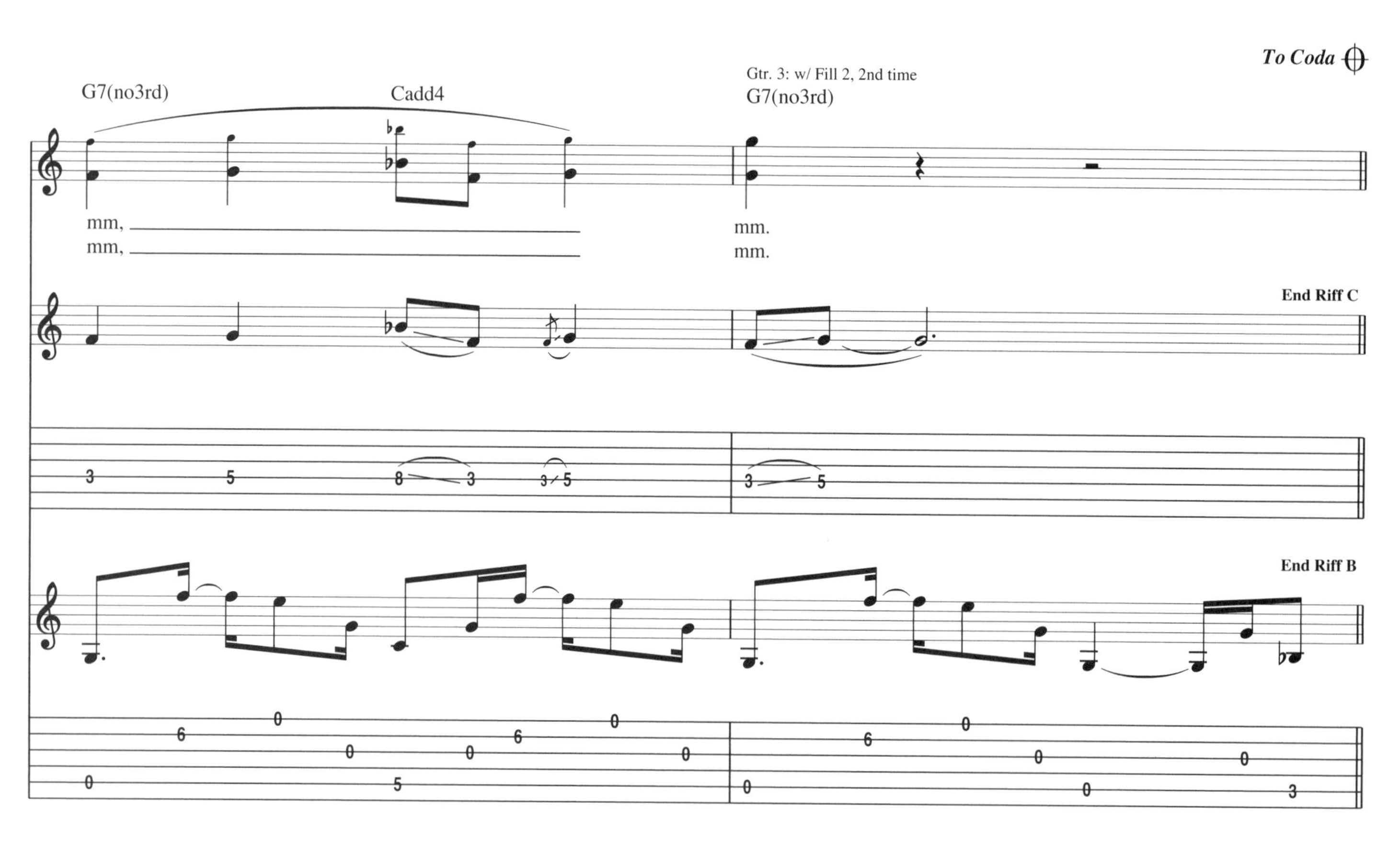
To Coda
Gtr. 3: w/ Fill 2, 2nd time
G7(no3rd)
Cadd4
G7(no3rd)
mm,
mm,
mm.
mm.
End Riff C
End Riff B

Fill 2
Gtr. 3

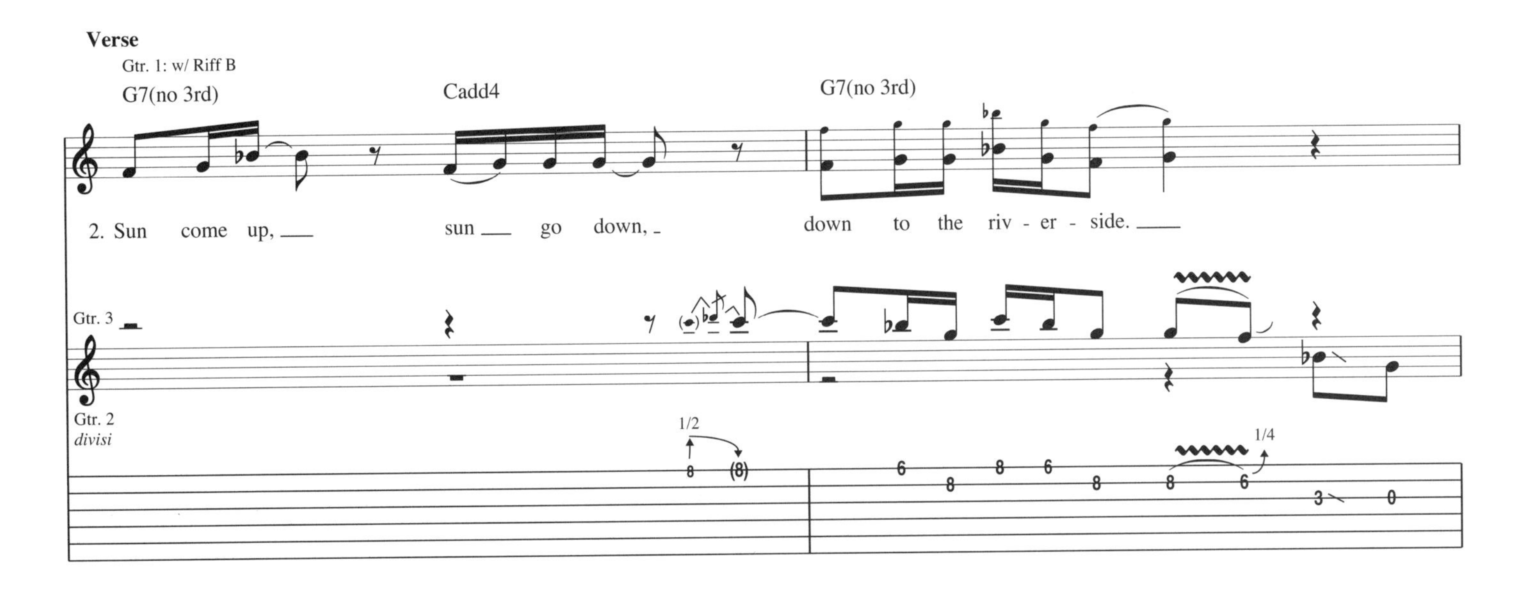
Verse
Gtr. 1: w/ Riff B
G7(no 3rd)
Cadd4
G7(no 3rd)
2. Sun come up, sun go down, down to the riv - er - side.
Gtr. 3
Gtr. 2
divisi
1/2
1/4

Cadd4
G7(no 3rd)
Sun jump in - to the riv' and drown, down to the riv - er - side.

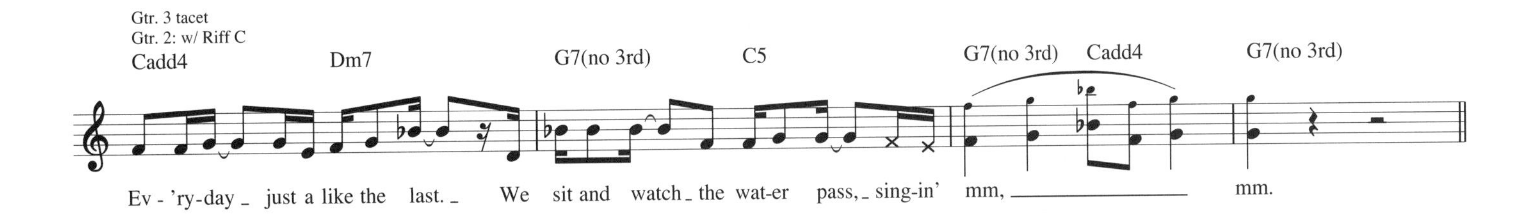
Gtr. 3 tacet
Gtr. 2: w/ Riff C
Cadd4
Dm7
G7(no 3rd)
C5
G7(no 3rd)
Cadd4
G7(no 3rd)
Ev - 'ry-day just a like the last. We sit and watch the wat-er pass, sing-in' mm, mm.

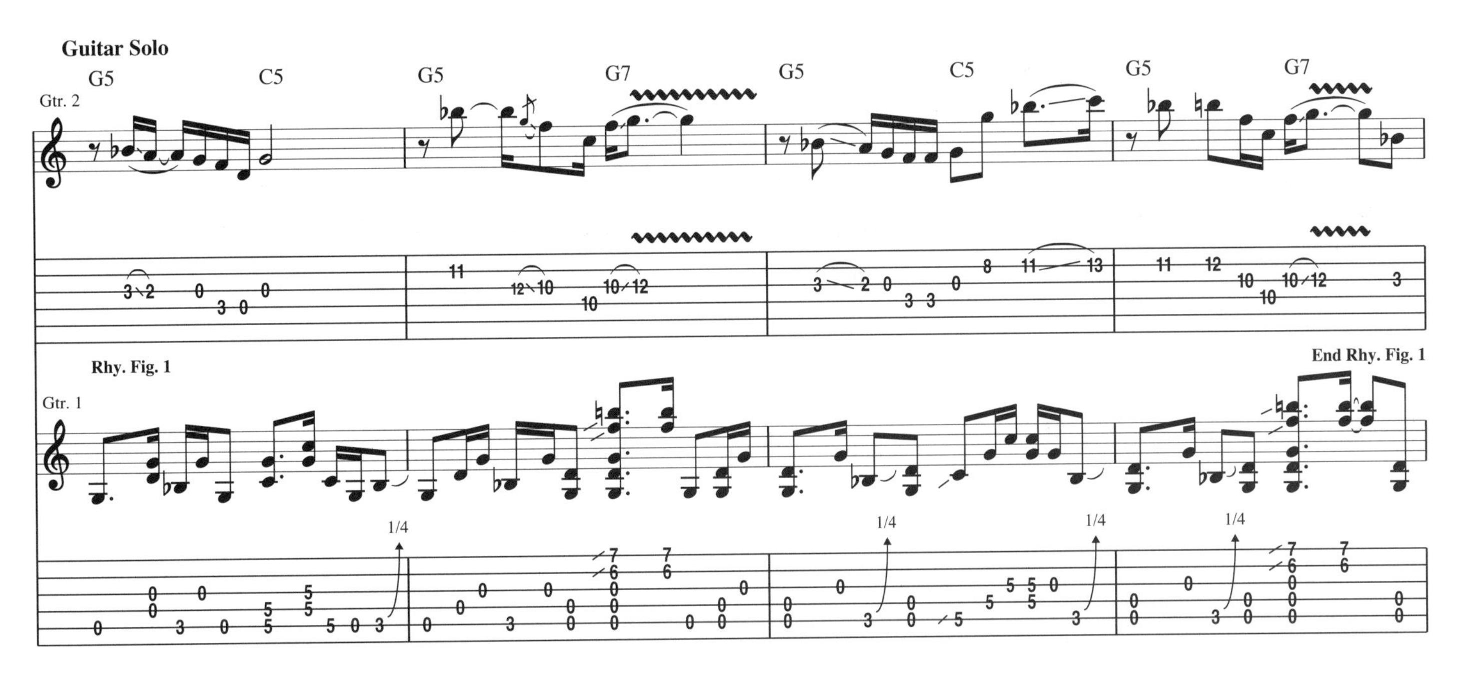
Guitar Solo
G5
C5
G5
G7
G5
C5
G5
G7
Gtr. 2
Rhy. Fig. 1
End Rhy. Fig. 1
Gtr. 1
1/4

Interlude

Verse

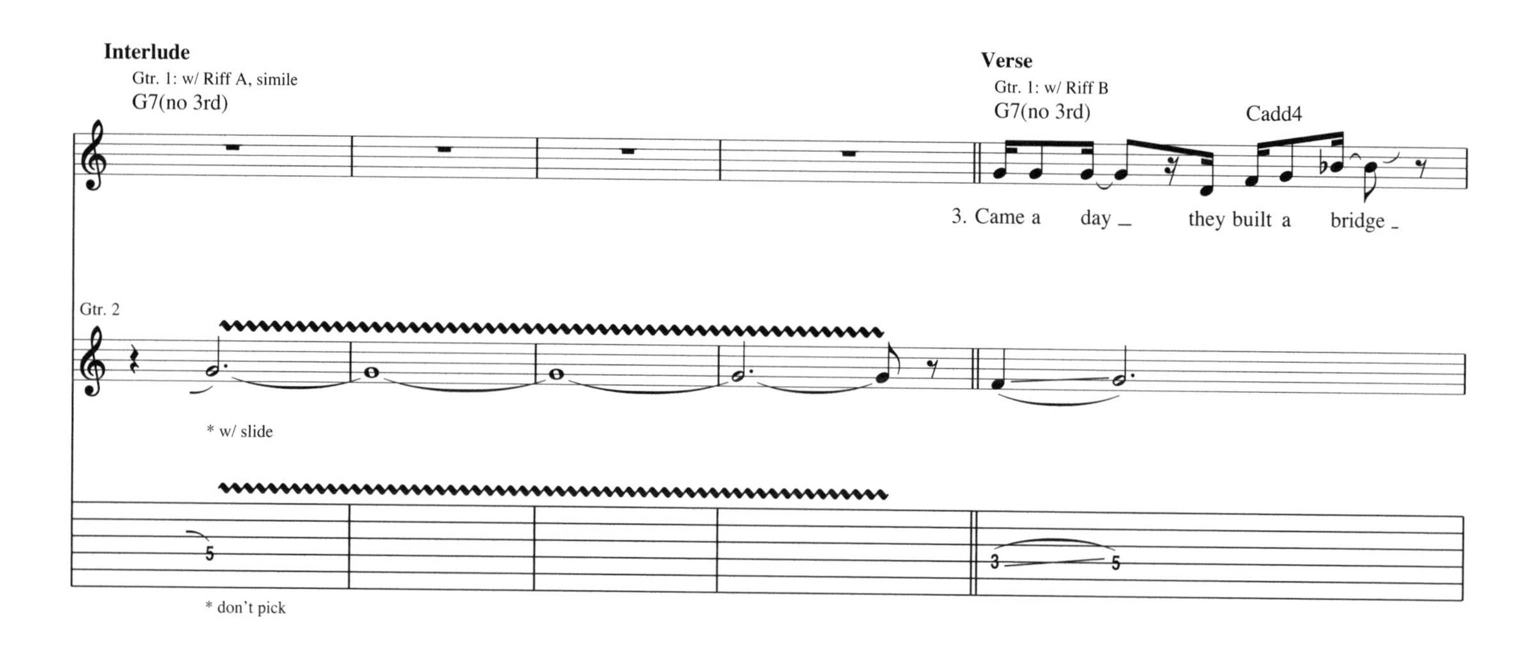

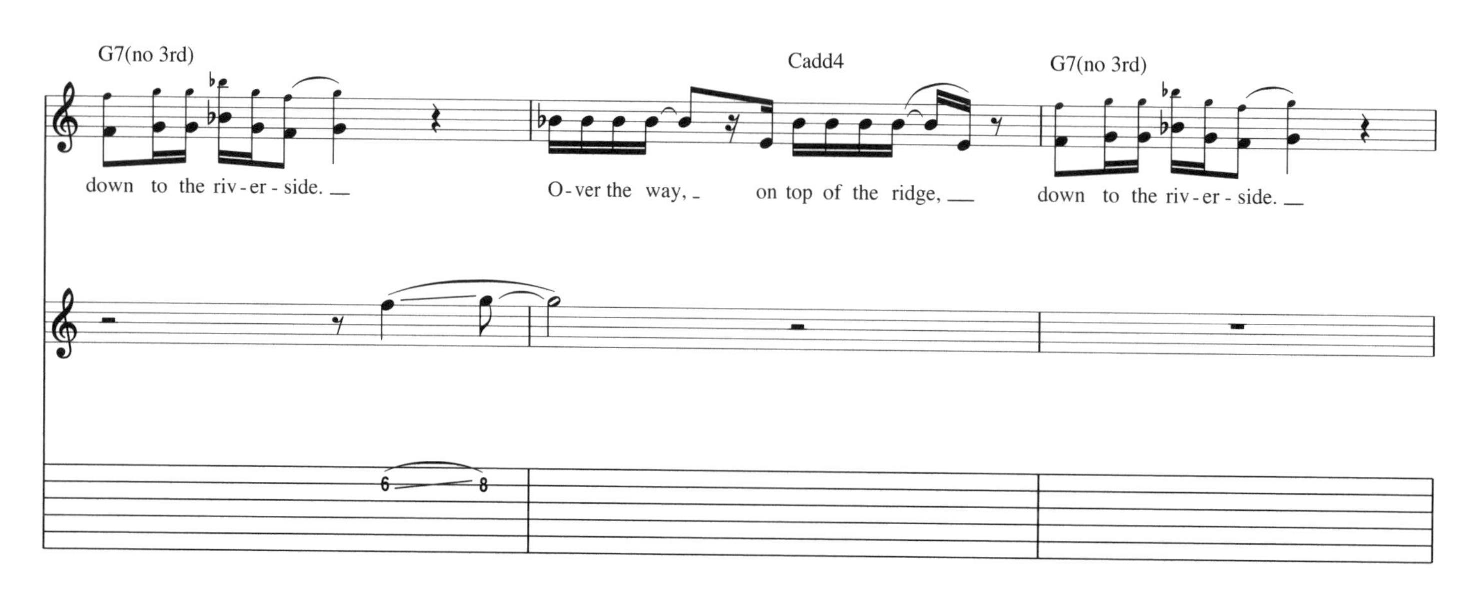

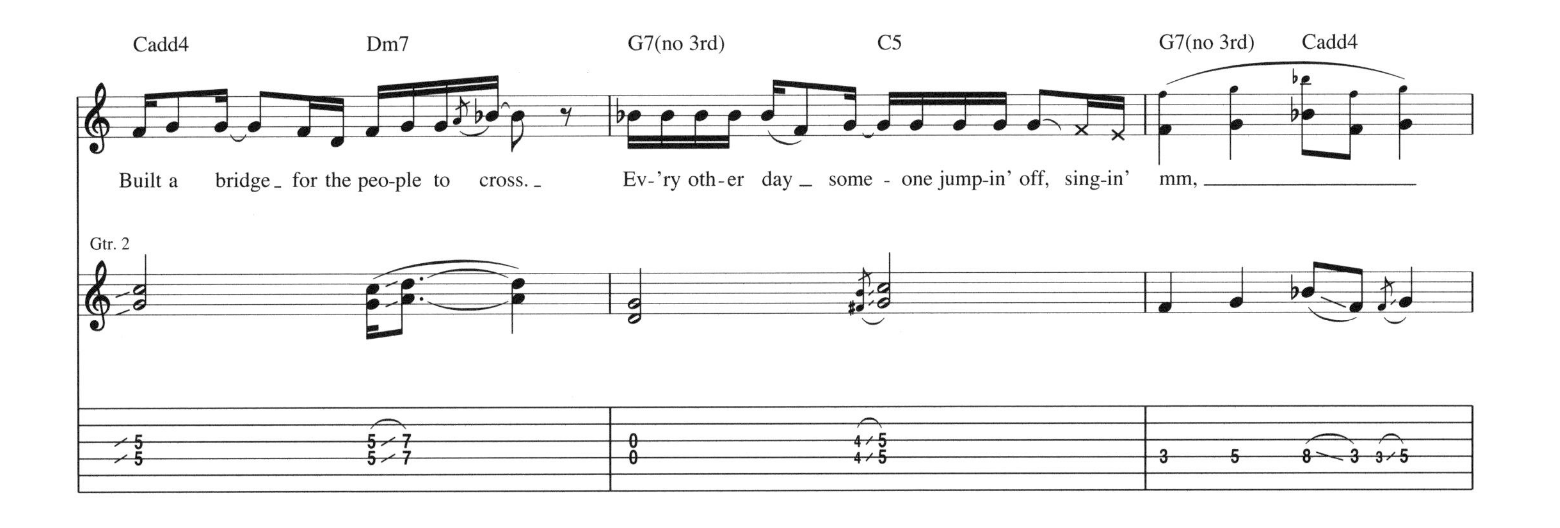
Cadd4
Dm7
G7(no 3rd)
C5
G7(no 3rd)
Cadd4
Built a bridge for the peo-ple to cross.
Ev-'ry oth-er day some - one jump-in' off, sing-in' mm,
Gtr. 2

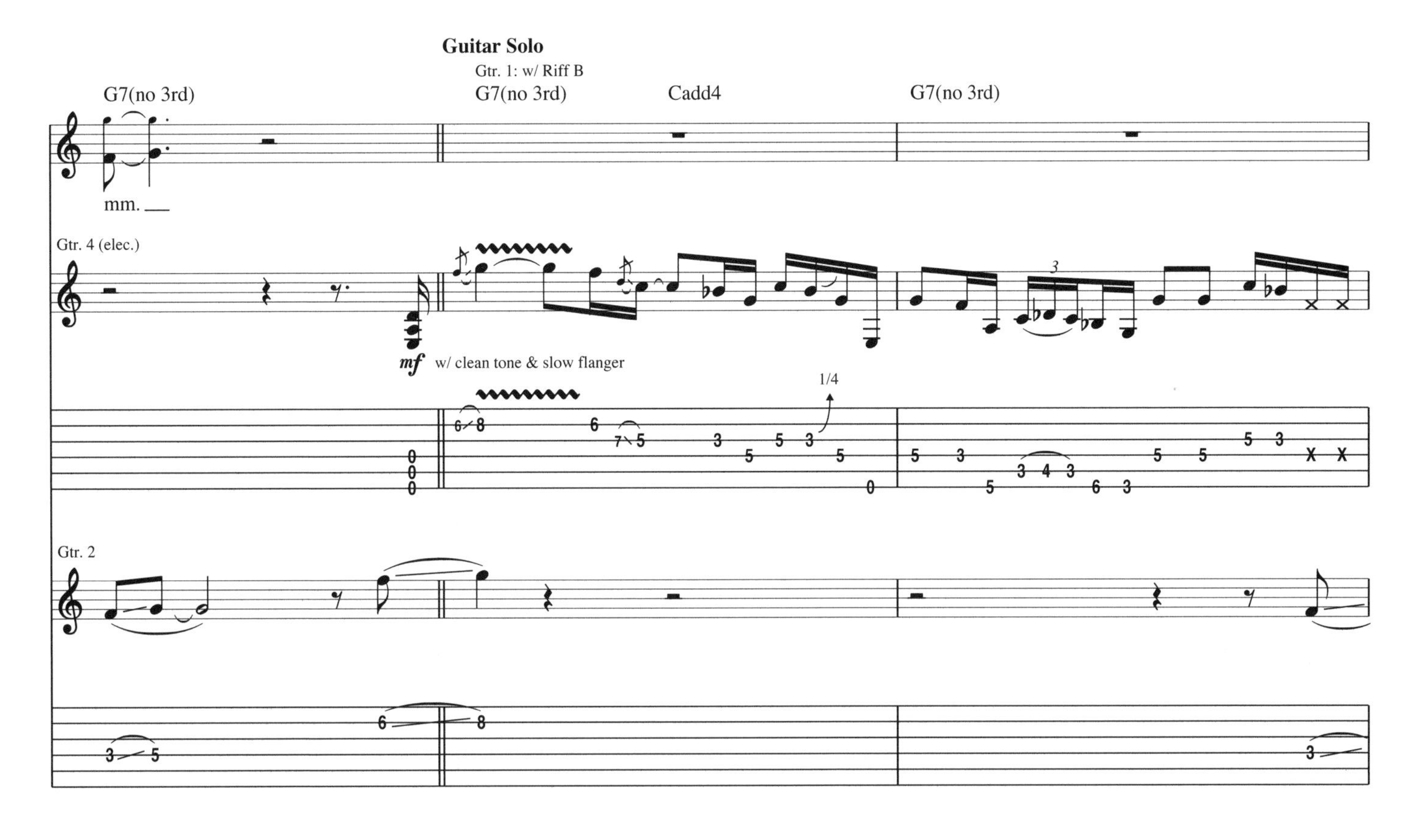
Guitar Solo
Gtr. 1: w/ Riff B
G7(no 3rd)
G7(no 3rd)
Cadd4
G7(no 3rd)
mm.
Gtr. 4 (elec.)
mf
w/ clean tone & slow flanger
1/4
Gtr. 2

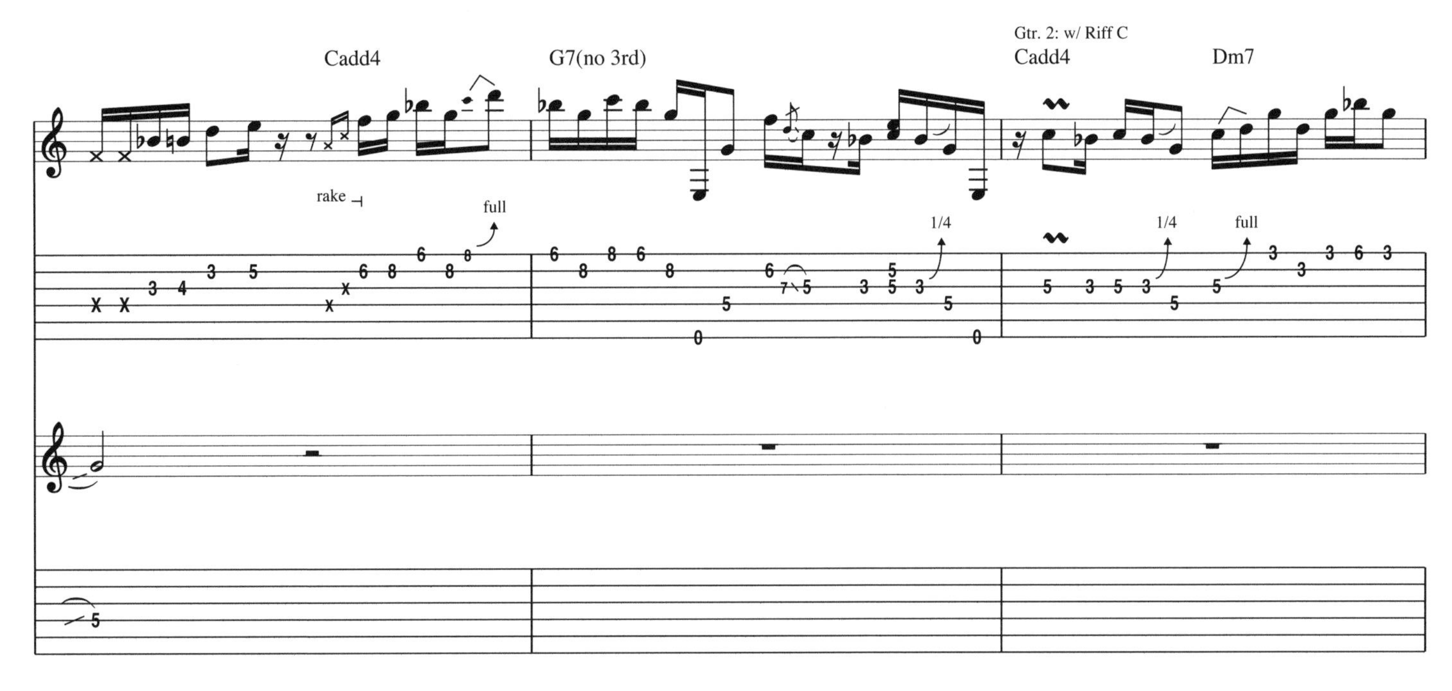
Gtr. 2: w/ Riff C
Cadd4
G7(no 3rd)
Cadd4
Dm7
rake
full
1/4
1/4
full

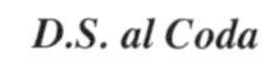
D.S. al Coda

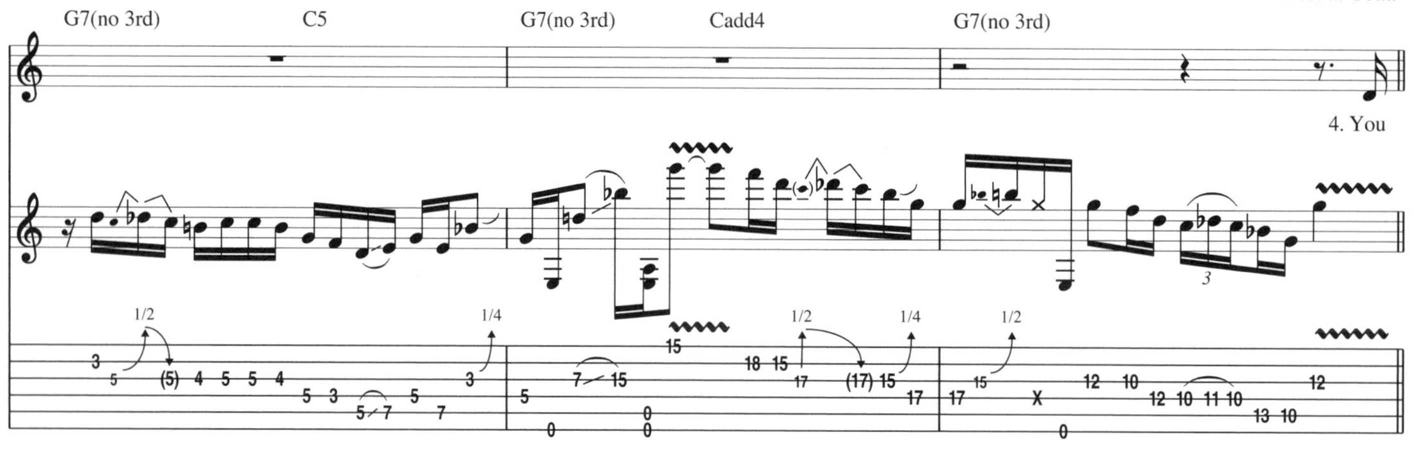
G7(no 3rd)
C5
G7(no 3rd)
Cadd4
G7(no 3rd)
4. You

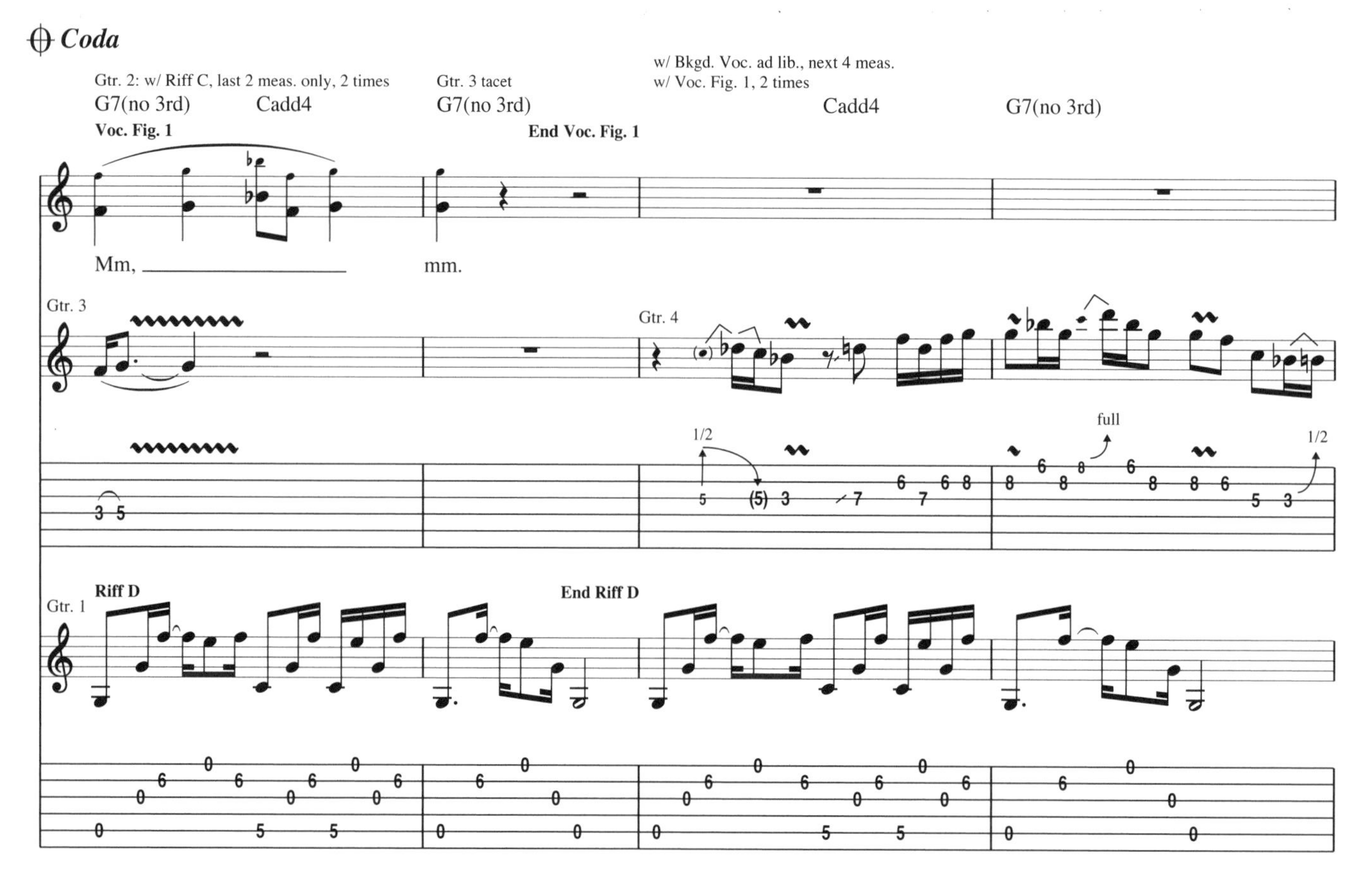
Coda
Gtr. 2: w/ Riff C, last 2 meas. only, 2 times
Gtr. 3 tacet
w/ Bkgd. Voc. ad lib., next 4 meas.
w/ Voc. Fig. 1, 2 times
G7(no 3rd)
Cadd4
G7(no 3rd)
Cadd4
G7(no 3rd)
Voc. Fig. 1
End Voc. Fig. 1
Mm,
mm.
Gtr. 3
Gtr. 4
Riff D
Gtr. 1
End Riff D

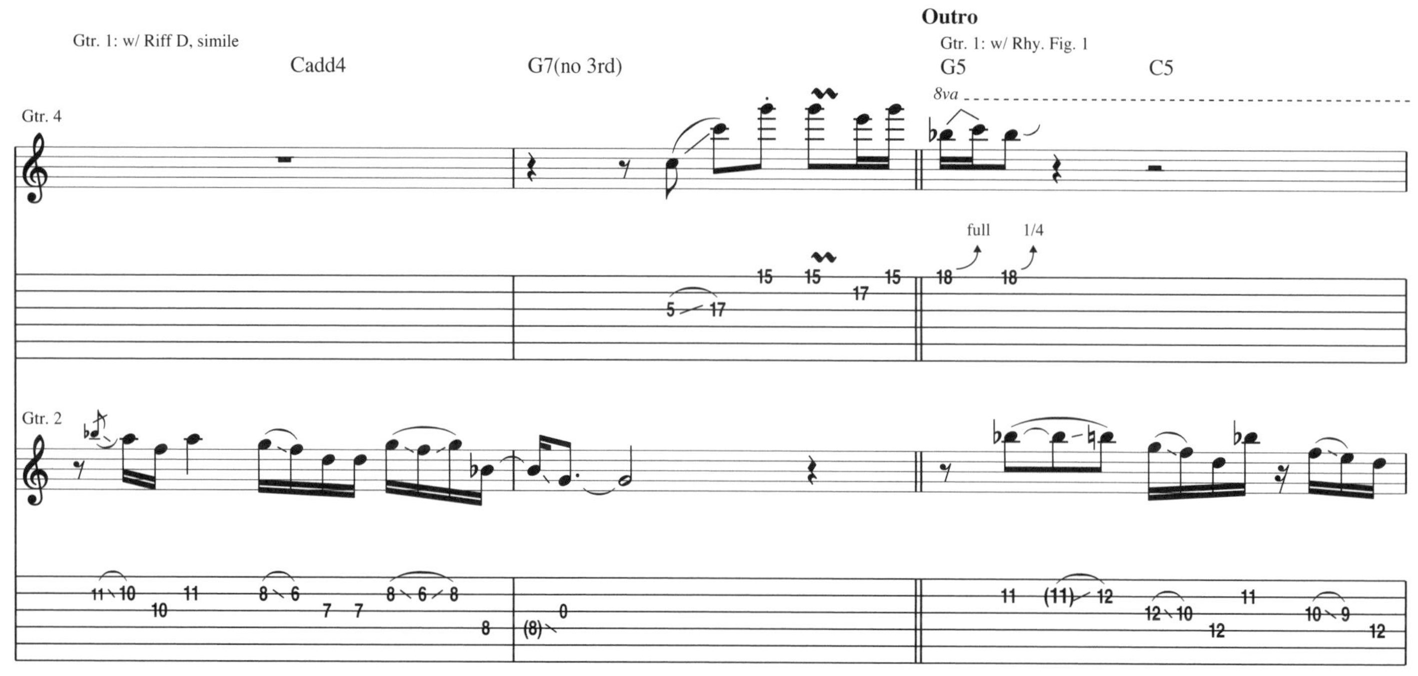
Gtr. 1: w/ Riff D, simile
Cadd4
G7(no 3rd)
Outro
Gtr. 1: w/ Rhy. Fig. 1
G5
C5
Gtr. 4
8va
Gtr. 2

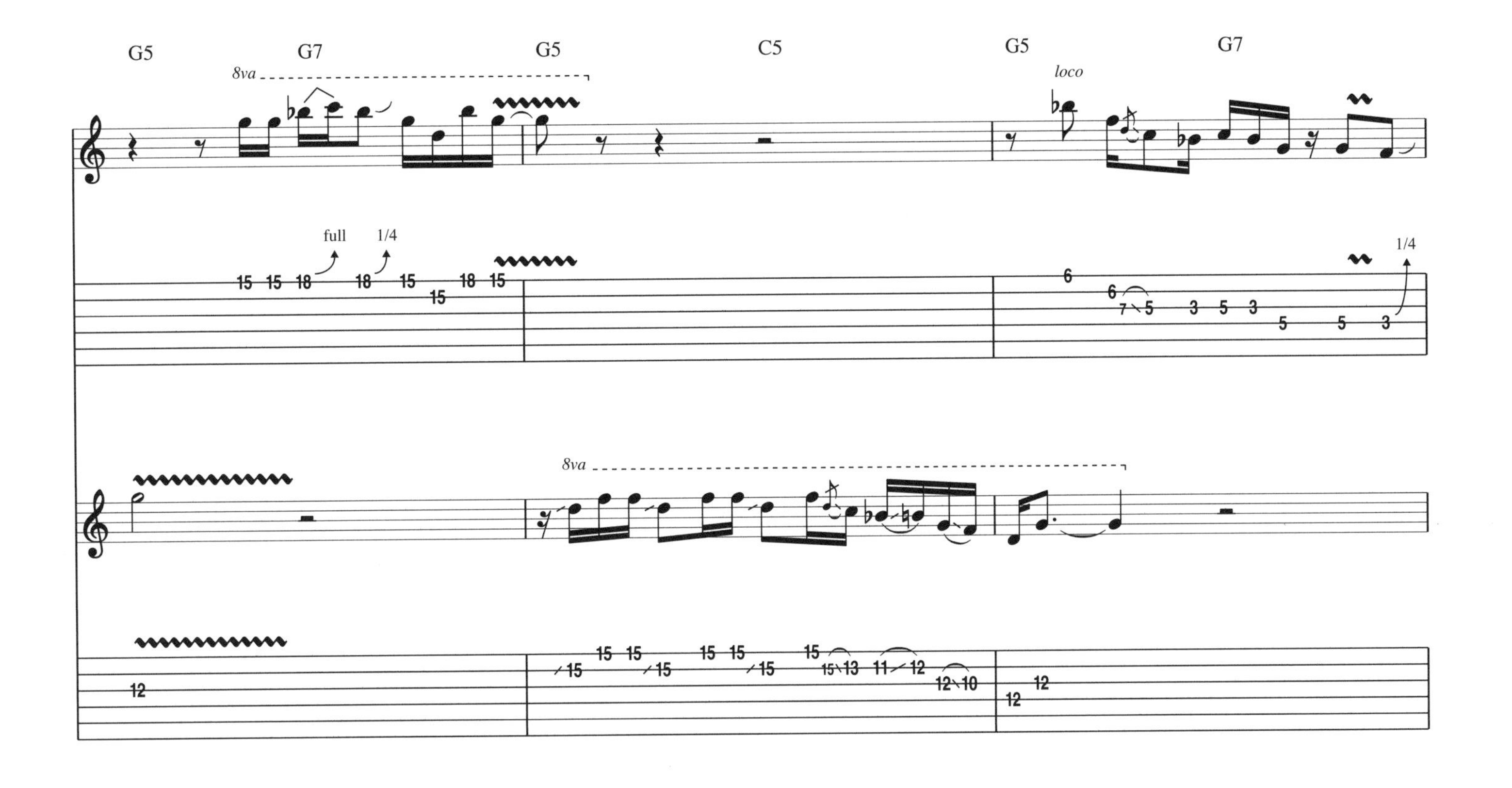
G5
G7
G5
C5
G5
G7
8va
loco
full
1/4
1/4
8va

Gtr. 4
B♭5
C5
D5
N.C.(F5)
G5
G7
B♭5
C5
D5
N.C.(F5)
G5
G7
1/4
Gtr. 2
loco
Gtr. 1

What's Goin' Down

Words and Music by Kenny Wayne Shepherd and Joe Nadeau

G
C
C♯
way?
D
Well, ev - 'ry-thing is chang - in' now.
Uh, now's the time and the time is now.
Uh pret - ty soon it's all gone a - way,
It's not the why, it's, it's just the how.
G
1.
C open
End Rhy. Fig. 1A
gone a - way.
End Rhy. Fig. 1

2.
G
C
C#
C
C# Bm
(cont. in slash)

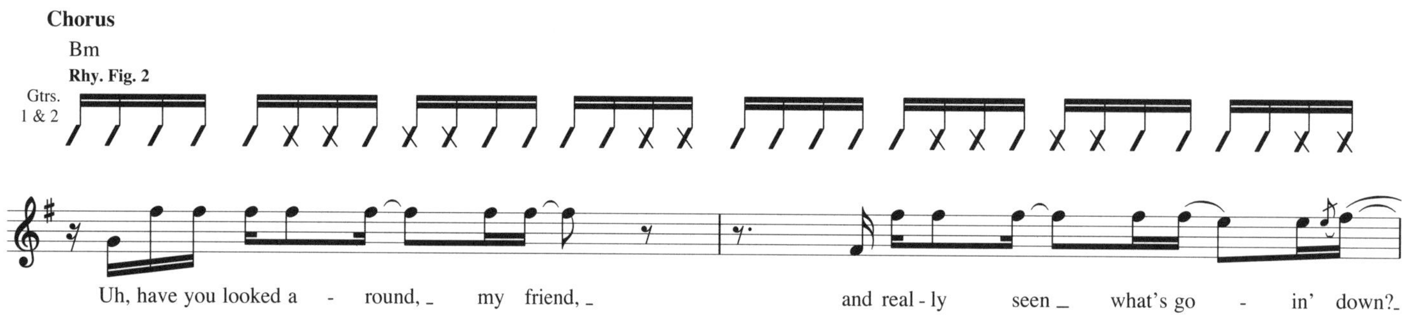
Chorus
Bm
Rhy. Fig. 2
Gtrs. 1 & 2
Uh, have you looked a - round, my friend, and real - ly seen what's go - in' down?

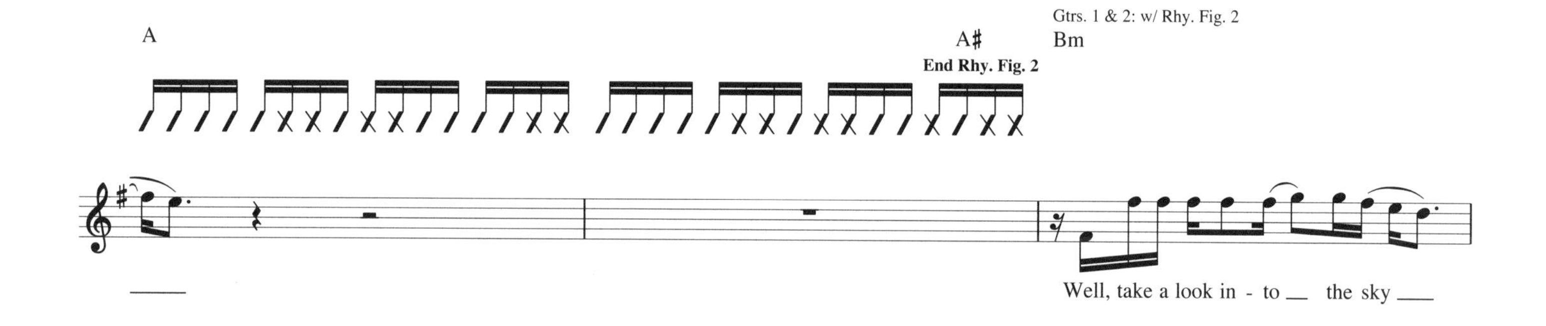
A
A#
End Rhy. Fig. 2
Gtrs. 1 & 2: w/ Rhy. Fig. 2
Bm
Well, take a look in - to the sky

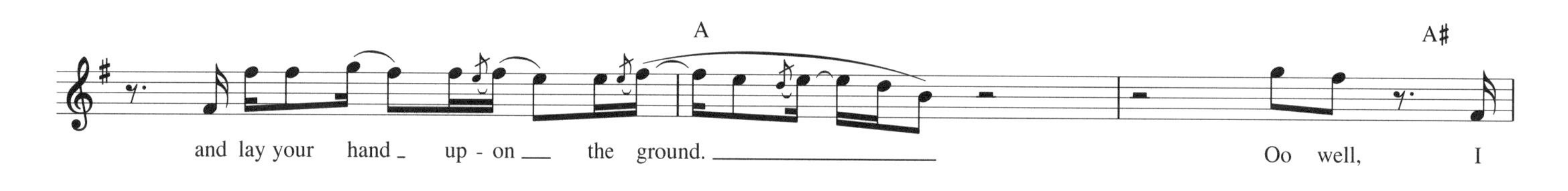
A
A#
and lay your hand up - on the ground. Oo well, I

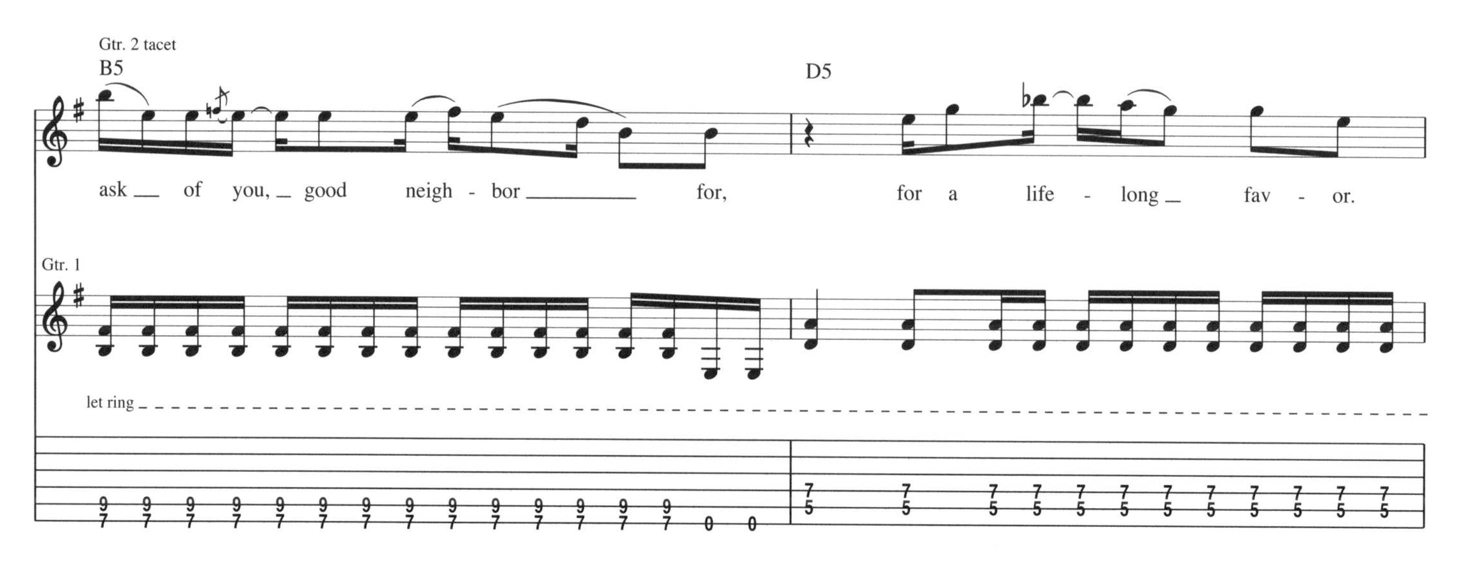
Gtr. 2 tacet
B5
D5
ask of you, good neigh - bor for, for a life - long fav - or.
Gtr. 1
let ring

* Chord symbols reflect overall tonality.

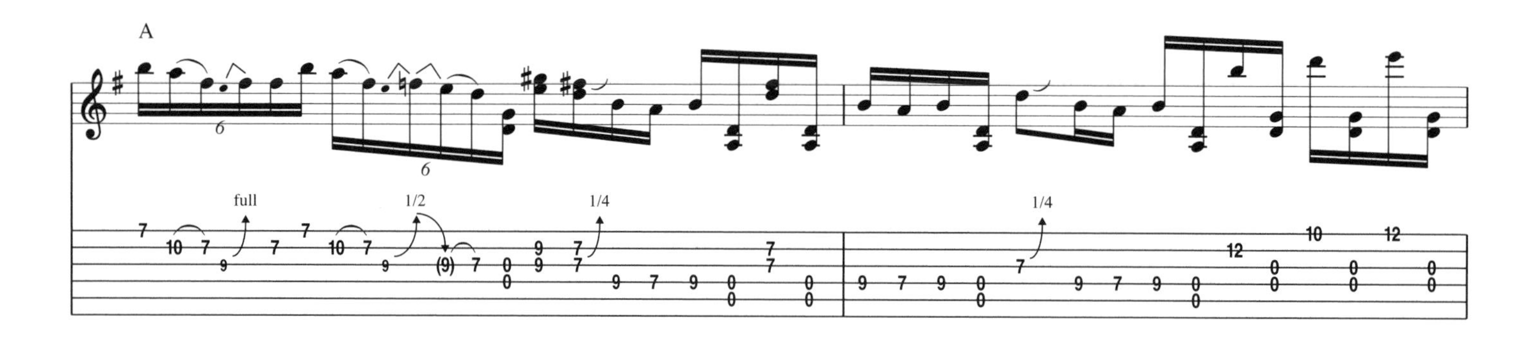
A
full
1/2
1/4
1/4

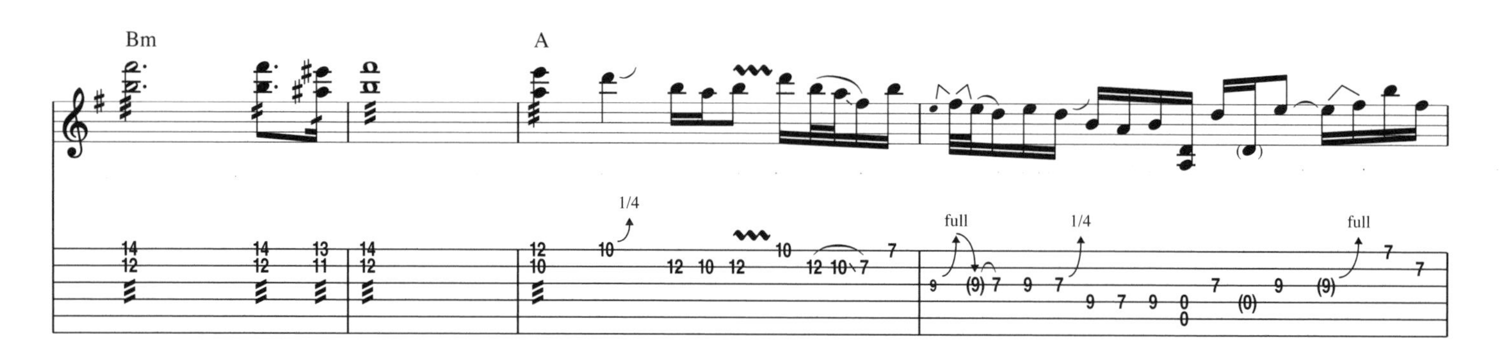
Bm
A
1/4
full
1/4
full

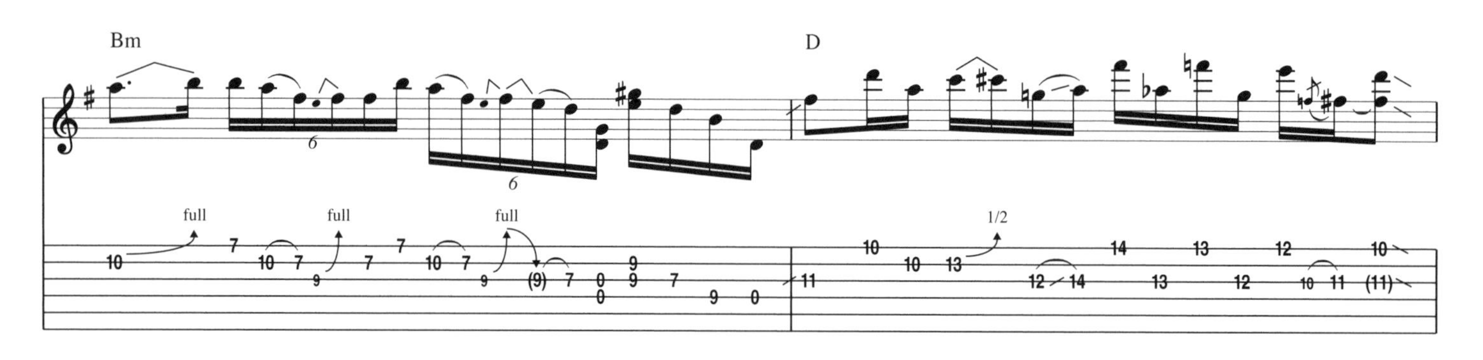
Bm
D
full
full
full
1/2

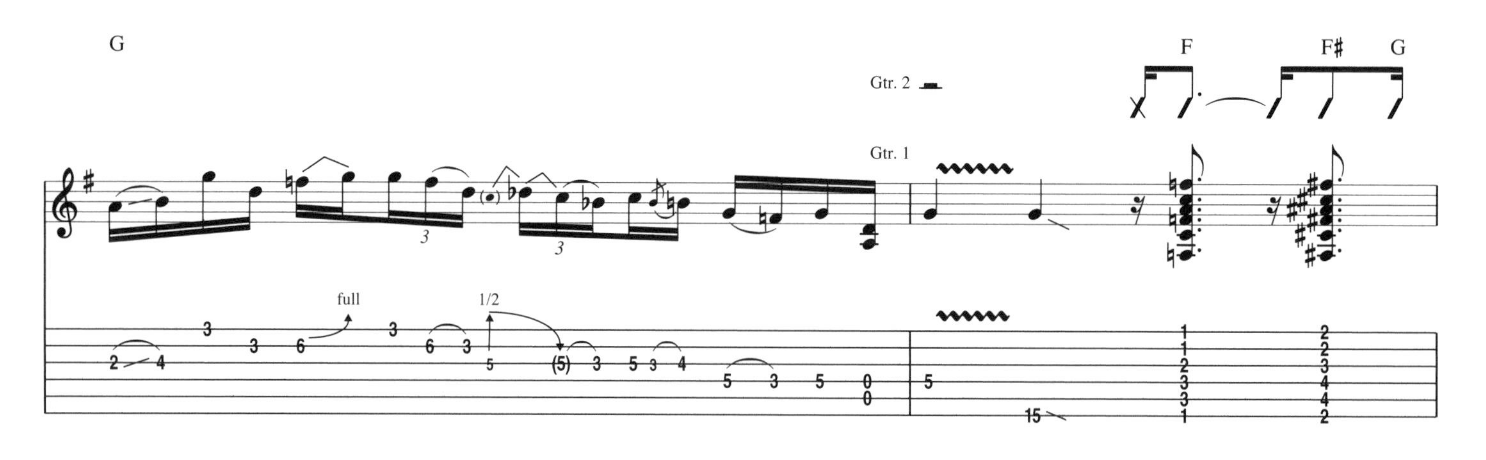
G
Gtr. 2
Gtr. 1
F
F#
G
full
1/2

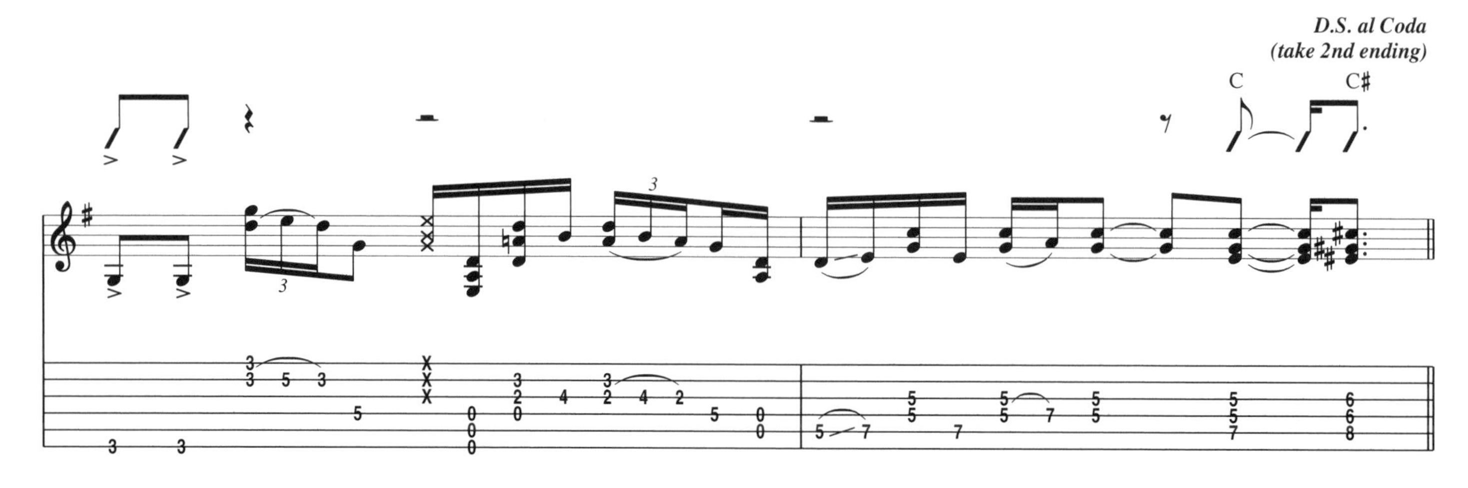
D.S. al Coda
(take 2nd ending)
C
C#

Coda
Interlude
F
F♯
G
3fr
Gtr. 2
Gtr. 1
w/ Voc. ad lib., next 6 meas.
G
Gtr. 2 tacet
C7
G
C7
Outro-Guitar Solo
w/ Voc. ad lib., next 8 meas.
G
Rhy. Fig. 3
Gtr. 2
Gtr. 1
f w/ dist.
* vol. swell
C open
End Rhy. Fig. 3
Gtr. 2: w/ Rhy. Fig. 3, 12 times, simile
G
full
1/2
1/4
full
full
full
1/2

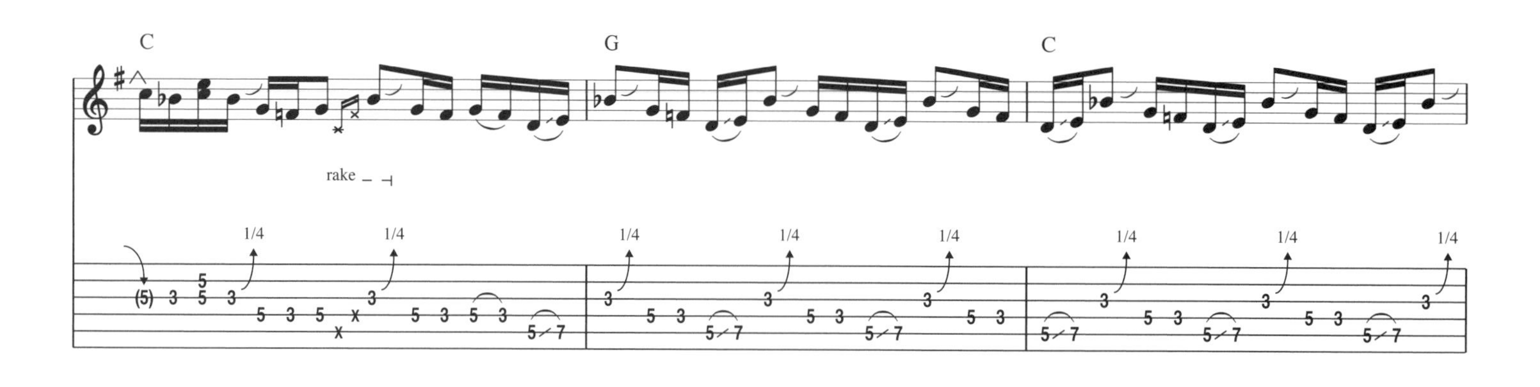
C
G
C
rake

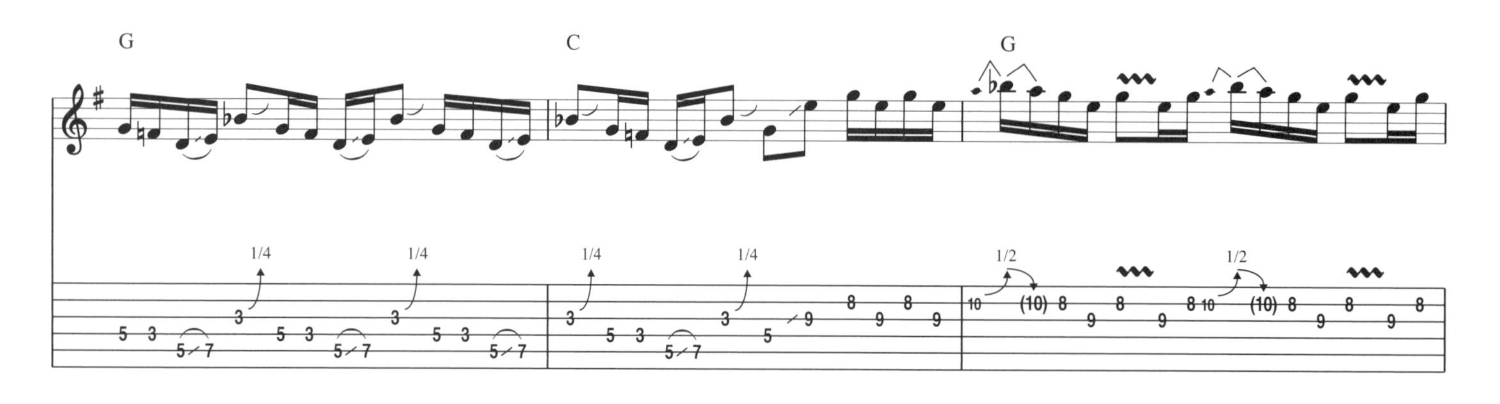
G
C
G

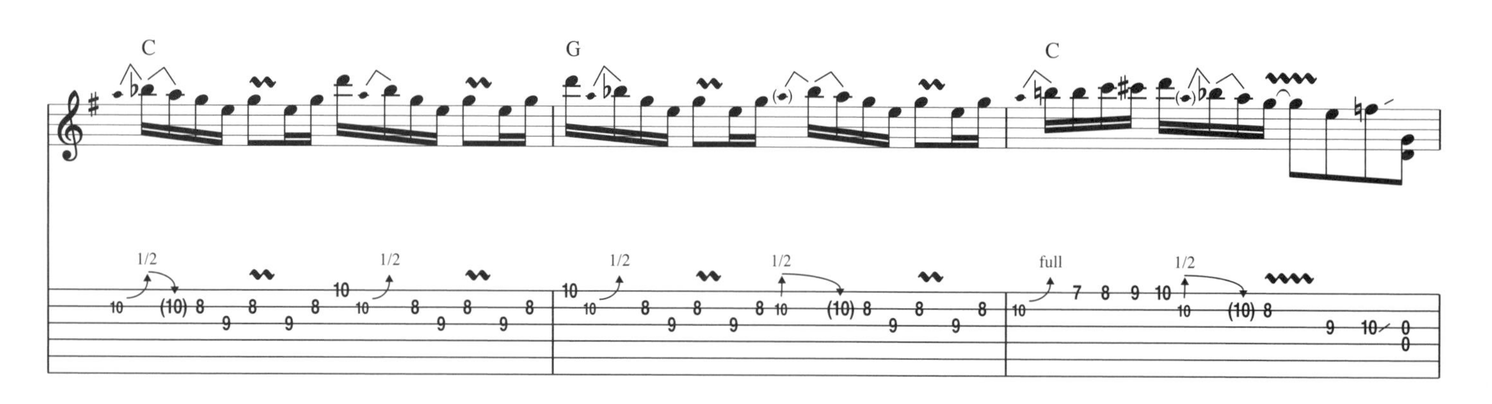
C
G
C
full

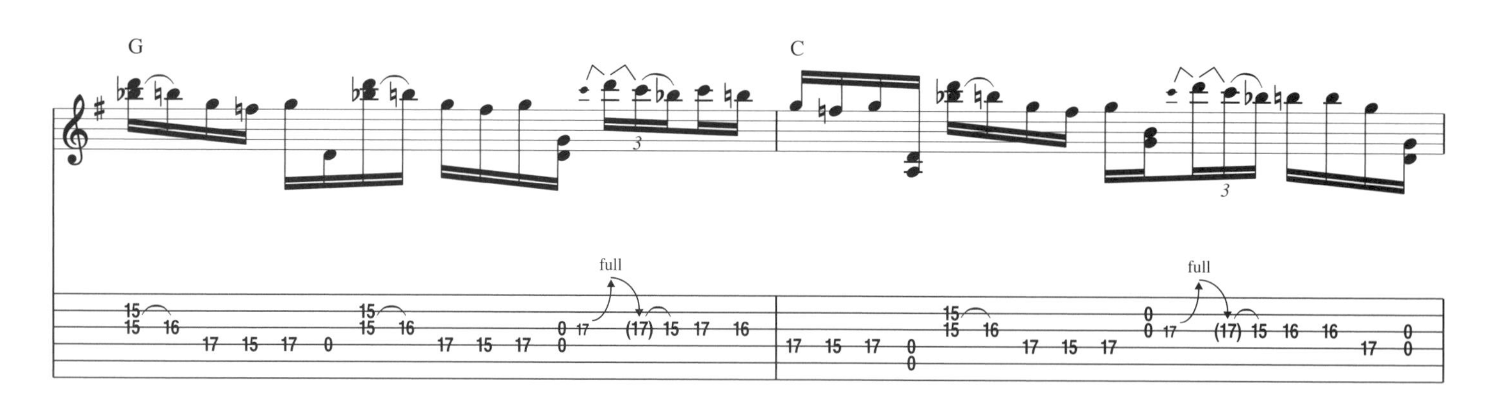
G
C
full
full

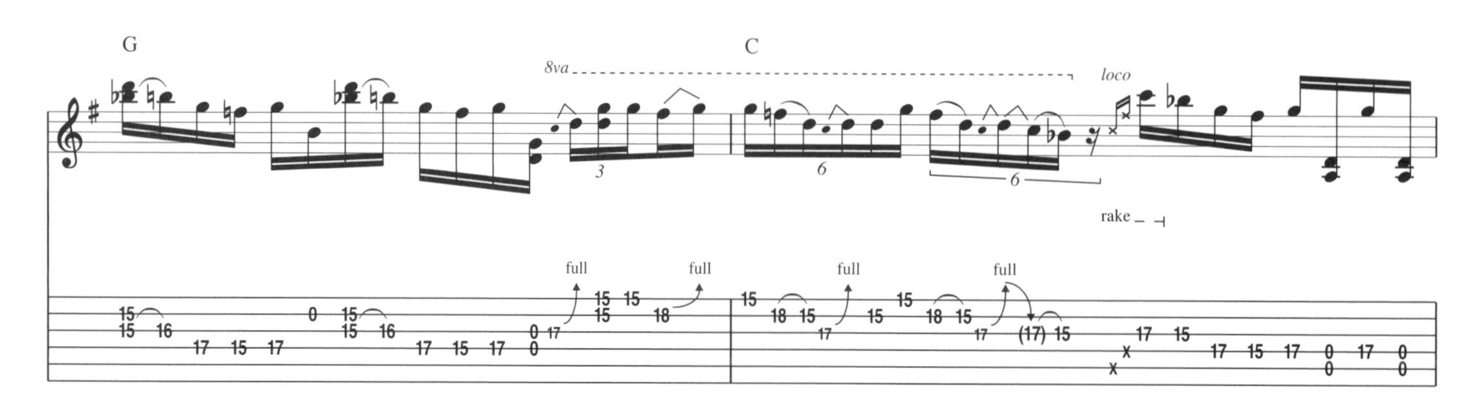
G
8va
C
loco
rake
full
full
full
full

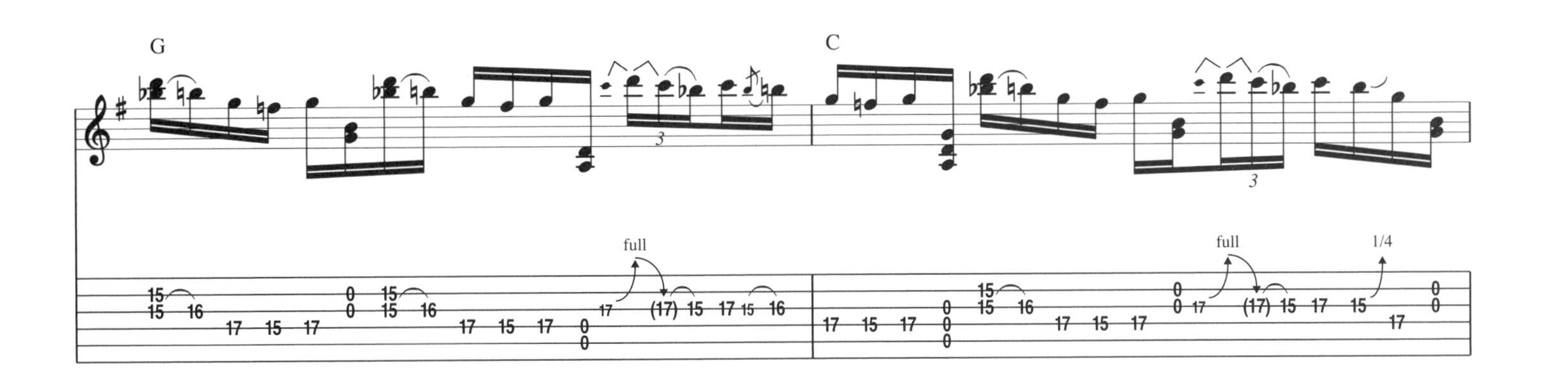
G
C
full
full
1/4

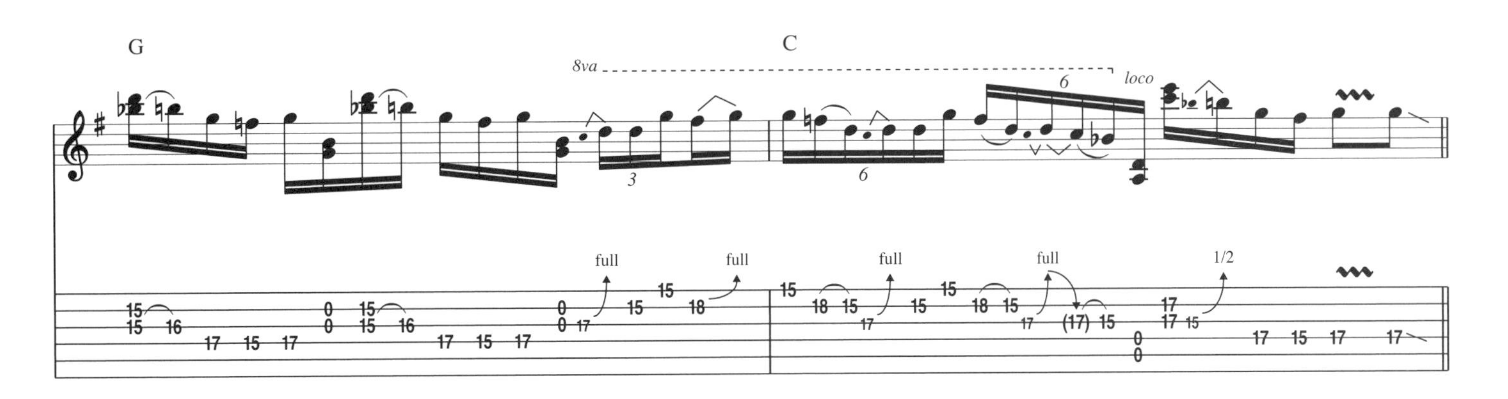
G
8va
C
loco
full
full
full
full
1/2

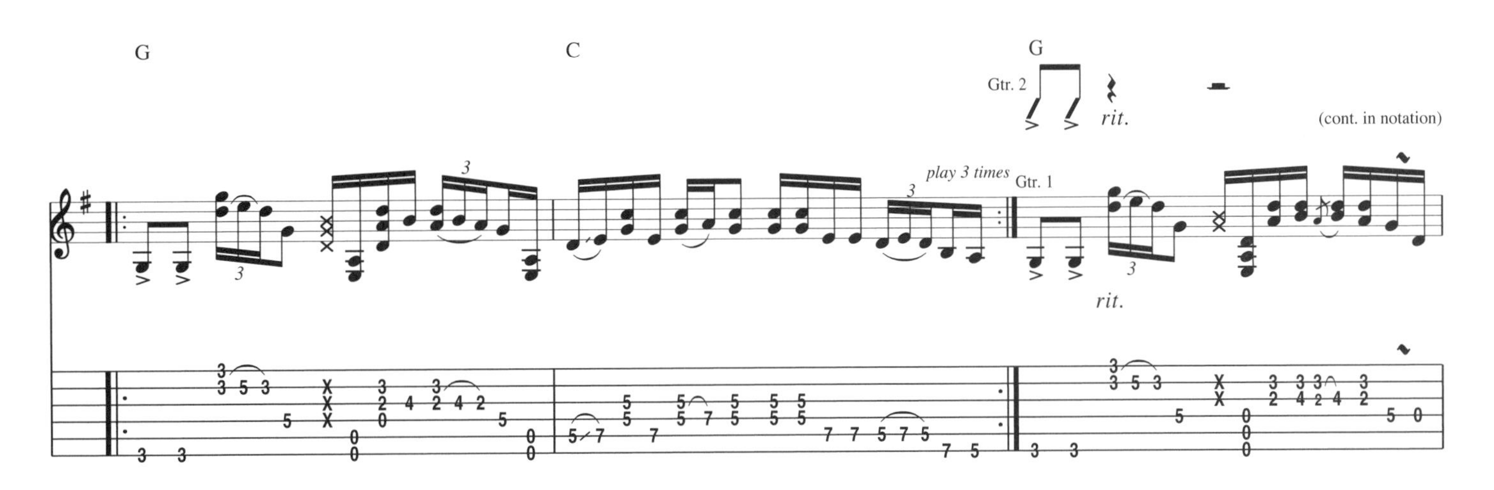
G
C
G
Gtr. 2
rit.
(cont. in notation)
play 3 times
Gtr. 1
rit.

Free Time
N.C.
G
Gtr. 1
let ring
Gtr. 2
let ring

Ledbetter Heights

By Kenny Wayne Shepherd

A7
1/2
1/2
E7
B7
let ring
A7
1/4
E7
B7
E7
rake
rake
1/2
3/4
1/2
1/2
full
rake
rake
1/2
1/2
A7
full
rake
1/2
E7
rake
1/4

B7
A7
E7
full
1/4
1/2
hold bend
let ring

* Played behind the beat.

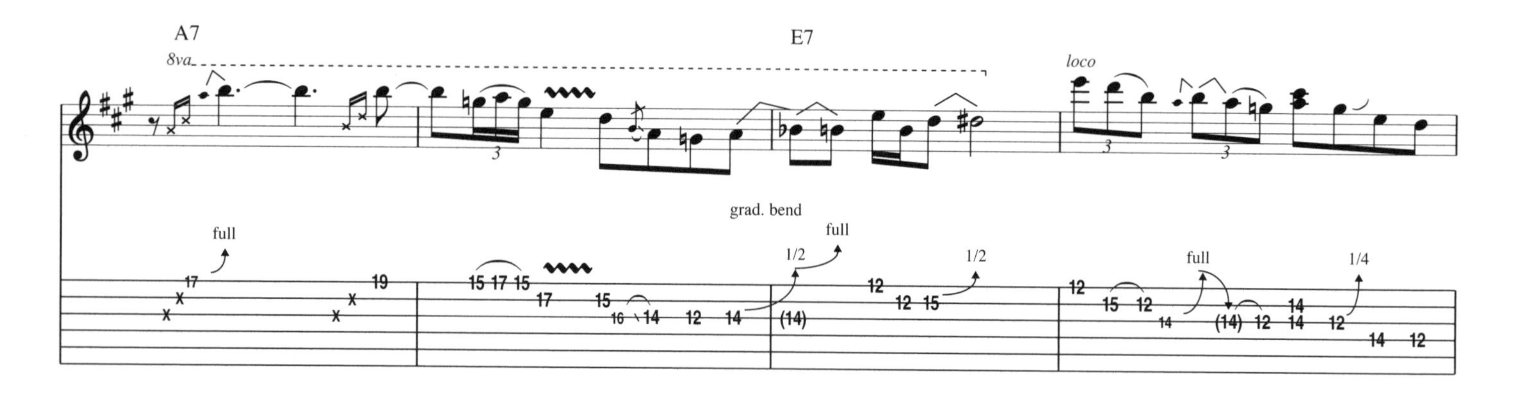
A7
8va
E7
loco
grad. bend
full
1/2
1/4

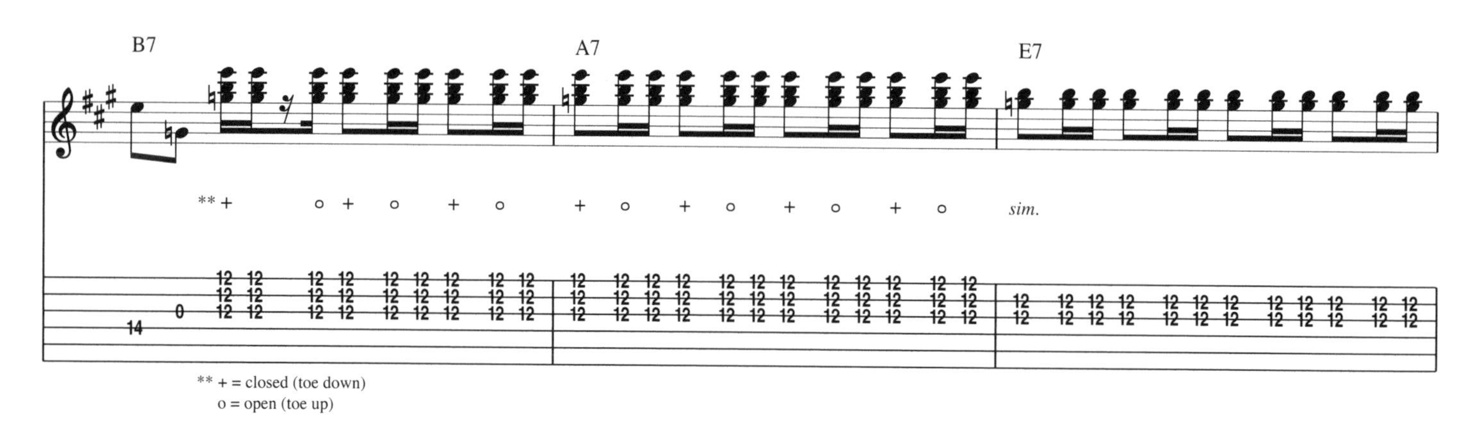
B7
A7
E7
sim.
** + = closed (toe down)
o = open (toe up)

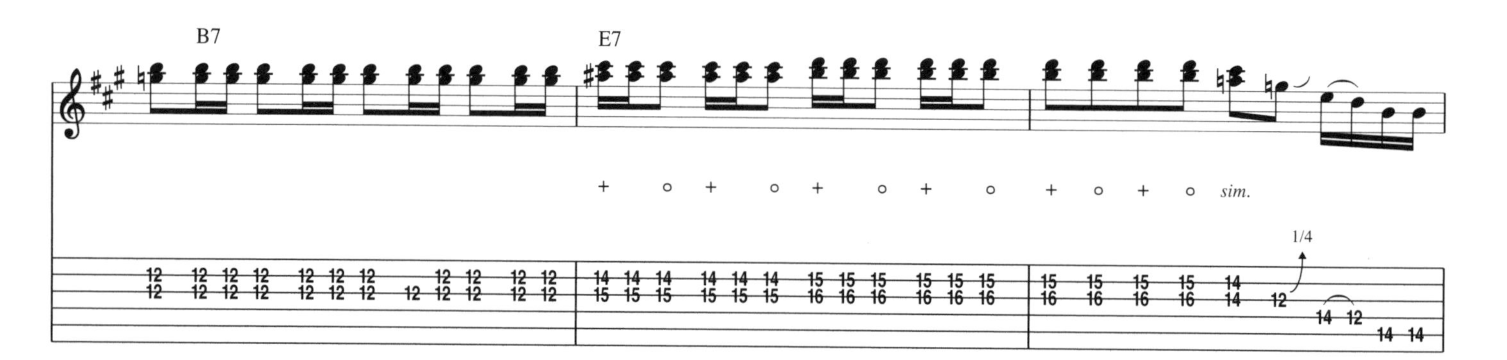
B7
E7
sim.
1/4

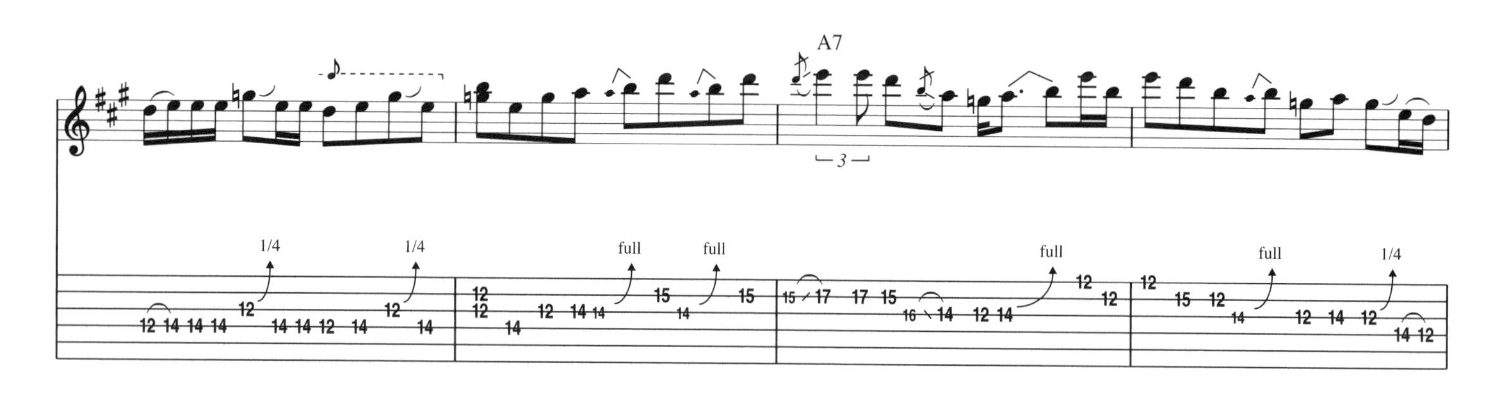
A7
1/4
full

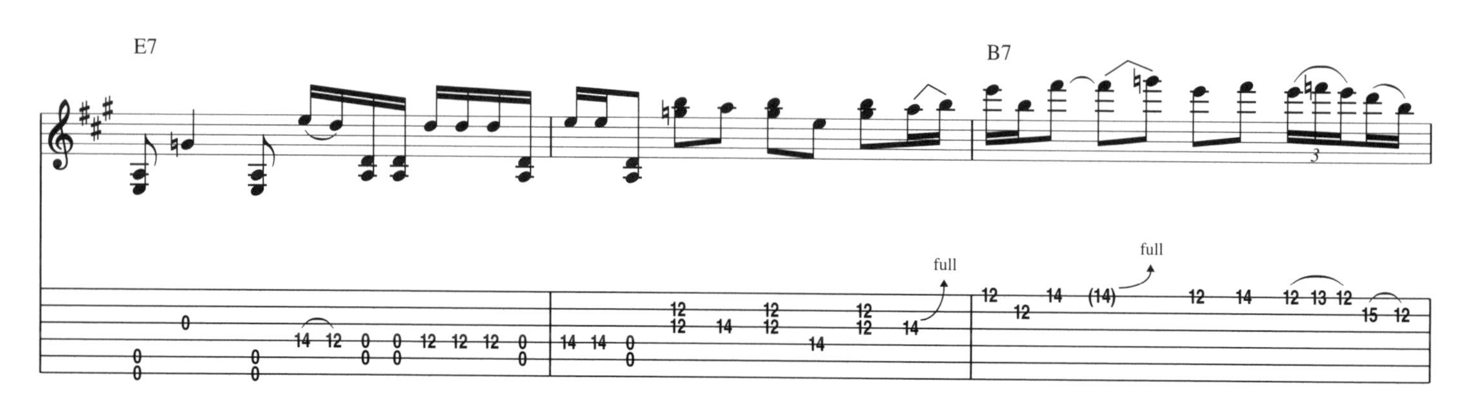
E7
B7
full

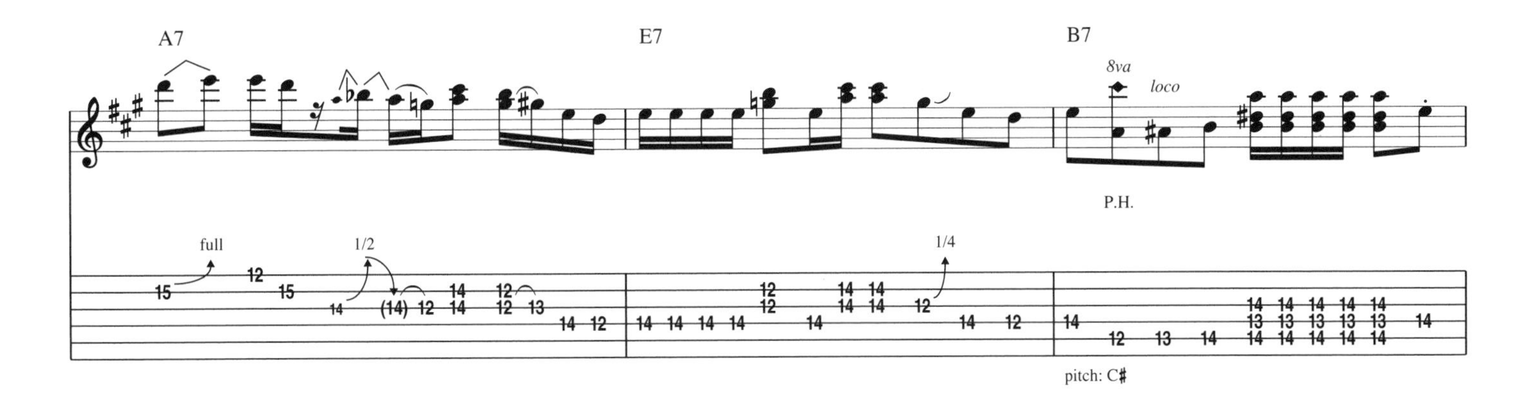
A7
E7
B7
8va
loco
P.H.
full
1/2
1/4
pitch: C#

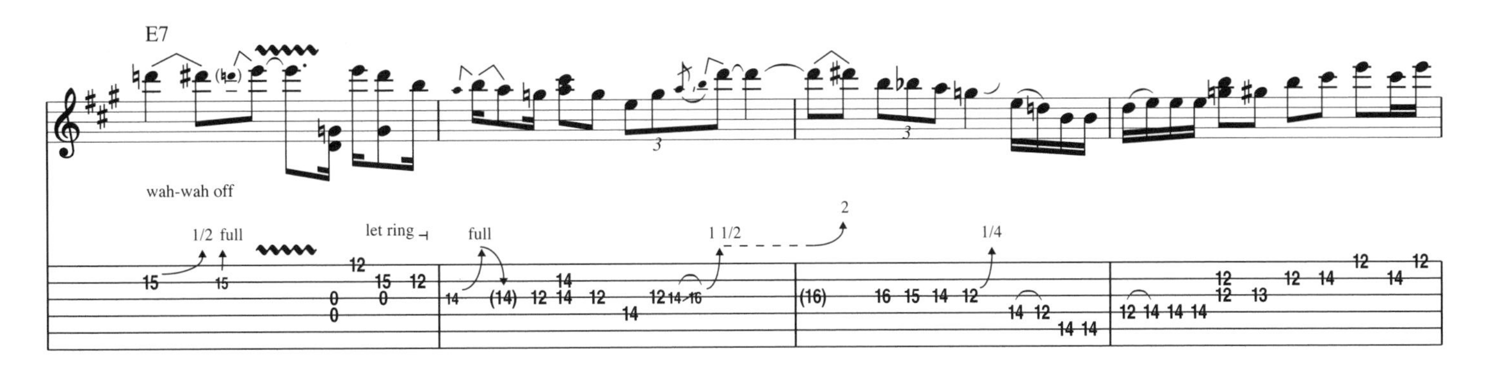
E7
wah-wah off
1/2 full
let ring
full
1 1/2
2
1/4

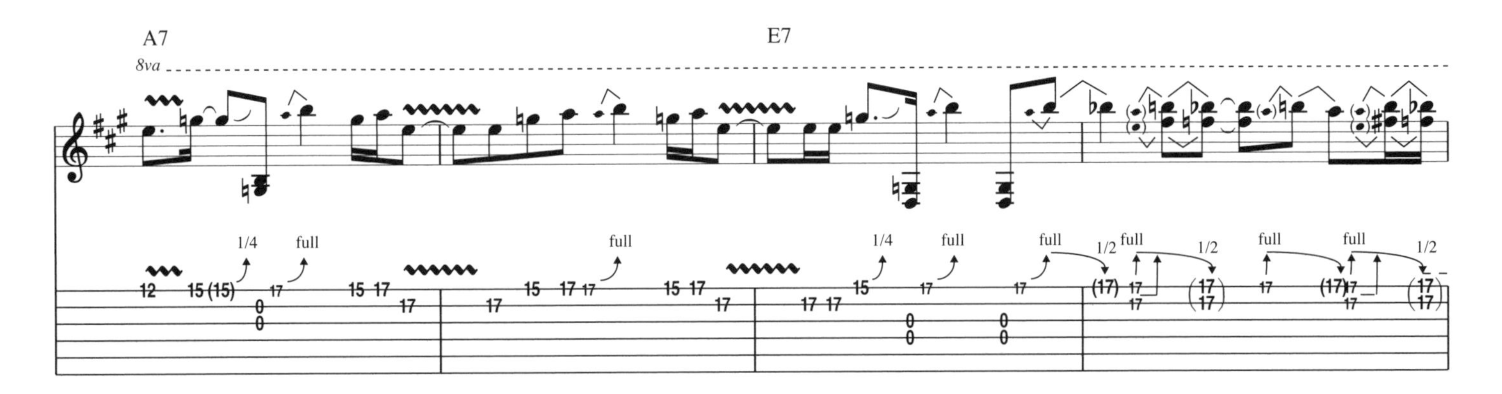
A7
E7
8va
1/4
full
1/2

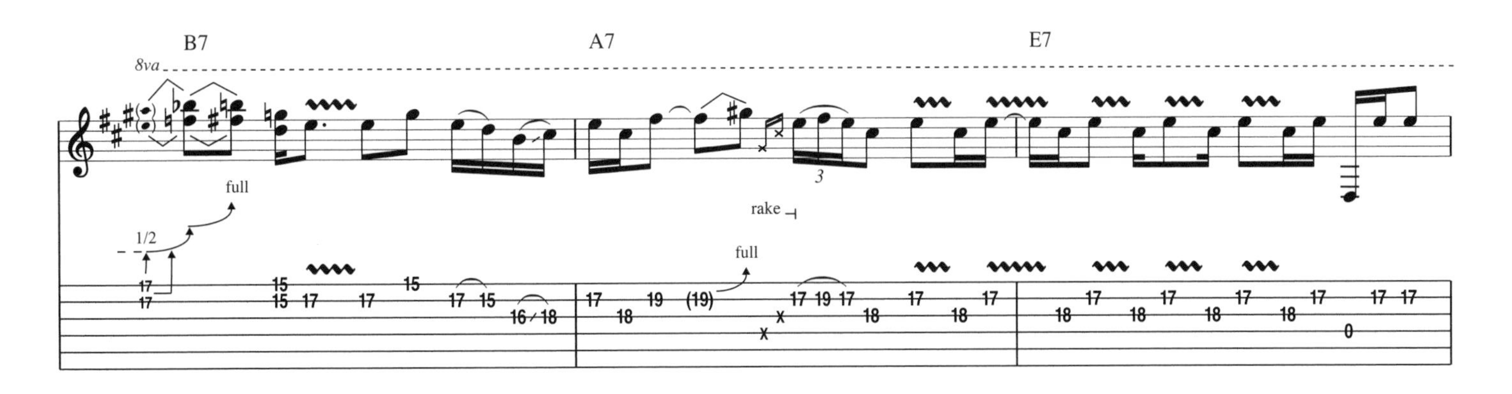
B7
A7
E7
8va
full
1/2
rake

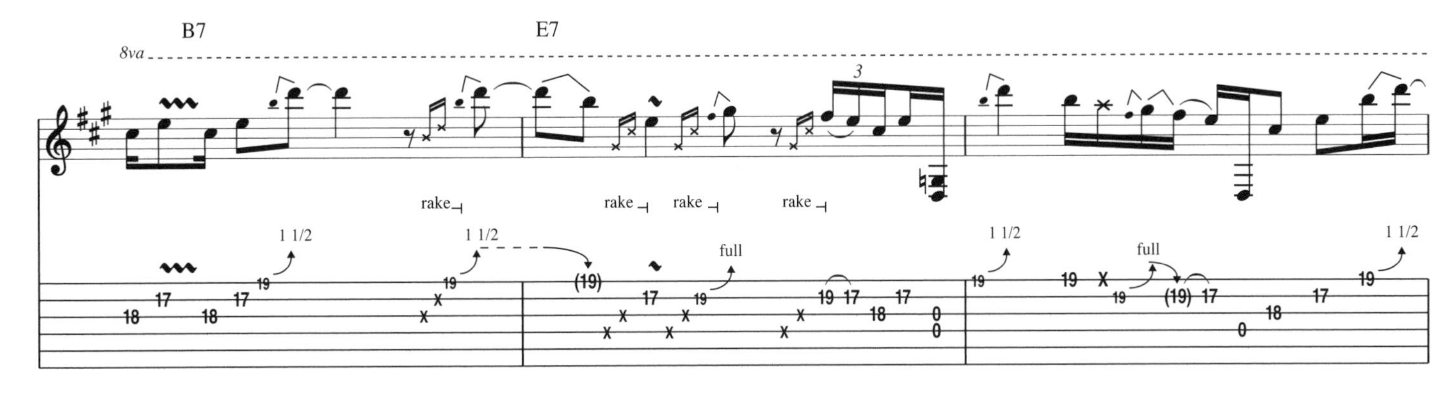
B7
E7
8va
rake
1 1/2
full

8va
A7
loco
grad. bend
full
let ring
E7
B7
A7
E7
B7
E7
A7

E7
B7
A7
E7
8va
B7
8va
E7
loco
1/2
full
1/2
1/4
1/4
full
1/2
1/4
1/4
A7
full
1/2
full
1/2
E7
1/4
1/4
full
B7
1/2
A7
E7
1/4

B7
E7
1/4
full
grad. bend
A7
1/2
E7
B7
D.S. al Coda
(take repeat)
A7
E7
B7
Coda
Free Time
E7
E9
w/ bar

GUITAR NOTATION LEGEND

Guitar music can be notated three different ways: on a *musical staff*, in *tablature*, and in *rhythm slashes*.

RHYTHM SLASHES are written above the staff. Strum chords in the rhythm indicated. Use the chord diagrams found at the top of the first page of the transcription for the appropriate chord voicings. Round noteheads indicate single notes.

THE MUSICAL STAFF shows pitches and rhythms and is divided by bar lines into measures. Pitches are named after the first seven letters of the alphabet.

TABLATURE graphically represents the guitar fingerboard. Each horizontal line represents a string, and each number represents a fret.

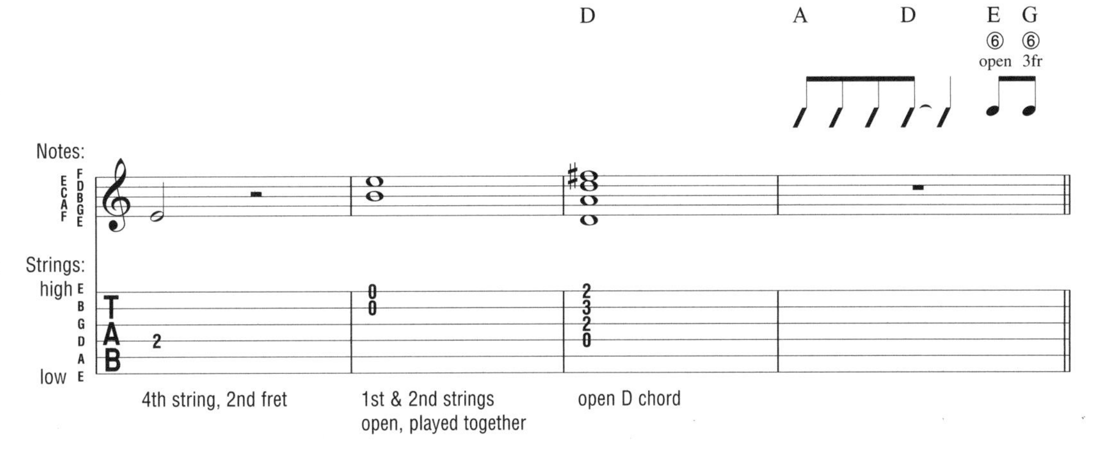

Definitions for Special Guitar Notation

HALF-STEP BEND: Strike the note and bend up 1/2 step.

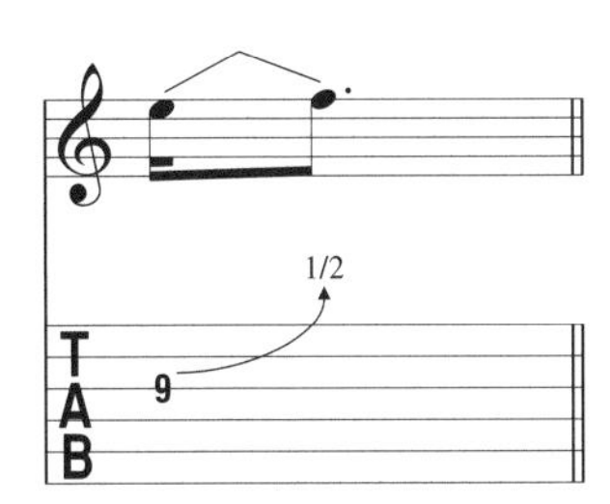

WHOLE-STEP BEND: Strike the note and bend up one step.

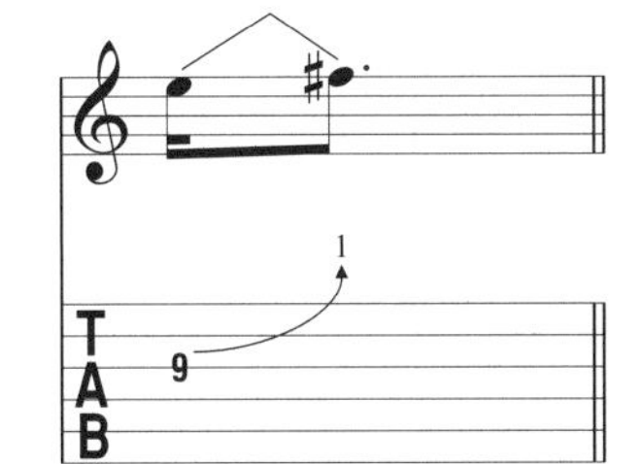

GRACE NOTE BEND: Strike the note and immediately bend up as indicated.

SLIGHT (MICROTONE) BEND: Strike the note and bend up 1/4 step.

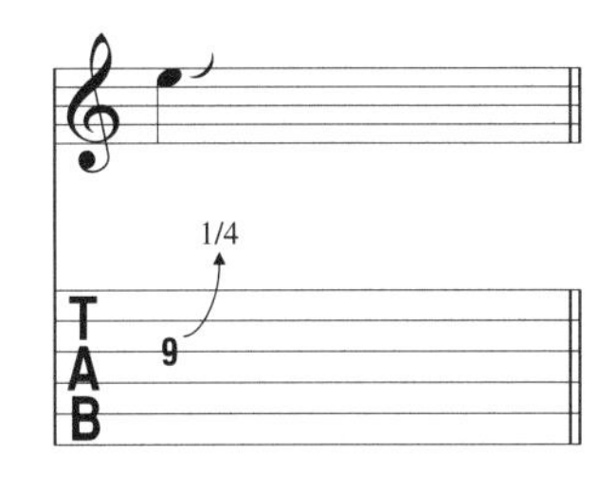

BEND AND RELEASE: Strike the note and bend up as indicated, then release back to the original note. Only the first note is struck.

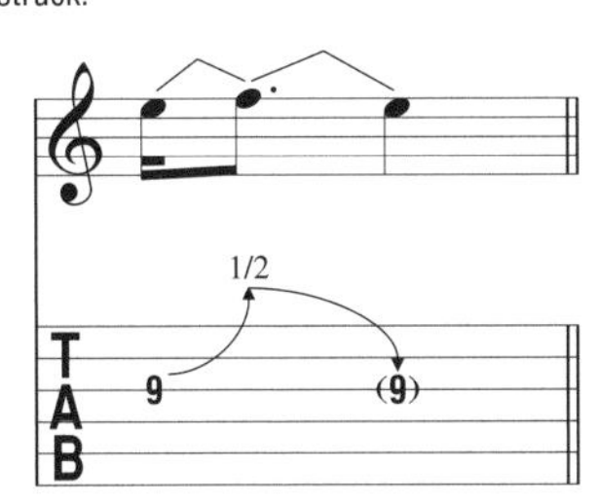

PRE-BEND: Bend the note as indicated, then strike it.

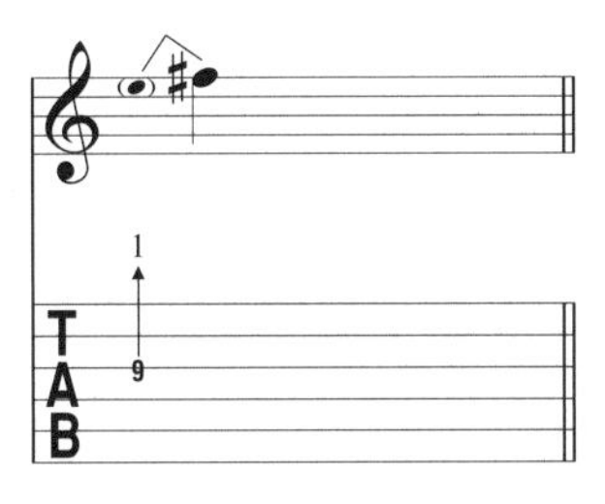

PRE-BEND AND RELEASE: Bend the note as indicated. Strike it and release the bend back to the original note.

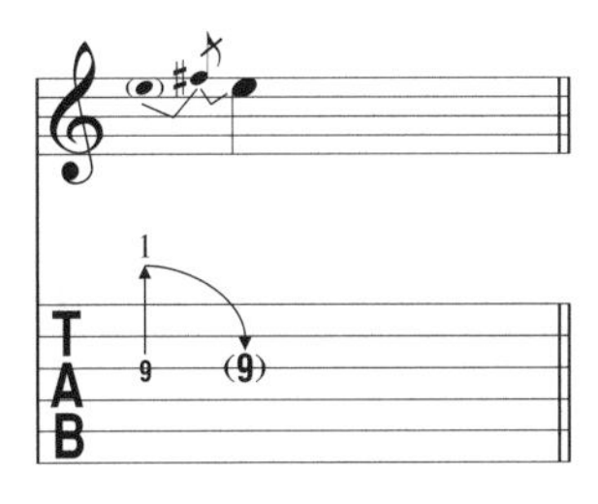

UNISON BEND: Strike the two notes simultaneously and bend the lower note up to the pitch of the higher.

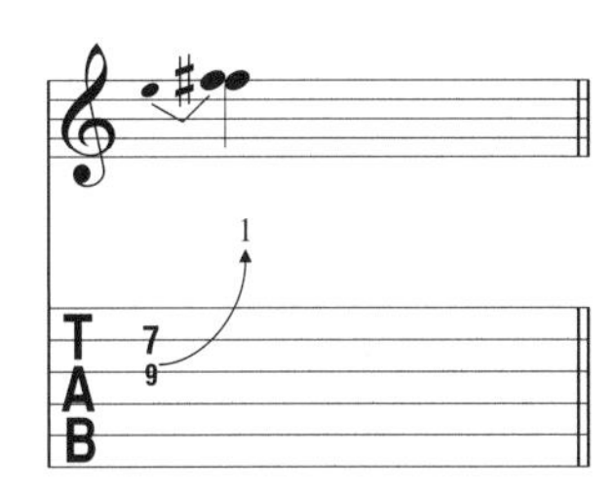

VIBRATO: The string is vibrated by rapidly bending and releasing the note with the fretting hand.

WIDE VIBRATO: The pitch is varied to a greater degree by vibrating with the fretting hand.

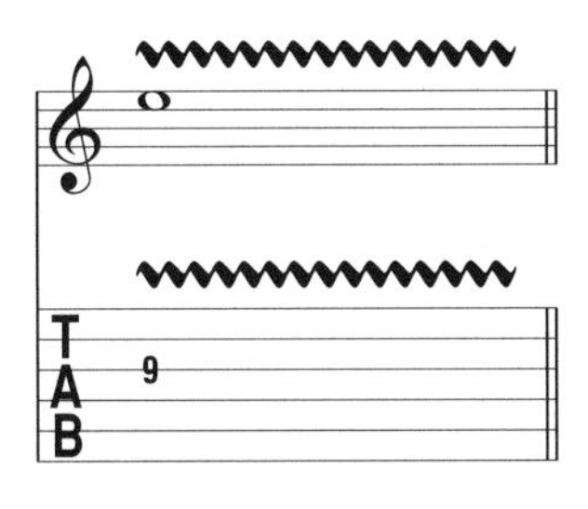

HAMMER-ON: Strike the first (lower) note with one finger, then sound the higher note (on the same string) with another finger by fretting it without picking.

PULL-OFF: Place both fingers on the notes to be sounded. Strike the first note and without picking, pull the finger off to sound the second (lower) note.

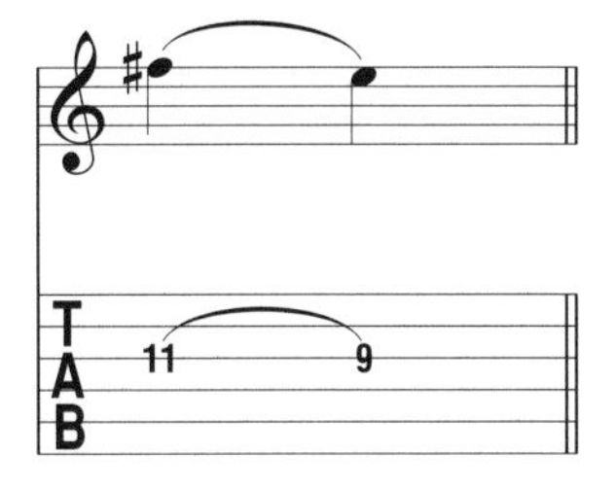

LEGATO SLIDE: Strike the first note and then slide the same fret-hand finger up or down to the second note. The second note is not struck.

SHIFT SLIDE: Same as legato slide, except the second note is struck.

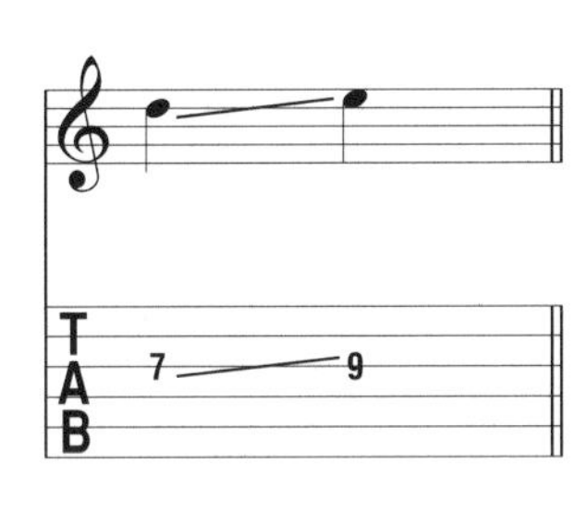

TRILL: Very rapidly alternate between the notes indicated by continuously hammering on and pulling off.

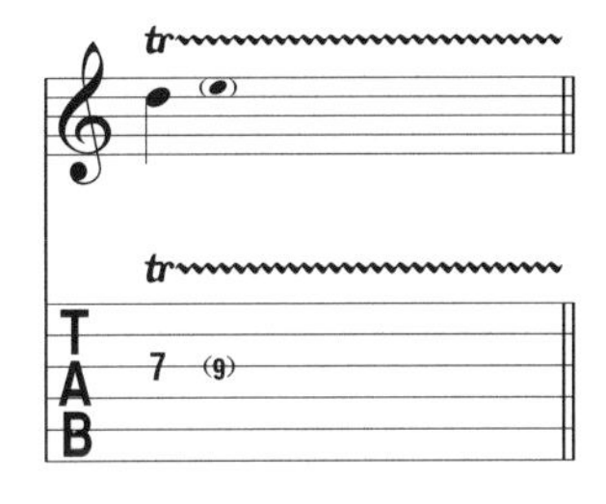

TAPPING: Hammer ("tap") the fret indicated with the pick-hand index or middle finger and pull off to the note fretted by the fret hand.

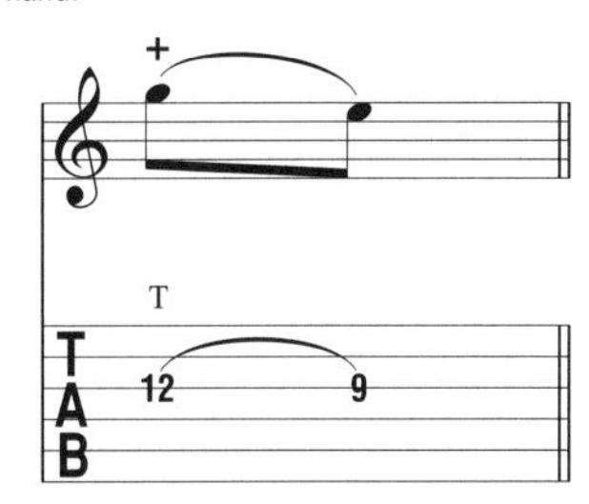

NATURAL HARMONIC: Strike the note while the fret-hand lightly touches the string directly over the fret indicated.

PINCH HARMONIC: The note is fretted normally and a harmonic is produced by adding the edge of the thumb or the tip of the index finger of the pick hand to the normal pick attack.

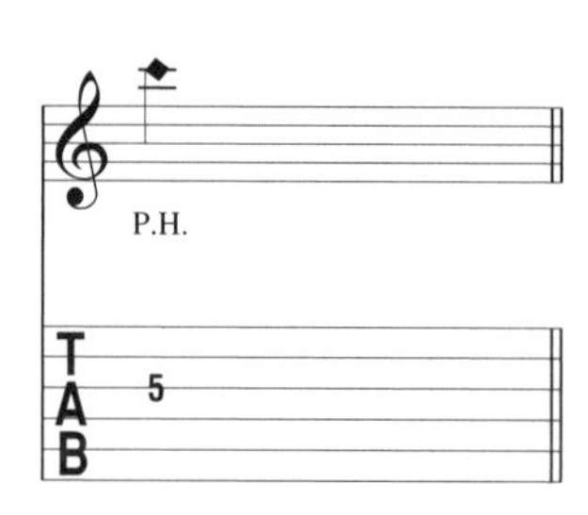

HARP HARMONIC: The note is fretted normally and a harmonic is produced by gently resting the pick hand's index finger directly above the indicated fret (in parentheses) while the pick hand's thumb or pick assists by plucking the appropriate string.

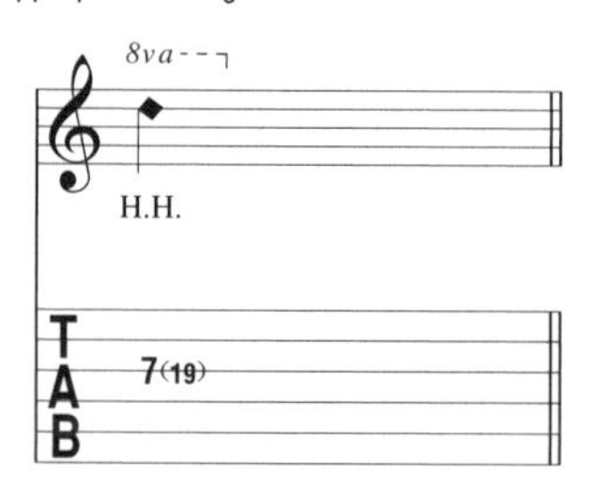

PICK SCRAPE: The edge of the pick is rubbed down (or up) the string, producing a scratchy sound.

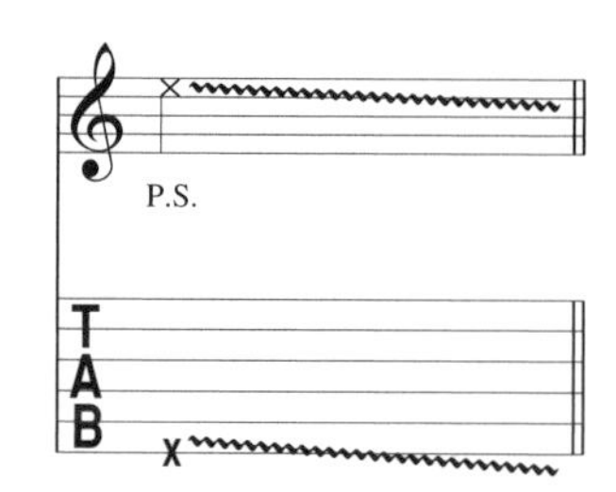

MUFFLED STRINGS: A percussive sound is produced by laying the fret hand across the string(s) without depressing, and striking them with the pick hand.

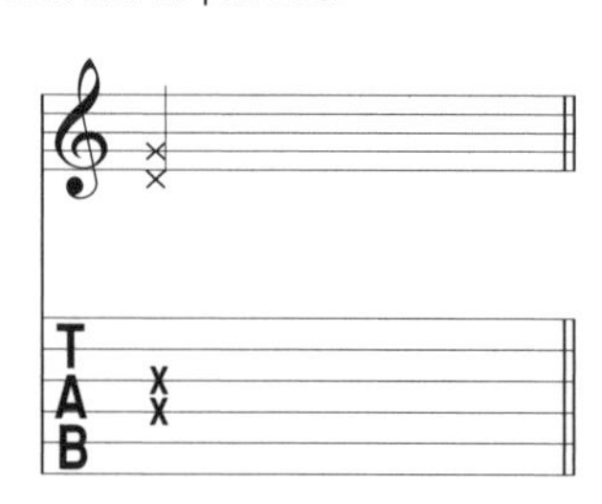

PALM MUTING: The note is partially muted by the pick hand lightly touching the string(s) just before the bridge.

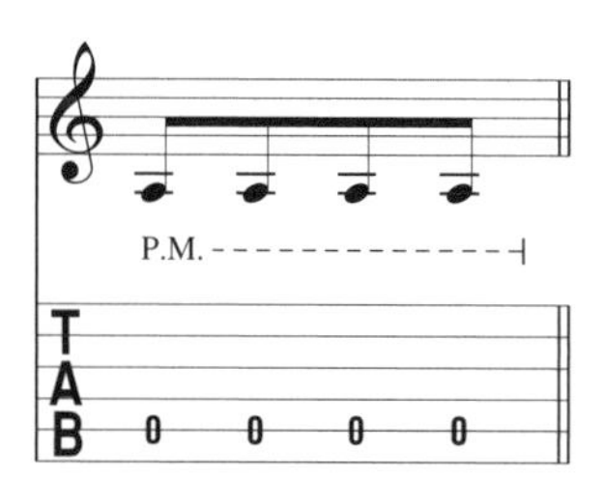

RAKE: Drag the pick across the strings indicated with a single motion.

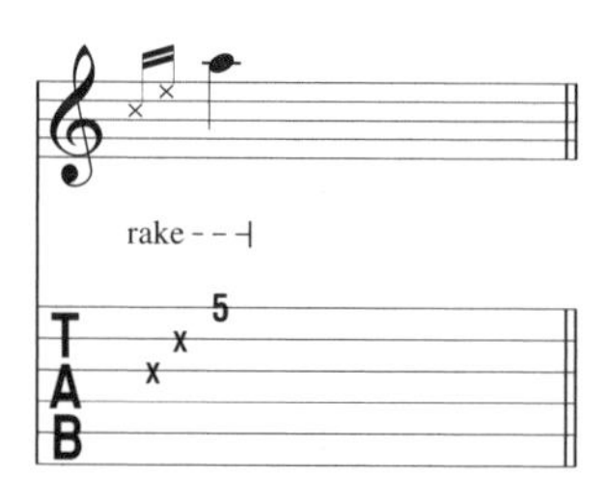

TREMOLO PICKING: The note is picked as rapidly and continuously as possible.

ARPEGGIATE: Play the notes of the chord indicated by quickly rolling them from bottom to top.

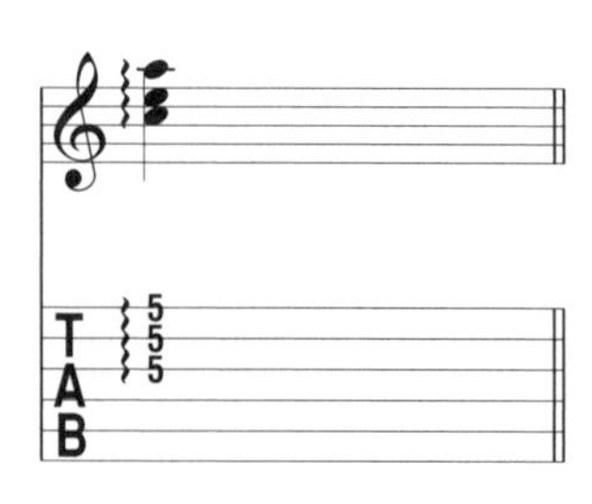

VIBRATO BAR DIVE AND RETURN: The pitch of the note or chord is dropped a specified number of steps (in rhythm), then returned to the original pitch.

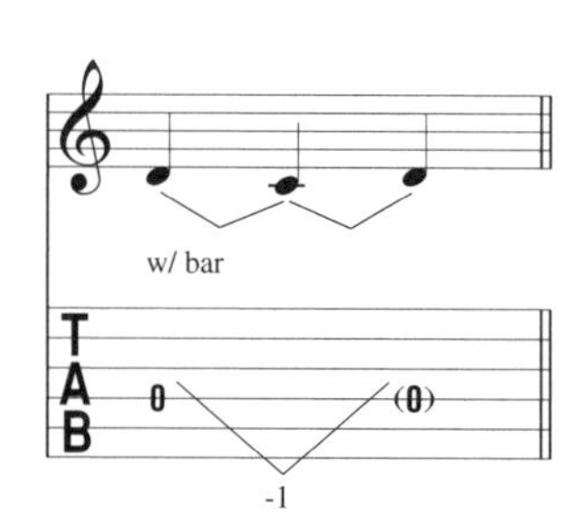

VIBRATO BAR SCOOP: Depress the bar just before striking the note, then quickly release the bar.

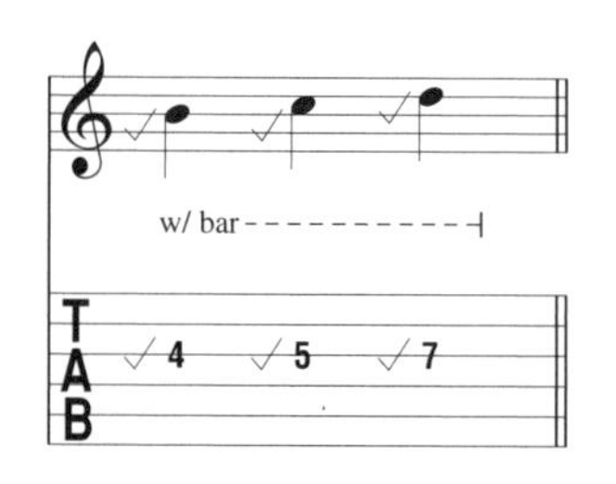

VIBRATO BAR DIP: Strike the note and then immediately drop a specified number of steps, then release back to the original pitch.

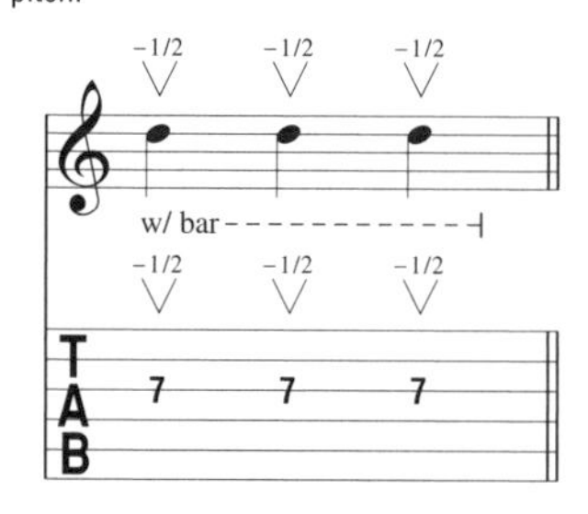

Additional Musical Definitions

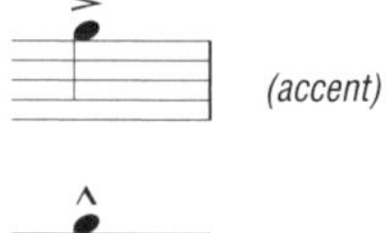 *(accent)* • Accentuate note (play it louder).

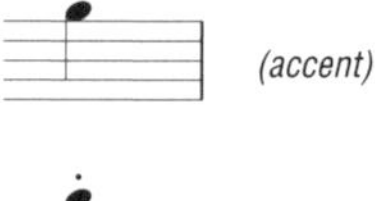 *(accent)* • Accentuate note with great intensity.

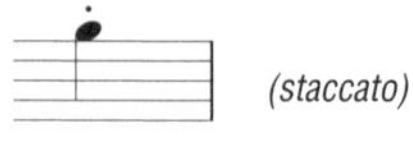 *(staccato)* • Play the note short.

 • Downstroke

 V • Upstroke

D.S. al Coda • Go back to the sign (𝄋), then play until the measure marked "***To Coda,***" then skip to the section labelled "**Coda.**"

D.C. al Fine • Go back to the beginning of the song and play until the measure marked "***Fine***" (end).

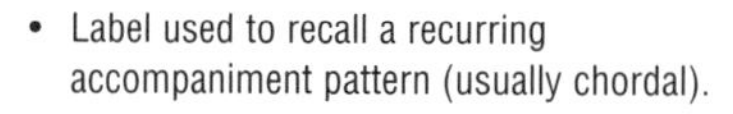

Rhy. Fig. • Label used to recall a recurring accompaniment pattern (usually chordal).

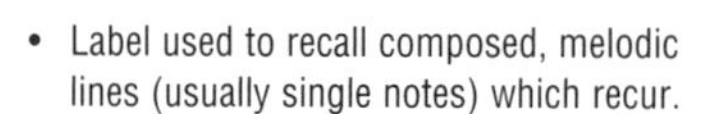

Riff • Label used to recall composed, melodic lines (usually single notes) which recur.

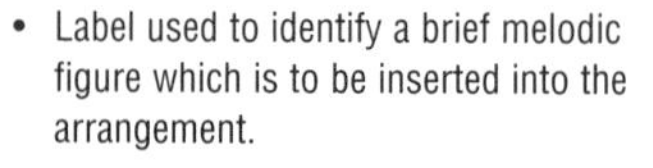

Fill • Label used to identify a brief melodic figure which is to be inserted into the arrangement.

Rhy. Fill • A chordal version of a Fill.

tacet • Instrument is silent (drops out).

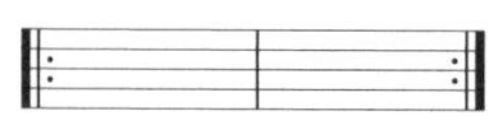 • Repeat measures between signs.

• When a repeated section has different endings, play the first ending only the first time and the second ending only the second time.

NOTE: Tablature numbers in parentheses mean:

1. The note is being sustained over a system (note in standard notation is tied), or
2. The note is sustained, but a new articulation (such as a hammer-on, pull-off, slide or vibrato) begins, or
3. The note is a barely audible "ghost" note (note in standard notation is also in parentheses).

GUITAR RECORDED VERSIONS®

Guitar Recorded Versions® are note-for-note transcriptions of guitar music taken directly off recordings. This series, one of the most popular in print today, features some of the greatest guitar players and groups from blues and rock to country and jazz.

Guitar Recorded Versions are transcribed by the best transcribers in the business. Every book contains notes and tablature. Visit **www.halleonard.com** for our complete selection.

14041344 The Definitive AC/DC Songbook $39.99
00690016 The Will Ackerman Collection $19.95
00690501 Bryan Adams – Greatest Hits $19.95
00690603 Aerosmith – O Yeah! (Ultimate Hits) $24.95
00690147 Aerosmith – Rocks $19.95
00690178 Alice in Chains – Acoustic $19.95
00694865 Alice in Chains – Dirt $19.95
00660225 Alice in Chains – Facelift $19.95
00694925 Alice in Chains – Jar of Flies/Sap $19.95
00690387 Alice in Chains – Nothing Safe: Best of the Box $19.95
00694932 Allman Brothers Band – Definitive Collection for Guitar Volume 1 ....$24.95
00694933 Allman Brothers Band – Definitive Collection for Guitar Volume 2 ....$24.95
00694934 Allman Brothers Band – Definitive Collection for Guitar Volume 3 ....$24.95
00690958 Duane Allman Guitar Anthology $24.99
00691071 Alter Bridge – AB III $22.99
00690945 Alter Bridge – Blackbird $22.99
00690755 Alter Bridge – One Day Remains $22.99
00123558 Arctic Monkeys – AM $22.99
00114564 As I Lay Dying – Awakened $22.99
00690158 Chet Atkins – Almost Alone $19.95
00694876 Chet Atkins – Contemporary Styles $19.95
00694878 Chet Atkins – Vintage Fingerstyle $19.95
00690609 Audioslave $19.95
00690804 Audioslave – Out of Exile $19.95
00690884 Audioslave – Revelations $19.95
00690926 Avenged Sevenfold $22.95
00690820 Avenged Sevenfold – City of Evil $24.95
00123216 Avenged Sevenfold – Hail to the King $22.99
00691065 Avenged Sevenfold – Waking the Fallen $22.99
00123140 The Avett Brothers Guitar Collection $22.99
00694918 Randy Bachman Collection $22.95
00690503 Beach Boys – Very Best of $19.95
00694929 Beatles: 1962-1966 ....$24.99
00694930 Beatles: 1967-1970 ....$24.95
00690489 Beatles – 1 ....$24.99
00694880 Beatles – Abbey Road $19.95
00691066 Beatles – Beatles for Sale $22.99
00690110 Beatles – Book 1 (White Album) $19.95
00690111 Beatles – Book 2 (White Album) $19.95
00690902 Beatles – The Capitol Albums, Volume 1 ....$24.99
00694832 Beatles – For Acoustic Guitar $22.99
00691031 Beatles – Help! $19.99
00690482 Beatles – Let It Be $17.95
00691067 Beatles – Meet the Beatles! $22.99
00691068 Beatles – Please Please Me $22.99
00694891 Beatles – Revolver $19.95
00694914 Beatles – Rubber Soul $22.99
00694863 Beatles – Sgt. Pepper's Lonely Hearts Club Band $22.99
00110193 Beatles – Tomorrow Never Knows $22.99
00691044 Jeff Beck – Best of Beck $24.99
00690632 Beck – Sea Change $19.95
00691041 Jeff Beck – Truth $19.99
00694884 Best of George Benson $19.95
00692385 Chuck Berry $22.99
00690835 Billy Talent $19.95
00690879 Billy Talent II $19.95
00129737 The Black Keys – Turn Blue $22.99
00690149 Black Sabbath $16.99
00690901 Best of Black Sabbath $19.95
00691010 Black Sabbath – Heaven and Hell $22.99
00690148 Black Sabbath – Master of Reality $16.99
00690142 Black Sabbath – Paranoid $16.99
14042759 Black Sabbath – 13 ....$19.99
00692200 Black Sabbath – We Sold Our Soul for Rock 'N' Roll $19.95
00690389 blink-182 – Enema of the State $19.95
00690831 blink-182 – Greatest Hits $19.95
00691179 blink-182 – Neighborhoods $22.99
00690523 blink-182 – Take Off Your Pants and Jacket $19.95
00690028 Blue Oyster Cult – Cult Classics $19.95
00690008 Bon Jovi – Cross Road $19.95
00691074 Bon Jovi – Greatest Hits $22.99
00139086 Joe Bonamassa – Different Shades of Blue $22.99
00690913 Boston $19.95
00690829 Boston Guitar Collection $19.99
00690491 Best of David Bowie $19.95
00690583 Box Car Racer $19.95
00691023 Breaking Benjamin – Dear Agony $22.99
00690873 Breaking Benjamin – Phobia $19.95
00690764 Breaking Benjamin – We Are Not Alone $19.95
00690451 Jeff Buckley Collection $24.95
00690957 Bullet for My Valentine – Scream Aim Fire $22.99
00119629 Bullet for My Valentine – Temper Temper $22.99
00690678 Best of Kenny Burrell $19.95
00691077 Cage the Elephant – Thank You, Happy Birthday $22.99
00691159 The Cars – Complete Greatest Hits $22.99
00690261 Carter Family Collection $19.95
00691079 Best of Johnny Cash $22.99
00690043 Best of Cheap Trick $19.95
00690171 Chicago – The Definitive Guitar Collection $22.95
00691011 Chimaira Guitar Collection $24.99
00690567 Charlie Christian – The Definitive Collection $19.95
00101916 Eric Church – Chief $22.99
00129545 The Civil Wars $19.99
00138731 Eric Clapton & Friends – The Breeze $22.99
00690590 Eric Clapton – Anthology $29.95
00692391 Best of Eric Clapton – 2nd Edition $22.95
00691055 Eric Clapton – Clapton $22.99
00690936 Eric Clapton – Complete Clapton $29.99
00690247 Eric Clapton – 461 Ocean Boulevard $19.99
00690010 Eric Clapton – From the Cradle $19.95
00690363 Eric Clapton – Just One Night $24.99
00694873 Eric Clapton – Timepieces $19.95
00694869 Eric Clapton – Unplugged $22.95
00690415 Clapton Chronicles – Best of Eric Clapton $18.95
00694896 John Mayall/Eric Clapton – Bluesbreakers $19.95
00690162 Best of the Clash $19.95
00690828 Coheed & Cambria – Good Apollo I'm Burning Star, IV, Vol. 1: From Fear Through the Eyes of Madness ..$19.95
00690940 Coheed and Cambria – No World for Tomorrow $19.95
00130786 Coldplay – Ghost Stories $19.99
00690494 Coldplay – Parachutes $19.95
00690593 Coldplay – A Rush of Blood to the Head $19.95
00690806 Coldplay – X & Y $19.95
00690855 Best of Collective Soul $19.95
00691091 The Best of Alice Cooper $22.99
00694940 Counting Crows – August & Everything After $19.95
00127184 Best of Robert Cray $19.99
00694840 Cream – Disraeli Gears $19.95
00690285 Cream – Those Were the Days $17.95
00690819 Best of Creedence Clearwater Revival $22.95
00690648 The Very Best of Jim Croce $19.95
00690572 Steve Cropper – Soul Man $19.95
00690613 Best of Crosby, Stills & Nash $22.95
00699521 The Cure – Greatest Hits $24.95
00690637 Best of Dick Dale $19.95
00690822 Best of Alex De Grassi $19.95
00690967 Death Cab for Cutie – Narrow Stairs $22.99
00690289 Best of Deep Purple $19.99
00690288 Deep Purple – Machine Head $17.99
00690784 Best of Def Leppard $22.99
00694831 Derek and the Dominos – Layla & Other Assorted Love Songs $22.95
00692240 Bo Diddley – Guitar Solos by Fred Sokolow $19.99
00690384 Best of Ani DiFranco $19.95
00690380 Ani DiFranco – Up Up Up Up Up Up $19.95
00690979 Best of Dinosaur Jr. $19.99
00690833 Private Investigations – Best of Dire Straits and Mark Knopfler $24.95
00695382 Very Best of Dire Straits – Sultans of Swing $22.95
00122443 Dream Theater $24.99
00690250 Best of Duane Eddy $16.95
00690909 Best of Tommy Emmanuel $22.99
00690555 Best of Melissa Etheridge $19.95
00690515 Extreme II – Pornograffitti $19.95
00691009 Five Finger Death Punch $19.99
00690664 Best of Fleetwood Mac $19.95
00690870 Flyleaf $19.95
00690808 Foo Fighters – In Your Honor $19.95
00691115 Foo Fighters – Wasting Light $22.99
00690805 Best of Robben Ford $22.99
00120220 Robben Ford – Guitar Anthology $24.99
00690842 Best of Peter Frampton $19.95
00694920 Best of Free $19.95
00694807 Danny Gatton – 88 Elmira St. $19.95
00690438 Genesis Guitar Anthology $19.95
00690753 Best of Godsmack $19.95
00120167 Godsmack $19.95
00690338 Goo Goo Dolls – Dizzy Up the Girl $19.95
00113073 Green Day – Uno $21.99
00116846 Green Day – ¡Dos! $21.99
00118259 Green Day – ¡Tré! $21.99
00691190 Best of Peter Green $19.99
00690927 Patty Griffin – Children Running Through $19.95
00690591 Patty Griffin – Guitar Collection $19.95
00690978 Guns N' Roses – Chinese Democracy $24.99
00691027 Buddy Guy Anthology $24.99
00694854 Buddy Guy – Damn Right, I've Got the Blues $19.95
00690697 Best of Jim Hall $19.95
00690840 Ben Harper – Both Sides of the Gun $19.95
00691018 Ben Harper – Fight for Your Mind $22.99
00694798 George Harrison Anthology $19.95
00690841 Scott Henderson – Blues Guitar Collection $19.95
00692930 Jimi Hendrix – Are You Experienced? $24.95
00692931 Jimi Hendrix – Axis: Bold As Love $22.95
00690304 Jimi Hendrix – Band of Gypsys $24.99
00690608 Jimi Hendrix – Blue Wild Angel $24.95
00694944 Jimi Hendrix – Blues $24.95
00692932 Jimi Hendrix – Electric Ladyland $24.95
00119619 Jimi Hendrix – People, Hell and Angels $22.99
00690602 Jimi Hendrix – Smash Hits $24.99
00691152 West Coast Seattle Boy: The Jimi Hendrix Anthology $29.99
00691332 Jimi Hendrix – Winterland (Highlights) $22.99
00690017 Jimi Hendrix – Woodstock $24.95
00690843 H.I.M. – Dark Light $19.95
00690869 Hinder – Extreme Behavior $19.95
00660029 Buddy Holly $22.99
00690793 John Lee Hooker Anthology $24.99
00660169 John Lee Hooker – A Blues Legend $19.95
00694905 Howlin' Wolf $19.95
00690692 Very Best of Billy Idol $19.95
00121961 Imagine Dragons – Night Visions $22.99
00690688 Incubus – A Crow Left of the Murder $19.95
00690136 Indigo Girls – 1200 Curfews $22.95
00690790 Iron Maiden Anthology $24.99
00691058 Iron Maiden – The Final Frontier $22.99
00690887 Iron Maiden – A Matter of Life and Death $24.95
00690730 Alan Jackson – Guitar Collection $19.95
00694938 Elmore James – Master Electric Slide Guitar $19.95
00690652 Best of Jane's Addiction $19.95
00690684 Jethro Tull – Aqualung $19.95
00690693 Jethro Tull Guitar Anthology $22.99
00691182 Jethro Tull – Stand Up $22.99
00690898 John 5 – The Devil Knows My Name $22.95
00690814 John 5 – Songs for Sanity $19.95
00690751 John 5 – Vertigo $19.95
00694912 Eric Johnson – Ah Via Musicom $19.95
00690660 Best of Eric Johnson $22.99
00691076 Eric Johnson – Up Close $22.99

00690169	Eric Johnson – Venus Isle	$22.95
00122439	Jack Johnson – From Here to Now to You	$22.99
00690846	Jack Johnson and Friends – Sing-A-Longs and Lullabies for the Film Curious George	$19.95
00690271	Robert Johnson – The New Transcriptions	$24.95
00699131	Best of Janis Joplin	$19.95
00690427	Best of Judas Priest	$22.99
00690277	Best of Kansas	$19.95
00690911	Best of Phil Keaggy	$24.99
00690727	Toby Keith Guitar Collection	$19.99
00120814	Killswitch Engage – Disarm the Descent	$22.99
00690504	Very Best of Albert King	$19.95
00124869	Albert King with Stevie Ray Vaughan – In Session	$22.99
00130447	B.B. King – Live at the Regal	$17.99
00690444	B.B. King & Eric Clapton – Riding with the King	$22.99
00690134	Freddie King Collection	$19.95
00691062	Kings of Leon – Come Around Sundown	$22.99
00690157	Kiss – Alive!	$19.95
00690356	Kiss – Alive II	$22.99
00694903	Best of Kiss for Guitar	$24.95
00690355	Kiss – Destroyer	$16.95
14026320	Mark Knopfler – Get Lucky	$22.99
00690164	Mark Knopfler Guitar – Vol. 1	$19.95
00690163	Mark Knopfler/Chet Atkins – Neck and Neck	$19.95
00690780	Korn – Greatest Hits, Volume 1	$22.95
00690377	Kris Kristofferson Collection	$19.95
00690834	Lamb of God – Ashes of the Wake	$19.95
00690875	Lamb of God – Sacrament	$19.95
00690977	Ray LaMontagne – Gossip in the Grain	$19.99
00690823	Ray LaMontagne – Trouble	$19.95
00691057	Ray LaMontagne and the Pariah Dogs – God Willin' & The Creek Don't Rise	$22.99
00690922	Linkin Park – Minutes to Midnight	$19.95
00699623	The Best of Chuck Loeb	$19.95
00114563	The Lumineers	$22.99
00690525	Best of George Lynch	$24.99
00690955	Lynyrd Skynyrd – All-Time Greatest Hits	$22.99
00694954	New Best of Lynyrd Skynyrd	$19.95
00690577	Yngwie Malmsteen – Anthology	$24.95
00690754	Marilyn Manson – Lest We Forget	$19.95
00694956	Bob Marley – Legend	$19.95
00690548	Very Best of Bob Marley & The Wailers – One Love	$22.99
00694945	Bob Marley – Songs of Freedom	$24.95
00690914	Maroon 5 – It Won't Be Soon Before Long	$19.95
00690657	Maroon 5 – Songs About Jane	$19.95
00690748	Maroon 5 – 1.22.03 Acoustic	$19.95
00690989	Mastodon – Crack the Skye	$24.99
00119220	Brent Mason – Hot Wired	$19.99
00691176	Mastodon – The Hunter	$22.99
00137718	Mastodon – Once More 'Round the Sun	$22.99
00690616	Matchbox Twenty – More Than You Think You Are	$19.95
00691942	Andy McKee – Art of Motion	$22.99
00691034	Andy McKee – Joyland	$19.99
00120080	The Don McLean Songbook	$19.95
00694952	Megadeth – Countdown to Extinction	$22.95
00690244	Megadeth – Cryptic Writings	$19.95
00694951	Megadeth – Rust in Peace	$22.95
00690011	Megadeth – Youthanasia	$22.99
00690505	John Mellencamp Guitar Collection	$19.95
00690562	Pat Metheny – Bright Size Life	$19.95
00691073	Pat Metheny with Christian McBride & Antonion Sanchez – Day Trip/Tokyo Day Trip Live	$22.99
00690646	Pat Metheny – One Quiet Night	$19.95
00690559	Pat Metheny – Question & Answer	$19.95
00118836	Pat Metheny – Unity Band	$22.99
00102590	Pat Metheny – What's It All About	$22.99
00690040	Steve Miller Band Greatest Hits	$19.95
00119338	Ministry Guitar Tab Collection	$24.99
00102591	Wes Montgomery Guitar Anthology	$24.99
00694802	Gary Moore – Still Got the Blues	$22.99
00691005	Best of Motion City Soundtrack	$19.99
00129884	Jason Mraz – Yes!	$22.99
00690787	Mudvayne – L.D. 50	$22.95
00691070	Mumford & Sons – Sigh No More	$22.99
00118196	Muse – The 2nd Law	$19.99
00690996	My Morning Jacket Collection	$19.99
00690984	Matt Nathanson – Some Mad Hope	$22.99
00690611	Nirvana	$22.95
00694895	Nirvana – Bleach	$19.95
00694913	Nirvana – In Utero	$19.95
00694883	Nirvana – Nevermind	$19.95
00690026	Nirvana – Unplugged in New York	$19.95
00120112	No Doubt – Tragic Kingdom	$22.95
00690226	Oasis – The Other Side of Oasis	$19.95
00307163	Oasis – Time Flies... 1994-2009	$19.99
00690818	The Best of Opeth	$22.95
00691052	Roy Orbison – Black & White Night	$22.99
00694847	Best of Ozzy Osbourne	$22.95
00690399	Ozzy Osbourne – The Ozzman Cometh	$22.99
00690933	Best of Brad Paisley	$22.95
00690995	Brad Paisley – Play: The Guitar Album	$24.99
00690939	Christopher Parkening – Solo Pieces	$19.99
00690594	Best of Les Paul	$19.95
00694855	Pearl Jam – Ten	$22.99
00690439	A Perfect Circle – Mer De Noms	$19.95
00690725	Best of Carl Perkins	$19.99
00690499	Tom Petty – Definitive Guitar Collection	$19.95
00690868	Tom Petty – Highway Companion	$19.95
00690176	Phish – Billy Breathes	$22.95
00691249	Phish – Junta	$22.99
00121933	Pink Floyd – Acoustic Guitar Collection	$22.99
00690428	Pink Floyd – Dark Side of the Moon	$19.95
00690789	Best of Poison	$19.95
00690299	Best of Elvis: The King of Rock 'n' Roll	$19.95
00692535	Elvis Presley	$19.95
00690925	The Very Best of Prince	$22.99
00690003	Classic Queen	$24.95
00694975	Queen – Greatest Hits	$24.95
00690670	Very Best of Queensryche	$19.95
00690878	The Raconteurs – Broken Boy Soldiers	$19.95
00109303	Radiohead Guitar Anthology	$24.99
00694910	Rage Against the Machine	$19.95
00119834	Rage Against the Machine – Guitar Anthology	$22.99
00690179	Rancid – And Out Come the Wolves	$22.95
00690426	Best of Ratt	$19.95
00690055	Red Hot Chili Peppers – Blood Sugar Sex Magik	$19.95
00690584	Red Hot Chili Peppers – By the Way	$19.95
00690379	Red Hot Chili Peppers – Californication	$19.95
00690673	Red Hot Chili Peppers – Greatest Hits	$19.95
00690090	Red Hot Chili Peppers – One Hot Minute	$22.95
00691166	Red Hot Chili Peppers – I'm with You	$22.99
00690852	Red Hot Chili Peppers – Stadium Arcadium	$24.95
00690511	Django Reinhardt – The Definitive Collection	$19.95
00690779	Relient K – MMHMM	$19.95
00690643	Relient K – Two Lefts Don't Make a Right ... But Three Do	$19.95
00690260	Jimmie Rodgers Guitar Collection	$19.95
00138485	Kid Rock – Guitar Tab Collection	$19.99
14041901	Rodrigo Y Gabriela and C.U.B.A. – Area 52	$24.99
00690014	Rolling Stones – Exile on Main Street	$24.95
00690631	Rolling Stones – Guitar Anthology	$27.95
00690685	David Lee Roth – Eat 'Em and Smile	$19.95
00690031	Santana's Greatest Hits	$19.95
00690796	Very Best of Michael Schenker	$19.95
00128870	Matt Schofield Guitar Tab Collection	$22.99
00690566	Best of Scorpions	$22.95
00690604	Bob Seger – Guitar Anthology	$22.99
00138870	Ed Sheeran – X	$19.99
00690803	Best of Kenny Wayne Shepherd Band	$19.95
00690750	Kenny Wayne Shepherd – The Place You're In	$19.95
00690857	Shinedown – Us and Them	$19.95
00122218	Skillet – Rise	$22.99
00691114	Slash – Guitar Anthology	$24.99
00690872	Slayer – Christ Illusion	$19.95
00690813	Slayer – Guitar Collection	$19.95
00690419	Slipknot	$19.95
00690973	Slipknot – All Hope Is Gone	$22.99
00690330	Social Distortion – Live at the Roxy	$19.95
00120004	Best of Steely Dan	$24.95
00694921	Best of Steppenwolf	$22.95
00690655	Best of Mike Stern	$19.95
14041588	Cat Stevens – Tea for the Tillerman	$19.99
00690949	Rod Stewart Guitar Anthology	$19.99
00690021	Sting – Fields of Gold	$19.95
00690520	Styx Guitar Collection	$19.95
00120081	Sublime	$19.95
00690992	Sublime – Robbin' the Hood	$19.99
00690519	SUM 41 – All Killer No Filler	$19.95
00691072	Best of Supertramp	$22.99
00690994	Taylor Swift	$22.99
00690993	Taylor Swift – Fearless	$22.99
00142151	Taylor Swift – 1989	$22.99
00115957	Taylor Swift – Red	$21.99
00691063	Taylor Swift – Speak Now	$22.99

00690767	Switchfoot – The Beautiful Letdown	$19.95
00690531	System of a Down – Toxicity	$19.95
00694824	Best of James Taylor	$17.99
00694887	Best of Thin Lizzy	$19.95
00690871	Three Days Grace – One-X	$19.95
00690891	30 Seconds to Mars – A Beautiful Lie	$19.95
00690233	The Merle Travis Collection	$19.99
00690683	Robin Trower – Bridge of Sighs	$19.95
00699191	U2 – Best of: 1980-1990	$19.95
00690732	U2 – Best of: 1990-2000	$19.95
00690894	U2 – 18 Singles	$19.95
00124461	Keith Urban – Guitar Anthology	$19.99
00690039	Steve Vai – Alien Love Secrets	$24.95
00690172	Steve Vai – Fire Garden	$24.95
00660137	Steve Vai – Passion & Warfare	$24.95
00690881	Steve Vai – Real Illusions: Reflections	$24.95
00694904	Steve Vai – Sex and Religion	$24.95
00110385	Steve Vai – The Story of Light	$22.99
00690392	Steve Vai – The Ultra Zone	$19.95
00700555	Van Halen – Van Halen	$19.99
00690024	Stevie Ray Vaughan – Couldn't Stand the Weather	$19.95
00690370	Stevie Ray Vaughan and Double Trouble – The Real Deal: Greatest Hits Volume 2	$22.95
00690116	Stevie Ray Vaughan – Guitar Collection	$24.95
00660136	Stevie Ray Vaughan – In Step	$19.95
00694879	Stevie Ray Vaughan – In the Beginning	$19.95
00660058	Stevie Ray Vaughan – Lightnin' Blues '83-'87	$24.95
00694835	Stevie Ray Vaughan – The Sky Is Crying	$22.95
00690025	Stevie Ray Vaughan – Soul to Soul	$19.95
00690015	Stevie Ray Vaughan – Texas Flood	$19.95
00690772	Velvet Revolver – Contraband	$22.95
00109770	Volbeat Guitar Collection	$22.99
00121808	Volbeat – Outlaw Gentlemen & Shady Ladies	$22.99
00690132	The T-Bone Walker Collection	$19.95
00694789	Muddy Waters – Deep Blues	$24.95
00690071	Weezer (The Blue Album)	$19.95
00690516	Weezer (The Green Album)	$19.95
00690286	Weezer – Pinkerton	$19.95
00691046	Weezer – Rarities Edition	$22.99
00117511	Whitesnake Guitar Collection	$19.99
00690447	Best of the Who	$24.95
00691941	The Who – Acoustic Guitar Collection	$22.99
00691006	Wilco Guitar Collection	$22.99
00690672	Best of Dar Williams	$19.95
00691017	Wolfmother – Cosmic Egg	$22.99
00690319	Stevie Wonder – Hits	$19.99
00690596	Best of the Yardbirds	$19.95
00690844	Yellowcard – Lights and Sounds	$19.95
00690916	The Best of Dwight Yoakam	$19.95
00691020	Neil Young – After the Goldrush	$22.99
00691019	Neil Young – Everybody Knows This Is Nowhere	$19.99
00690904	Neil Young – Harvest	$29.99
00691021	Neil Young – Harvest Moon	$22.99
00690905	Neil Young – Rust Never Sleeps	$19.99
00690443	Frank Zappa – Hot Rats	$19.95
00690624	Frank Zappa and the Mothers of Invention – One Size Fits All	$22.99
00690623	Frank Zappa – Over-Nite Sensation	$22.99
00121684	ZZ Top – Early Classics	$24.99
00690589	ZZ Top – Guitar Anthology	$24.95
00690960	ZZ Top Guitar Classics	$19.99

7777 W. Bluemound Rd. P.O. Box 13819 Milwaukee, WI 53213

Complete songlists and more at **www.halleonard.com**

Prices, contents, and availability subject to change without notice.

0515